Global Histories of Education

Series Editors

Christian Ydesen [iD]
Department of Culture and Learning
Aalborg University
Aalborg, Denmark

Eugenia Roldan Vera
Cinvestav-Coapa
Mexico City, Estado de México, Mexico

Klaus Dittrich
Literature and Cultural Studies
Education University of Hong Kong
Hong Kong, China

Linda Chisholm [iD]
Education Rights and Transformation
University of Johannesburg
Johannesburg, Gauteng, South Africa

We are very pleased to announce the ISCHE Global Histories of Education book series. The International Standing Conference for the History of Education has organized conferences in the field since 1978. Thanks to our collaboration with Palgrave Macmillan we now offer an edited book series for the publication of innovative scholarship in the history of education.

This series seeks to engage with historical scholarship that analyzes education within a global, world, or transnational perspective. Specifically, it seeks to examine the role of educational institutions, actors, technologies as well as pedagogical ideas that for centuries have crossed regional and national boundaries. Topics for publication may include the study of educational networks and practices that connect national and colonial domains, or those that range in time from the age of Empire to decolonization. These networks could concern the international movement of educational policies, curricula, pedagogies, or universities within and across different socio-political settings. The 'actors' under examination might include individuals and groups of people, but also educational apparatuses such as textbooks, built-environments, and bureaucratic paperwork situated within a global perspective. Books in the series may be single authored or edited volumes. The strong transnational dimension of the Global Histories of Education series means that many of the volumes should be based on archival research undertaken in more than one country and using documents written in multiple languages. All books in the series will be published in English, although we welcome English-language proposals for manuscripts which were initially written in other languages and which will be translated into English at the cost of the author. All submitted manuscripts will be blind peer-reviewed with editorial decisions to be made by the ISCHE series editors who themselves are appointed by the ISCHE Executive Committee to serve three to five year terms.

Full submissions should include: (1) a proposal aligned to the Palgrave Book Proposal form (downloadable here); (2) the CV of the author(s) or editor(s); and, (3) a cover letter that explains how the proposed book fits into the overall aims and framing of the ISCHE Global Histories of Education book series. Proposals and queries should be addressed to bookseries@ische.org. Preliminary inquiries are welcome and encouraged.

Sotiria Grek • Joakim Landahl
Martin Lawn • Christian Lundahl

The World as a Laboratory

Torsten Husén and the Rise of Transnational Research in Education 1950s–1990s

Sotiria Grek
University of Edinburgh
Edinburgh, UK

Joakim Landahl
Stockholm University
Stockholm, Sweden

Martin Lawn
University of Edinburgh
Edinburgh, UK

Christian Lundahl
Örebro University
Örebro, Sweden

ISSN 2731-6408   ISSN 2731-6416   (electronic)
Global Histories of Education
ISBN 978-3-031-68089-2   ISBN 978-3-031-68090-8   (eBook)
https://doi.org/10.1007/978-3-031-68090-8

© The Editor(s) (if applicable) and The Author(s), under exclusive license to Springer Nature Switzerland AG 2024, corrected publication 2024

This work is subject to copyright. All rights are solely and exclusively licensed by the Publisher, whether the whole or part of the material is concerned, specifically the rights of translation, reprinting, reuse of illustrations, recitation, broadcasting, reproduction on microfilms or in any other physical way, and transmission or information storage and retrieval, electronic adaptation, computer software, or by similar or dissimilar methodology now known or hereafter developed.
The use of general descriptive names, registered names, trademarks, service marks, etc. in this publication does not imply, even in the absence of a specific statement, that such names are exempt from the relevant protective laws and regulations and therefore free for general use.
The publisher, the authors and the editors are safe to assume that the advice and information in this book are believed to be true and accurate at the date of publication. Neither the publisher nor the authors or the editors give a warranty, expressed or implied, with respect to the material contained herein or for any errors or omissions that may have been made. The publisher remains neutral with regard to jurisdictional claims in published maps and institutional affiliations.

This Palgrave Macmillan imprint is published by the registered company Springer Nature Switzerland AG.
The registered company address is: Gewerbestrasse 11, 6330 Cham, Switzerland

If disposing of this product, please recycle the paper.

Preface and Acknowledgements

This book focuses on the internationalisation of education research for policy in the second half of the twentieth century. The research has been supported by the Swedish Research Council under Grant [dnr/ref] 2019-03653, *The disembedded laboratory—Torsten Husén and the internationalisation of educational research for policy*. The following scholars have been affiliated to the project, Professor Christian Lundahl (Principal Investigator), Örebro University, Professor Sotiria Grek, University of Edinburgh, Professor Joakim Landahl, Stockholm University, Professor Emeritus Martin Lawn, University of Edinburgh.

The project was possible thanks to the rich research archive of Torsten Husén at the National Archive (Riksarkivet) in Stockholm. Despite the access difficulties caused by COVID-19, we were able to obtain a significant amount of material for our analysis. We would like to acknowledge the assistance we received from the staff members at Riksarkivet in acquiring all the necessary data. Our gratitude also extends to the staff members at the Linnaeus University Library in Växjö, where the Husén Library is held, and to the archivists at the Hoover Institution Library & Archives. We are also grateful to PhD and archivist Germund Larsson for his help in collecting, systematising, and digitising the data, with the assistance of students Moa Insulander and Emma Hagberg. We also acknowledge the work of PhD student Sophie Winkler at Örebro University, who served as a project assistant and provided valuable assistance in several ways, including formatting this book.

The manuscript of this book was reviewed in its final state by Professor Jenny Ozga at the Department of Education, Oxford University. Her wise

vi PREFACE AND ACKNOWLEDGEMENTS

and challenging comments have been greatly appreciated. Finally, we are grateful to Görel Strömkvist, daughter of Torsten Husén, for sharing documents, micro tapes, memories, and thoughts on the worklife of Torsten Husén. Her open interest and curiosity towards the project are greatly appreciated. Görel and her brother, Mats Husén, have also read the final version of the book and provided valuable reflections and comments. They have also given their permission to print some pictures in the book.

Although this book is a collaborative work, each chapter has a main author. Christian Lundahl is the main author of the Prologue, Chap. 6 on the International Encyclopedia of Education, the Epilogue, and Appendix A on the Husén archive and overarching methodological points of departure. Martin Lawn is the author of Chaps. 1 and 2, which concern the early formation of transnational research networks. Chapter 3, concerning the work of the International Association for Educational Achievement (IEA), and Chap. 7, on international writing and publishing strategies, were authored by Joakim Landahl. Chapter 4, which deals with the International Institute for Educational Planning (IIEP), and Chap. 5, which discusses futurological thinking in education research and policy work, were authored by Sotiria Grek.

Edinburgh, UK
Stockholm, Sweden
Ludlow, UK
Örebro, Sweden
March 8, 2024

Sotiria Grek
Joakim Landahl
Martin Lawn
Christian Lundahl

CONTENTS

1 **Organising the Future of Educational Research in Post-war Europe and Beyond**   1
Networking   5
Disembedded   9
Governing   13
International Actors, Networks, and the Modernisation of Education   14

2 **Forming Transnational Networks: The Early 1950s in Europe**   17
A First Major Education Conference   20
A Post-war Borderless Research Area in Europe   24
The First Education Expert Conferences in the 1950s   28
The First International Conference on Educational Research 1956   31
New Research Institutes and Their Networking   34
School Evaluation 1957/1958   36
Husén at the End of the 1950s   38
A New Form of Comparative Research   40
A Transnational Connector of Research   42

vii

viii CONTENTS

3 Collecting International Data: Husén and the International
Association for the Evaluation of Educational Achievement 45
Statistics: National and International Data 47
Introducing IEA 49
Relocating the Headquarters 50
Data Processing 55
Electing a Chairman 59
Recruiting Countries 63
The Dream of Global Knowledge 67

4 The Rise of a Global Expert Network: The International
Institute for Educational Planning, 1963–1973 69
A Brief History of the IIEP 71
The Husén Archive on the IIEP 75
*The IIEP Governing Board Meetings: Research and
Internationalisation* 79
The IIEP Internship Scheme: Educating the Educators 84
The Epistemic Power of Socialisation 87

5 Education Futuramas: Torsten Husén and Futurological
Thinking in Education 91
The Politics of Prediction 92
Torsten Husén's 'Future Think': The Aspen/Berlin Seminars and
The School in Question (*1979*) 95
Aspen/Berlin Seminars: A Timeline 96
Torsten Husén's The School in Question: A Comparative Study
of the School and Its Future in Western Societies (*1979*) 101
*Futures Thinking and Utopia as a New Mode of Political
Imagination in Education* 105

6 Editing the *International Encyclopedia of Education*,
1980–1994 109
What Constitutes an Encyclopaedia? 112
The International Encyclopaedia of Education Takes Form 114
Producing and Indexing the Content 114
Deciding upon Section Editors 118
*A World of Educational Knowledge and Knowledge of the
Educational World* 120

CONTENTS   ix

World 'Facts': The Country System Reports   125
Unwrapping International Encyclopaedic Knowledge   128

**7   Words for the World: Writing and Publishing Strategies
      for an International Book Market**   133
Making Use of International and International Experiences:
Three Major Phases   134
   From Germany to Sweden   134
   World-wide Expert on Sweden   137
   Overview of the World   140
Writing Practices   142
   Breaking the Language Barrier   142
   An Atlantic Crossing: Bringing the Typewriter to the US   144
   Time and Space for Writing   147
Dissemination   148
   Finding Publishers and Making Translations   148
   Reprints and Other Ways of Spreading Publications   150
Knowledge Strategies and Publications in Times of Change   152

**Correction to: The Rise of a Global Expert Network: The
International Institute for Educational Planning, 1963–1973**   C1

Epilogue: The Disembedded Laboratory   155

**Appendix A: Torsten Husén and His Archive as a
Disembedded Laboratory**   165

Appendix B   179

Source Material   181

Bibliography   189

Index   199

PROLOGUE

This book is about the construction of an international and comparative education research community in the 1950s–1990s, and the growth of its 'disembedded laboratory' creating cross-border knowledge with policy implications. Drawing on Science and Technology Studies (STS), we approach knowledge-making through the prism of 'laboratory studies,' that is, the cultural, symbolic, and political construction of knowledge, not at the point when it is 'set' (i.e. accepted as truth), but in the *process* of its production. The notion of 'disembeddedness' is used to show that the kinds of education knowledge we investigate were not being produced at a single site; rather, they were the product of parallel 'constructions' in multiple sites, spaces, and networks, including the moments (or rather, the long journeys of the time) of travel and translation. In the book the disembedded laboratory of international and comparative education research takes different shapes. The chapters describe, for example, the context of its appearance during a post-war context, the growth of actor and organisation networks, the development of data technologies, the rise of experts and the consolidation and dissemination of knowledge.

The book explores shifting and heterogenous transnational networks that contribute to the development of social science research beyond fixed time and space dimensions, and that extends science beyond individual ideas, researchers, environments, institutions, and universities. It follows a sociology of science theoretical framework. STS is a field of knowledge that has developed in the post-war period, in particular through historical and sociological studies, where what is studied is the interaction between

xii PROLOGUE

science, technology, and society. Nowadays, the STS field consists of interdisciplinary studies that often work in the borderland between traditional humanistic and natural science/technological disciplines, and which have a close relationship with post humanist and neo-materialist theories. Within social science disciplines we find STS studies, for example, with feminist, historical, economic, and legal perspectives. Also, within educational science research, STS has grown increasingly stronger.[1]

Empirically, the book originates in an extraordinary research archive, that of the Swedish internationally renowned educational scholar Torsten Husén (1916–2009). Further details of Husén's biography are presented in Appendix A, but in brief he was a key figure in the establishment of comparative education as a field of research, from the late 1950s until the 1990s. For example, he served as the chairman of the International Association for the Evaluation of Educational Achievement (IEA) between 1962 and 1978. Additionally, he served as chairman of the governing board of the International Institute for Educational Planning (IIEP) from 1970 to 1980. He authored more than 1200 publications between 1940 and 2008. The Husén archive contains what seems to be an entire set of documents, letters, and cards that crossed Husén's desk at the university. These academic notes bear witness to over 50 years of work with global educational research through one of its key players. We have drawn on this resource to illustrate, through the work of a key actor in international and comparative education, how ideas were developed, how they moved and changed, how the material conditions of knowledge production altered, and how geo-politics shaped priorities and tied knowledge closer to educational policy. Husén, then, is for us more an exemplar of—and guide to—developments in education research, rather than the subject of a biographical study. The level of detail in the archive allows us to comprehend

---

[1] E.g. Jan Nespor, *Knowledge in Motion: Space, Time and Curriculum in Undergraduate Physics and Management* (London: Routledge, 1994); Christian Lundahl, *Viljan att veta vad andra vet: Kunskapsbedömning i tidigmodern, modern och senmodern skola.* (Stockholm: Arbetslivsinstitutet, 2006); Tara Fenwick and Richard Edwards, *Actor-Network Theory and Education* (London: Routledge, 2010); Tara Fenwick and Richard Edwards, eds., *Researching Education through Actor-Network Theory* (Oxford: Wiley-Blackwell, 2012); Radhika Gorur, 'Policy as Assemblage,' *European Educational Research Journal* 10, no. 4 (2011); Radhika Gorur, 'Situated, Relational and Practice-Oriented: The Actor-Network Theory Approach,' in *Educational Policy and Contemporary Theory: Implications for Research*, ed. Kalervo N. Gulson et al. (London: Routledge, 2015); Radhika Gorur et al., 'Politics by Other Means? STS and Research in Education,' *Discourse: Studies in the Cultural Politics of Education* 40, no. 1 (2019).

the social processes of research in several ways. The sheer volume of more than 200,000 pages of documents demonstrates the centrality of correspondence, the production and circulation of texts, and the exchange of ideas and information in a strict material way. A thorough examination of the content reveals a wealth of information about the context and processes of academic work. These include attending conferences, reading, writing, and reviewing texts, as well as editorial work and social networking. Consequently, we regard the archive as an invitation to an historical and ethnographical understanding of social sciences in general and international and comparative educational research in particular as a 'laboratory.'

International and comparative education is an interdisciplinary research field where representatives of various humanities and social sciences disciplines conduct research on international aspects of education.[2] To be strictly comparative, in the sense that two or more countries are studied, has paradoxically not been the dominant feature of this research. The majority of the studies that have been published study education within the framework instead of a single national context. The comparative aspect thus gets seen as the combined effect of what the research field as a whole is doing.[3] Early comparativists (such as Michael Sadler 1861–1943, Paul Monroe 1869–1947, and Isaac Kandel 1881–1965) saw the nation-state as the 'dominant unit of analysis.'[4] Research in comparative education has

---

[2] The field of international and comparative pedagogy has its roots in the early nineteenth century when Marc-Antoine Jullien, a Frenchman, developed guidelines for international education comparisons. However, the institutionalization of the research field with its own journals, societies, and university courses only occurred during the twentieth century, particularly in the post-war period. Internationally speaking, the research field originally went by the name comparative education. Later, they also spoke of international education as a related field of research and nowadays they are called often together as comparative and international education. The basic idea behind this name change is, among other things, that comparative education is not always international in nature. International education has also partly dealt with other issues, such as the special educational needs of developing countries. The boundaries between the two however, the research fields are fluid (see further Pella Kaloyannaki and Andreas M. Kazamias, 'The Modernist Beginning of Comparative Education: The Proto-Scientific and the Reformist-Meliorist Administrative Motif,' in *International Handbook of Comparative Education*, ed. Robert Cowen and Andreas M. Kazamias (Dordrecht; Springer, 2009); Joakim Landahl and Christian Lundahl, eds., *Bortom PISA: Internationell och jämförande pedagogik* (Stockholm: Natur och Kultur, 2017).

[3] Landahl and Lundahl, *Bortom PISA.*

[4] Mark Bray, 'The WCCES and Intercultural Dialogue: Historical Perspectives and Continuing Challenges,' *International Review of Education* 54, no. 3/4 (2008): 305.

asked questions such as: how and why do different countries' schools differ in terms of content and results, and how can we study, and explain, these differences? What this book describes about the IEA and *The International Encyclopedia of Education* in Chaps. 3 and 6 is very much about this. Another common orientation within comparative education deals with international or transnational influences. Here, for example, interest has been directed towards the development and dissemination of certain type of educational ideas across national and cultural borders.

One of the most significant orientations in international and comparative education in recent years has centred around the concept of policy borrowing,[5] and how international organisations contribute to transnational trends in education policy.[6] Chapter 4 on the International Institute for Educational Planning and Chap. 5 on Futures thinking describe events in line with this research. Research on international and comparative education per se is less common.[7] Issues concerning the formation of the field, how researchers find each other and organise for collaboration, how standards are set for data collection and text production, and how global dissemination of results is carried out have not been extensively studied. Several books exist on various aspects of comparative education, although they do not focus on the work of scholars in the field.[8] Following an alternative angle, this book views comparative education by bringing in an STS perspective. In utilising an STS lens on comparative education, we find that we can attend more closely to the socio-material construction of the

---

[5] Gita Steiner-Khamsi, ed., *The Global Politics of Educational Borrowing and Lending* (New York; Teachers College Press, 2004); Gita Steiner-Khamsi and Florian Waldow, eds., *Policy Borrowing and Lending in Education* (London: Routledge, 2012); David Phillips and Kimberly Ochs, eds., *Educational Policy Borrowing: Historical Perspectives* (Oxford: Symposium Books, 2004).

[6] E.g. Maren Elfert and Christian Ydesen, Global Governance of Education: The Historical and Contemporary Entanglements of UNESCO, the OECD and the World Bank (London: Springer, 2023); Sotiria Grek, The New Production of Expert Knowledge: Education, Quantification and Utopia (London: Springer, 2024).

[7] Cf. Eckhardt Fuchs, and Eugenia Roldán Vera, eds. *The Transnational in the History of Education: Concepts and Perspectives* (Cham: Palgrave Macmillan, 2019); Oren Pizmony-Levy, "Testing for All: The Emergence and Development of International Assessment of Student Achievement, 1958–2012" (PhD diss., Indiana University, 2013).

[8] See however Martin Carnoy, Transforming Comparative Education: Fifty Years of Theory Building at Stanford (Stanford: Stanford University Press, 2019); J. Wesley Null, Peerless Educator: The Life and Work of Isaac Leon Kandel (New York: Peter Lang, 2007); Christian Ydesen, The OECD's Historical Rise in Education: The Formation of a Global Governing Complex (London: Palgrave Macmillan, 2020).

PROLOGUE xv

field of educational research, as well as explore its embodiment in the work and transactions of its key actors, like Torsten Husén.

The idea of the disembedded laboratory draws attention to spatially oriented histories of scientific thought and practice, symbolised in Husén's wide spaces of work, where knowledge is produced in the interaction of humans, objects, places, and spaces.[9] Both STS and comparative education work with ideas around transfer, adaptation, and translation; as already evidenced in scholarly literature, the movement of educational practices and objects involves processes of translation and is done in the context of specific interests and power relations.[10] We argue that such socio-historical and socio-material analyses can contribute to a more complex understanding of the formation of national and international policy as an interdependent process.

Additionally, the book relates to three vital research fields: the history of knowledge, the transnational history of science, and the history of educational research. The history of knowledge has in recent years emerged as a powerful research field.[11] While the meanings of the term are contested and the relationship to previous research on science is debated,[12] it is a field that has resulted in a broader understanding of how knowledge can be studied. Basically, history of knowledge focus on how something 'becomes knowledge.' Knowledge is seen as a socially anchored form of knowing, and in its construction more or less changeable, dispersed, and used in different places and at different times.[13] By studying processes of knowledge and fact construction in the past, we will get a better understanding of scholarly processes also of today.

A fundamental contribution of the field and with a particular relevance to this book is its perspectives on how knowledge travels; how and why

---

[9] Martina Merz, "Nobody Can Force You When You Are across the Ocean': Face to Face and E-mail Exchanges between Theoretical Physicists,' in *Making Space for Science: Territorial Themes in the Shaping of Knowledge*, ed. Crosbie Smith and Jon Agar (London: Palgrave Macmillan, 1998); David N. Livingstone, *Putting Science in its Place: Geographics of Scientific Knowledge* (Chicago: University of Chicago Press, 2003).

[10] Gita Steiner-Khamsi, 'Transferring education, Displacing Reforms,' *Discourse Formation in Comparative Education*, ed. Jürgen Schriewer (Frankfurt am Main: Peter Lang, 2009).

[11] E.g. Peter Burke, *What Is the History of Knowledge?* (Hoboken, New Jersey: Wiley, 2015).

[12] Lorraine Daston, 'The History of Science and the History of Knowledge,' *KNOW: A Journal on the Formation of Knowledge* 1, no. 1 (2015).

[13] Johan Östling and David Larsson Heidenblad, *The History of Knowledge* (Cambridge: Cambridge University Press, 2023).

xvi PROLOGUE

knowledge circulates and with what effects.[14] As we consider expert activity in networks, meetings, data use, publications, seminars and teaching, and so forth, how knowledge travels, how it is made to travel becomes topics that are threaded through all of the chapters of the book. Paradoxically, given the international nature of science,[15] traditional accounts of the history of science used to take the national unit for granted. Recently, more and more scholars have tried to analyse the history of science from the perspective of transnational connections. This has resulted in a richer understanding of how science is produced, disseminated, and transformed as it travels, and the respective power relations that determine the evolution of research.[16] Scholars have focused on the role of American influence. The role of philanthropic foundations in funding of research, not least during the Cold War and the reconstruction of Europe, has been detailed in several studies.[17] While this focus on America's hegemonic role is justifiable, it can be argued that it carries the risk of obscuring the role of smaller nations, resulting ultimately in a one-sided view of how science internationalises.

[14] James A. Secord, 'Knowledge in Transit,' *Isis* 95, no. 4 (2004); Johan Östling et al., eds., *Circulation of Knowledge: Explorations in the History of Knowledge* (Lund: Nordic Academic Press, 2018); Östling and Larsson Heidenblad, *History of Knowledge*; Wiebke Keim et al., eds., *Global Knowledge Production in the Social Sciences: Made in Circulation* (Farnham: Ashgate, 2014).

[15] Pierre Bourdieu, 'The Social Conditions of the International Circulation of Ideas,' in *Bourdieu: A Critical Reader*, ed. Richard Shusterman (Oxford: Blackwell, 1999).

[16] Heilbron et al., eds., *The Social and Human Sciences in Global Power Relations* (Cham: Palgrave Macmillan, 2018); Simone Turchetti, Néstor Herran and Soraya Boudia, 'Introduction: Have We Ever Been 'Transnational'? Towards a History of Science Across and Beyond Borders,' *British Journal for the History of Science* 45, no. 3 (2012); David Rodogno, Bernhard Struck and Jakob Vogel, *Shaping the Transnational Sphere: Experts, Networks and Issues from the 1840s and 1930s* (New York, Berghahn Books, 2015); Livingstone, *Putting Science in Its Place*; John Krige, ed., *How Knowledge Moves: Writing the Transnational History of Science and Technology* (Chicago: University of Chicago Press, 2019); John Krige, ed., *Knowledge Flows in a Global Age: A Transnational Approach* (Chicago: University of Chicago Press, 2022).

[17] Christian Fleck, *A Transnational History of the Social Sciences: Robber Barons, the Third Reich and the Invention of Empirical Social Research* (London: Bloomsbury Academic, 2011); Kristi Niskanen, 'Snille efterfrågas! Rockfeller Foundation, forskarpersona och kön vid Stockholms högskola under mellankrigstiden,' *Scandia* 83, no. 2 (2017); John Krige, *American Hegemony and the Postwar Reconstruction of Science in Europe* (Cambridge: MIT Press, 2008).

PROLOGUE   xvii

In the last few decades, we have witnessed an interest in the history of educational research. Special issues on the historical development of educational research and its current status have been published in the *Oxford Review of Education*, *Paedagogica Historica*, and the *European Educational Research Journal*.[18] The importance of international networks and other distribution mechanisms have been considered, such as the role of research institutes and international conferences.[19] Here transnational history of education focus on educational research as an *entangled* movement of international actors, cross-border phenomena, and processes.[20]

The historical context is crucial to this book. We examine the decades that saw the slow yet methodical construction of comparative education data for policymaking, the rise of cross-border and international comparisons and the role of a modern, comprehensive education in these processes. Through a detailed analysis of the interactions of a range of actors, materials, and institutions, we explore the socio-cognitive processes that saw education as the sole pathway towards the governing of a 'better society.' Such imaginaries of education have been in existence for centuries, nevertheless, the notion that education science can and should be informing the making of education policy was a novel idea in the twentieth century.

Torsten Husén saw the world as a laboratory, a kind of organised beehive, but our project goes beyond this and shows the work which

[18] Martin Lawn and John Furlong, 'The Disciplines of Education in the UK: Between the Ghost and the Shadow,' *Oxford Review of Education* 35, no. 5 (2009); Rita Hofstetter and Bernard Schneuwly, 'Introduction: Educational Sciences in Dynamic and Hybrid Institutionalization,' *Paedagogica Historica* 40, no. 5/6 (2004); Rita Hofstetter and Bernhard Schneuwly, 'Institutionalisation of Educational Sciences and the Dynamics of Their Development,' *European Educational Research Journal* 1, no. 1 (2002).

[19] For international networks see Martin Lawn, ed., *An Atlantic Crossing? The Work of the International Examinations Inquiry: Its Researchers, Methods and Influence* (Oxford: Symposium Books, 2008); for the role of research institutes see Gary McCulloch, 'Fred Clarke and the Internationalization of Studies and Research in Education,' *Paedagogica Historica* 50, no. 1/2 (2014); for the role of international conferences see e.g. Eckhardt Fuchs, 'Educational Science, Morality and Politics: International Educational Congresses in the Early Twentieth Century,' *Paedagogica Historica* 40, no. 5/6 (2004); see also Joakim Landahl and Anna Larsson, 'Pedagogy and the Humanities: Changing Boundaries in the Academic Map of Knowledge 1860s–1960s', in *The Humanities and the Modern Politics of Knowledge: The Impact and Organization of the Humanities in Sweden 1800–2020*, ed. Anders Ekström and Hampus Östh Gustafsson (Amsterdam: Amsterdam University Press, 2022).

[20] Eckhardt and Roldán Vera, *The Transnational*.

xviii   PROLOGUE

underpins it, that is the actual labouring over time and space, by large numbers of experts, acting in coordination, and then continues into an exploration of subsequent projects, logically extending, as the world changed fast, into world encyclopaedia, future studies, and connected areas. The laboratory metaphor grew. They were not just studying the world but being challenged by it;

the world of education as a natural laboratory in which different countries were experimenting with different strategies of teaching and learning; considering it as an experiment, so to speak, that enabled us to study the effects of the various observed 'treatments.'[21]

The book in particular discusses the place of quantitative research, the landscape of comparative education research in a post-war Europe and the growth of a community of experts and follows key scientific worker within it. We show how this community as it became more ambitious in the scope of its work and trying to shape the future of education worldwide. The use of the term 'networking' is specific here and relates to the conditions in Europe at this time, and the distant but interwoven influence of the US, across the Atlantic. It is a term referring to common interests, diverse possibilities of interactions, and the scarcity of funding. Networking as an idea and practice embraces the 'invisible college' of like-minded researchers; additionally, it may involve networks intended to accumulate knowledge to inform and change policy. Finally, the concept of disembeddedness draws attention to problems of working across distances and related technologies.

---

[21] Rainer Lehmann, 'The Scientific Contributions of Torsten Husén and Neville Postlethwaite to the Development of International Comparative Research on Educational Achievement,' in *IEA 1958–2008: 50 Years of Experiences and Memories*, vol. 1, ed. Constantinos Papanastasiou, Tjeerd Plomp and Elena C. Papanastasiou (Amsterdam: International Association for the Evaluation of Educational Achievement, 2011), 518. The idea of an educational laboratory was also expressed by other co-workers at IEA. Alan C. Purves wrote about comparative education that it is 'a laboratory in which the end is the improvement of education and learning for all. It is a laboratory in which each of the systems of education is an equal researcher and in which all are asking questions that can help the others. It is a laboratory which recognizes the similarities and differences among cultures, nations, and their educational systems and seeks to avoid cultural imperialism in educational solutions. It does assume that there is a global definition of learning and schooling, a broad definition with room for variation according to the particular history and aspirations of each participating system of education. This is a view of education and learning that allows for diversity within a larger global unity', Alan C. Purves, 'The world as an educational laboratory." *IEA Guidebook* (1991), 40.

PROLOGUE   xix

Although Torsten Husén and his work is reflected in all the chapters, the impetus for writing the book is the understanding of educational science as both situated and spatial, as both national and international, as well as actor-driven and net/worked. With its starting point in the collection of the work of a single actor, born, living, and working in Sweden, yet constantly connected, travelling, and translated globally, we deconstruct, analyse, and understand processes of knowledge making and its use in policy. Checking accounts, both primary and secondary, allowed us to analyse the micro processes of science, from a wider sociohistorical and transnational view, and their effects. The book is based on the material in the Torsten Husén's archive[22] in Stockholm but also on linked archive material in the IEA archive at Stanford University as well as on Husén's library at Linneaus University in Växjo. We also, of course, make use of Husén's own large range of publications in the analyses. A new element in this discussion is research on the shifting nature of educational expertise in the later post-war period: scholars and researchers move out of investigation into rule making, from independent functions into coordinated investigation, from scholarly inquiry into governing advice, and from individual interests into national policy. Husén was a significant actor in this period, and following his activities, we can view the emergence of post-war European research networking and its connection with an American and global networking.

THE CONTENT OF THE BOOK

The book is structured in seven chapters that shed light on the internationalisation of education research with a particular focus on research that for the first time was produced with the explicit aim of informing policy. We explore the work carried out in 'the disembedded laboratory' in relation to conditions for assessing, describing, and comparing national education systems. For this we use a few carefully selected cases which, respectively, but also in complementary ways, represent aspects of international networking, testing, planning, and publishing. A common feature of the cases is that they all contribute to a hitherto mostly untold story of the development of the field of international and comparative education.

---

[22] Formally the archive reference is SE/RA/720869 but will hereafter in the text be referred to as The Husén archive. However, the formal reference is used in the books reference list.

On a general level, all cases describe the various ways 'the laboratory' is developed and organised, and how it produces and disseminates comparative knowledge on education.

Chapter 1, Organising the Future of Educational Research in Post-war Europe and Beyond, discusses the rise of transnational research in education, and its close connection to the emerging field of global education and knowledge production and policy. The concept of the 'disembedded laboratory' draws attention to spatially oriented histories of scientific thought and practice, where knowledge is produced in the interaction of humans, objects, and spaces, and in constant practices. In this context, the chapter also elaborates on the concepts of networking and of governing.

Chapter 2, Forming Transnational Networks: The Early 1950s in Europe, follows the early years of the growth of a national and post-national education research community in Europe, and the foundation of new national research institutes in education, as well as the creation and exchange of scientific data between scholars and the importance of international congresses (especially in the psychology of education). The post-war significance of the American support for this form of educational research is followed from the American Zone in Germany, American exchanges and sponsored visits to the USA, their support for systematic comparative research data, and linked innovations in schooling, all of which Husén was closely connected with.

Chapter 3, Collecting International Data: Husén and the International Association for the Evaluation of Educational Achievement, discusses Husén's role in the rise of international large-scale assessments. Focusing on IEA, the organisation that Husén chaired for 17 years, the chapter discusses how the production of international data relied on ongoing negotiations about how the organisation should be governed. Questions such as electing a chairman, relocating headquarters and data processing, as well as recruiting countries were essential part of how collaboration across borders was organised.

Chapter 4, The Rise of a Global Expert Network: The International Institute for Educational Planning, 1963–1973, links the formation of the IIEP, formed by the UNESCO, the World Bank and the Ford Foundation, to further the development of the internationalisation of education research. The IIEP had the mission to create and build capacity for educational planning in countries of the Global South, with a particular focus on research capacity-building and the training of education professionals and experts.

Chapter 5, Education Futuramas: Torsten Husén and Futurological Thinking in Education, examines the Aspen/Berlin seminars in the 1970s as focal points in the study of the role of expertise in solving educational crises. The chapter discusses the function of 'futurology' to construct broader norms and understandings about the 'learning society.' This process required comparative analyses, blue-skies-thinking, interdisciplinarity and above all, the production of a high-level consensus on the purpose of education as a dual endeavour: the making of future citizens and workers. The concept which emerged, the 'learning society,' became the basis for Husén's thinking on the role of educational research in informing policymaking.

Chapter 6, Editing of the *International Encyclopaedia of Education*, 1980–1994, analyses how Husén used his wide network of worldwide educational experts to move beyond the creation of research knowledge, the subject of his earlier work, to its description and publication across world settings. The monumental task he directed, the International Encyclopaedia of Education (IEE), was to make a first attempt to describe the shaping of post-war educational research—reinstated in many national settings, using an important range of influential actors, and their methods, texts, and procedures. In addition, the chapter describes the problems in overcoming the challenges of scholarly editing in international knowledge production, and the problems of objectivity and bias.

Chapter 7, Words for the World: Writing and Publishing Strategies for an International Book Market, discusses Husén's academic writings. Focusing on his international publications and experiences, the chapter is divided into three parts. The first discusses the various ways in which Husén used his international experience, either to strengthen his position at home or on the international stage. The second part focuses on Husén's writing practices and the third part on dissemination strategies.

Finally, the epilogue revisits our thesis, the construction of an expert international research community and the growth of its disembedded laboratory (networks, spaces, materiality, travelling, translations), the creation of large-scale assessment, transnational organisations, and new (international) knowledge practices.

xxii   PROLOGUE

This book would not have been possible without access to Torsten Husén's research archive, unique in size and detail. We argue that the archive invites us to do textual ethnography of the internationalisation of educational research; to historically make observations of the 'disembedded laboratory.' This includes revealing actors, networks, places and spaces, materiality, and other conditions in creating cross-border knowledge with policy implications. In Appendix A, we open this archive, stretching over Husén's more than 50-year long career and briefly describe Husén, his major work and influence. We also discuss some theoretical and methodological concerns, strengths, and limitations, of viewing the archive as an ethnographic invitation to a research laboratory.

LIST OF FIGURES

Fig. 3.1 Document showing proposals for a new name of the IEA that would strengthen the role of the UNESCO Institute for Education. The pencil notes indicate that the reader of the document disagrees with the proposal. (The Husén archive, 2.237)   52

Fig. 4.1 Table showing the 'Statistical Summary of IIEP Training Programmes during the Last Four Academic Years' (International Institute for Educational Planning, '10th Session of the Governing Board,' November 22–24, 1971, Santiago de Chile (The Husén archive, 2.53), 30)   82

Fig. 4.2 Table showing the IIEP's 'Financial Resources Available in 1972 and 1973' (International Institute for Educational Planning, '11th Session of the Governing Board,' November 28–30, November, Paris (The Husén archive, 2.56), 24)   83

Fig. 4.3 'The diverse origins of the 131 trainees who have successfully completed courses of six months or longer at the Institute since 1965 are geographically illustrated in the map … which shows the 68 countries from which they have come' (International Institute for Educational Planning, *IIEP 1972* (Paris: UNESCO, 1972), 6–7)   84

Fig. 4.4 'The discussion is usually lively when educational planning experts come to an IIEP seminar to exchange experiences and to catch up on new developments in research and methodology' (IIEP, *IIEP 1972*, 13)   86

Fig. 6.1 Word count average in Europe, Asia, and the Americas and the Caribbean, depending on official or university author   126

xxiii

xxiv   LIST OF FIGURES

Fig. 6.2   Average mentions of the term 'evaluation' in 1985 and 1994   128
Fig. 7.1   Comparativist and expert on Sweden. The quest for Husén's writings in the field of comparative education was initially related to his expertise on Swedish educational policy. This 1961 report was published by the US Office of Education   139
Fig. 7.2   Husén's portable typewriter Erika. (Photo: Mats Husén. According to his children, he typed all his work using only two fingers)   145
Fig. 7.3   Dedication to Jackie and Frank Sutton in Husén's bibliography *Tryckta skrifter: 1940–1975*, in which he refers to his 'bad habit of thinking at the type-writer.' Frank Sutton was deputy vice president of the Ford Foundation, a major funder of the IEA (private photo)   152
Fig. A.1   Torsten Husén in his office. (Photo Yukiko Sawano 2001. With courtesy of the Husén family)   166
Fig. A.2   Number of publications by Husén 1940–2008, based on Husén 1981, 1996, and a library search (Torsten Husén, ed., *Torsten Husén: Tryckta skrifter 1940–1980* (Uppsala: Almqvist & Wiksell, 1981); Torsten Husén, ed., *Torsten Husén: Printed Publications 1981–1995* (Stockholm: Institute of International Education, 1996))   167
Fig. A.3   This thematic overview of Husén's writings between 1940 and 2008 is based on Husén 1981, 1996, and a library search. (Husén, *Tryckta skrifter*; Husén, *Printed Publications*.) Some publications are classified under more than one theme. The total number of classifications are 1619   168

LIST OF TABLES

Table A.1   Husén's publications between 1940 and 2008 in different
             languages, based on Husén 1981, 1996, and a library search   169
Table A.2   Thematic overview of the Torsten Husén archive, *Riksarkivet*
             Stockholm   172

CHAPTER 1

Organising the Future of Educational Research in Post-war Europe and Beyond

The contemporary field of educational research reflects the fact that it is interwoven across Europe, organised through journals, transnational exchanges and collaborations, and funded projects. It is a space in which researchers in many locations with multiple purposes can join in common fields of understanding and practice, based around shared concepts and problems. It is such a widespread field, yet it is global and self-referential. It is substantial and so it may seem to be beyond time, as if it has always been there. This chapter builds on the early stages of European and US scholars discovering each other and working together, how they were contacted and what they contributed, and places them in their national and international contexts. It starts in the shattered Europe of the late 1940s where relations and contacts grew slowly out of scientific conferences, American support and through the formation of embryo international associations. The foci of this cooperation and its productive and sharp end of which Husén was a part were the new technologies of assessment and testing, interwoven with the necessity of school reform. Educational research in early post-war Europe was locally based, and with imprecise and infrequent relations, nationally and across borders. A sense of transnationality seems to flicker with irregular movement. European countries had quite different histories of research work and research personnel, but they shared a condition of unstable funding and uneven conditions often without significant knowledge accumulation. As William D. Wall observes, after a career based in Europe and the UK:

© The Author(s), under exclusive license to Springer Nature Switzerland AG 2024
S. Grek et al., *The World as a Laboratory*, Global Histories of Education, https://doi.org/10.1007/978-3-031-68090-8_1

1

2 S. GREK ET AL.

prior to the 1939–45 war research in education and related sciences was artisanal in character. Most of the empirical work was done by university teachers in time left aside from their lecturing and tutorial duties, and by students, the majority of them working part time for higher degrees. Outside the United States, with a few conspicuous exceptions ... little support was given from public or private funds. Hence prior to 1945 in Europe, we find research addressing itself principally to the rather limited issues which can be handled by one person over a brief period of time.[1]

A serious prewar attempt at a funded European research project on assessment was disrupted by European political instability and the very different ways these scholars, drawn from nine countries, had of understanding knowledge, schools and assessment and, creating common meanings and standards. The work of the International Examinations Inquiry (IEI) in the 1930s had tried to understand and overcome this problem by engaging psychologists and comparativists in supportive exchanges and in proximity over some years, and in so doing produced a novel international space of understanding.[2] Their common interest in the new problems of assessment and expanding secondary education enabled them to clarify the term, engage in critical discussion, produce a series of linked projects, and publish their work internationally. Although this effect persisted in several countries, wartime disrupted the IEI personnel and its tasks, and it never reconvened. It appeared to model or at least presage a spate of post–Second World War international studies and the establishing of common epistemic communities, which loosely integrated professional, academic, and policy actors' networks. The Second World War gave a powerful impetus to changes which had been under way before but especially ideas concerning the responsibility of the state towards its less fortunate citizens, and reflected the citizens' demands upon the state. So, by the late 1940s, European states saw the necessity for social reform, and educational policy was a key element in this reform. Most European governments had to intervene more actively in the lives of their citizens in the period of reconstruction and several countries (UK, Denmark, Norway, Sweden, Belgium, Finland, German Federal Republic) had set up commissions and organisations of varying degrees of independence concerned with the conduct and

---

[1] William D. Wall, 'Research and educational action,' *International Review of Education* 16, no. 4 (1970): 484–5.

[2] Martin Lawn, ed., *An Atlantic Crossing? The Work of the International Examinations Inquiry: Its Researchers, Methods and Influence* (Oxford: Symposium Books, 2008).

1   ORGANISING THE FUTURE OF EDUCATIONAL RESEARCH IN POST-WAR...   3

fostering of educational research directly concerned with policymaking. A community of experts working across diverse statist jurisdictions, network organisations, and politics tended to seek outside experience and common understandings.

This chapter is focused on the formation of significant educational research networking, its ideas and tools, and joint activities in its early years. The idea of networking is used here to describe this early stage in the rise of transnational relations in educational research containing heterogenous sites, spatial communications, material technologies and procedures, and a disrupted social environment. This network, overall and in its constituent parts, and its production of knowledge, we refer to overall as *a disembedded laboratory*. It is stabilised by its membership which tends to share value and professional judgements, and a sense of professional enterprise, drawn from similar backgrounds in assessment, quantitative research, and similar emerging policy responsibilities. In other words, this is an early formation of a distinctive 'invisible college,' an epistemic community, sharing texts, references, and mail. As an idea and a practice, we refer to the way that Torsten Husén was active in its creation.

Post-war and until 1956, Torsten Husén had hosted mainly American (Fulbright supported) scholars visiting Stockholm and attended international psychological congresses in Europe. In that year, he began to attend the annual UNESCO seminars held at the UNESCO institute for Education in Hamburg. They were a beneficial meeting place for European academics interested in curriculum, innovation, and education. In 1956, he was appointed director of the newly established Department of Educational and Psychological Research at Stockholm School of Education, which was founded by an Act of the Swedish Parliament, and reflected a new recognition that educational research should relate to practical school situations and education policy, and that Sweden needed more trained educational researchers.[3] This institute was involved in a number of research and evaluation projects related to the Swedish School Reform legislation. This was an important appointment in educational research in Sweden and Husén was at the centre of inquiry and advice, working with one or two main colleagues. Very soon, his Stockholm office seems to be overshadowed by his travelling and communications with his European and international colleagues. Early every morning he began

---

[3] Council of Europe, *Educational Research, European Survey*, vol. 1 (Strasbourg: Documentation Centre for Education of Europe, 1968), 90–99.

4   S. GREK ET AL.

writing on his typewriter, a machine that stayed with him throughout his life, and if anything, it was the machine, wherever it was, that was his place of work.[4] In the post-war period, place wasn't a mutable concept for researchers, it was stable and determined. Letters were sent, telephone used locally, train journeys were made, but it was a slow process, open to misunderstandings and delays. Husén was at the centre of the organisation of Swedish research and the energetic hub of activity took place either at his research centre, his office, or at his home in central Stockholm. As his responsibilities increased into transnational projects and depended on intensive labour in different loci across the project world, mainly in Europe and the US, and a relatively simple mix of mechanical and electro-mechanical machines.[5] His position in Sweden and in school reform gave his networking position some significance, leading to numerous travel flights and different centres of important communication.

The approach taken in this project is encapsulated in the following quotation, focused on circulation, distance, and materiality.

> there is the geographical understanding of circulation, which has been used to analyse how knowledge travels over vast distances. Second, there is a social interpretation in which circulation represents an alternative to a uni-directional model where knowledge is spread to passive consumers and audiences. Finally, there is a material approach to circulation, focusing on the movement of objects that underpin and transfigure knowledge.[6]

This approach is not a neat ordering of social interaction, especially within an increasingly complex series of related projects, nor is it a mere rough guide to unfolding sets of international events, personnel and places or a set of easily bordered periods. A new theoretical concept from historical sociology acknowledges the complex histories of ideas, goods, period, and place, the idea of 'entanglement' acknowledges how each of these 'elements also have their own history and how narratives fix these histories.'

---

[4] Thomas F. Gieryn, 'A Space for Place in Sociology,' *Annual Review of Sociology* 26 (2000).

[5] Wiebe Bijker, Thomas P. Hughes and Trevor Pinch, eds., *The Social Construction of Technological Systems: New Directions in the Sociology and History of Technology* (Cambridge: MIT Press, 1987).

[6] Johan Östling and David Larsson Heidenblad, 'Fulfilling the Promise of the History of Knowledge: Key Approaches for the 2020s,' *Journal for the History of Knowledge* 1, no. 1 (2020): 3.

1 ORGANISING THE FUTURE OF EDUCATIONAL RESEARCH IN POST-WAR... 5

Entangled history addresses issues of convergence, contingency, diverse, and unexpected collisions of forces and effects, which are all features of such entanglement. This orientation that acknowledges interlocking flows and forces has gained traction across the social sciences and humanities.[7] A history of the time and places which Husén travels through, and effects, which we have organised in an institutional way, should not obscure their entangled history.

NETWORKING

Consequently, a key feature of the post-war period, which increased in scope and complexity over time, is networking. Leading practitioners in educational research, mainly in the US, came out of the dominant tradition of quantitative research and the psychology of testing in the twentieth century. For Husén in Sweden in the mid-1940s, these researchers were often not contemporaries, they were an earlier generation, but, like other Europeans, he was their disciple. He had been cut off from their publications and contacts by the war but as it ended, he subscribed again to scientific publications, wrote letters, and went to the first of the post-war congresses, the 12th International Congress of Psychology in Edinburgh in 1948. The academics who attended these Congresses often worked alone or with an assistant. They were geographically distant from Stockholm and from each other, but Husén assumed a scientific collegiality with academics who had published their research or who he might have met on visits or on scholarly leave. He wrote to them, sent, and received published texts, answered queries, and hosted their Stockholm visits. An embryo network, it could develop in some cases to incorporate stronger links and become an 'invisible college' and include European and American scholars, in the person or by public or private communication. They constituted a reference group for each other. The concept of the 'invisible college' is based on bibliometrics, revealing scientific production between scientists who were often geographically distant from each other, but it also included informal relations and correspondence between them.[8] The

---

[7] Terri Seddon, Julie McLeod and Noah W. Sobe, 'Reclaiming Comparative Historical Sociologies of Education,' *Uneven Space-Times of Education: Historical Sociologies of Concepts, Methods and Practices (World Yearbook of Education 2018)*, ed. Julie McLeod, Noah W. Sobe and Terri Seddon (London: Routledge, 2017), 9.

[8] Alesia Zuccala, 'Modelling the Invisible College,' *Journal of the American Society for Information and Technology* 57, no. 2 (2006); Derek J. de Solla Price and Donald Beaver, 'Collaboration in an Invisible College,' *American Psychologist* 21, no. 11 (1966); Derek J. de Solla Price, *Little Science, Big Science*. (New York: Columbia University Press, 1963).

6   S. GREK ET AL.

'college' becomes more obvious when they achieve financial support, have joint activities, and may be able to meet.

Husén worked in the one area, which had a powerful and consistent tradition of experimental research, but increasingly he did so with an interest in comparing national data across borders. A sound methodology in research united his field of work and allowed entry into it, but he was restless with its limitations.[9] Husén was a student of empirical research, and it was part of his research mission to reinforce this approach to research. In the 1940s and 1950s, education as a discipline in most quarters in Europe had very remote ties with the behavioural sciences. So, although he had a thorough grounding in quantitative research, and a publication record within it, Husén desired to widen the scope of this work from studies of national intelligence or testing methods and break away from 'the unique or particular features of the country and the national system of education where the researchers were based.'[10] He was on a mission. Widening the perspective on knowledge from school requirements to the broad social, political, and cultural context of its production also meant that he would avoid the 'very nature of education as a field of practice,' which by its nature is provincial.[11] His career as a researcher moved towards comparative questions and inter-disciplinary interests. Travel became one of his key methods. Yet, he was able to do this because of a scientific research background which was international in character, with documented methods, and tests for reliability and validity, but which had, until that point, only been able to produce national (yet significant) results. For Husén, this was a new form of comparative education yet to be developed. It used internationally recognised quantitative methods of work with a wider remit and transgressing of national confines. The scientific background and operations of research networking, as it was gradually established, are of interest here, but equally, so are the social relations of the project and its researchers. Danziger, in his study of the field of psychology and its social relations, explained their indivisibility, the conceptual is embedded in the social:

[9] Torsten Husén, 'Talent, Opportunity, and Career: A Twenty-Six-Year Follow-Up,' *The School Review*, 76, no. 2 (1968).
[10] Torsten Husén, 'The International Context of Educational Research,' *Oxford Review of Education* 9, no. 1 (1983): 24.
[11] Husén, 'International Context,' 23.

1 ORGANISING THE FUTURE OF EDUCATIONAL RESEARCH IN POST-WAR... 7

the pattern of social relations among investigators and their subjects, the norms of appropriate practices in the relevant research community, the kinds of knowledge interests that prevail at different times and places, and the relations of the research community within the broader social context that sustains it.[12]

The boundaries of this work are not clear cut, they are 'ambiguous, flexible, historically changing, contextually variable, internally inconsistent, and sometimes disputed.'[13] So, Husén's career, with its wide range of contexts, varied means and circumstances of production, and over time, diverse academic and policy contexts, does not allow for a simple narrative of routine actions and chronological accounts or a naïve version of the life worlds of Husén and his colleagues. Torsten Husén through his writings and actions appears to have been a catalyst and enabler, he was omnipresent, yet his roles and actions were constantly shifting. Depending on the angle, the context, and the time, Husén appears to shape shift. He is not a different person, but he presents in diverse ways. He appears to be, and to represent, the diversity of the research meetings, tasks, and times in the emergence of educational research. With his colleagues, he had to manage the increasing problematics of an advanced, long-distance project. The historical context here is a crucial backdrop to our work, and the decades that saw the slow yet methodical construction of education, comparative data for policymaking, the rise of cross-border and international comparisons and the role of a modern, comprehensive education in these processes. At this time, they are associated with a field of educational research which saw itself as the pathway towards the governing of 'a better society.' Such imaginaries of education have been in existence for centuries, nevertheless, the notion that education science can and should be informing the making of education policy was an innovative idea in the mid-twentieth century. Husén is both a significant actor in, and an exemplar and symbol of, the growth of educational research and policy in the late twentieth century.

Similarly innovative was the concept of cross-border research. Although ideas had always travelled, post-war Europe education science—with Husén at its helm—becomes systematic, organised, and institutionalised;

---

[12] Kurt Danzinger, *Constructing the Subject: Historical Origins of Psychological Research* (Cambridge: Cambridge University Press, 1990), 5.

[13] Thomas F. Gieryn, *Cultural Boundaries of Science: Credibility on the Line.* (Chicago: University of Chicago Press, 1999), 792.

8   S. GREK ET AL.

it is materialised through the controversies and consensus of expert networks; and it becomes legitimised in institutions, through the successful set-up of education research organisations like the IEA (International Association for the Evaluation of Educational Achievement) which still influence the education research arena. As it organised, its purposes change. While individual researchers in their national 'institutes' seem initially to work with like-minded quantitative researchers, who they were familiar with in various ways, this altered as they began to accumulate new partners and research data. Their ambitions grew closer to Husén's own aims and experience. They saw their work as affecting policy and not research data alone. Thus, they were transformed into what Stone calls policy networks. They are characterised by:

> *shared scientific understanding* as their prime motivation is to create and advance knowledge as well as to share, spread and often use that knowledge to inform policy and apply to practice. The expertise, scientific knowledge, data and method analysis and evaluations that help constitute knowledge networks provide the experts within them with some authority to inform policy.[14]

The practice of a network may consolidate and begin to increase its ambitions into a knowledge system, with aims that went beyond data collection towards policy change: in Stone's view, research becomes clearly coordinated, large amounts of data are amassed, and its results are disseminated. The network is changed by the pressures upon it for results for policy, and it is amassing large amounts of data. In addition, searching for funds means it must show policy change and not just intellectual endeavour.

> Global knowledge networks create and transfer knowledge—scientific, community-based and policy relevant—as well as the necessary hardware and finances to support acquisition and implementation ... such as knowledge networks operate within a shared system of knowledge creation and transmission, while the practices of individual members are informed by the histories, politics, and ecologies of the national and local places in which they work.[15]

---

[14] Diane Stone, *Knowledge Actors and Transnational Governance. The Private Public Policy Nexus in the Global Agora* (London: Palgrave Macmillan, 2013), 6.

[15] Janice Gross Stein and Richard Stren, 'Knowledge Networks in Global Society: Pathways to Development,' in *Networks of Knowledge: Collaborative Innovation in International Learning*, ed. Janice Grosse Stein et al. (Toronto: University of Toronto Press, 2001), 6–7.

DISEMBEDDED

There is no necessary progression between networks and knowledge networks as the latter may develop as experience, opportunity, and national circumstance allow. Husén moves between research and policy, across knowledge networks, at different points in his work. Our particular concern here is with the rise of the international knowledge networking through a focus on the technical, value-based, political, and cognitive processes that brought previously dispersed scientists into an organised, cosmopolitan, and—crucially—legitimate disembedded scientific laboratory that slowly began to emerge for policy during the post-war years. It is possible to describe advanced networks, distinguishable from 'an invisible college' or a research community, by the need for classification, standardisation and expert training, and the complex technologies and work, in the following ways. This next stage of networking need commodities, including self-help manuals, training texts or expert systems; organisations, with the detailed division of tasks and the ordering of their performance according to bureaucratic rules and procedures; and individuals, highly trained and socialised in accordance with an agreed ethical and disciplinary code.[16] Most importantly, it has to operate with the local and central management of complexity over distance with speed. The greater the distance between members, the more essential are the network features described by Merz which makes the point that laboratories are located in a physical space but that they exist within a 'disembedded' space as well, created through communications and travel it is determined by the interactive and manipulative practices which accumulate around a research project.

What is a laboratory in a theoretical science? And what then, is its 'place'? The notion of a laboratory developed in laboratory studies centres around the 'local context' of scientific work [the 'local situatedness' of research practices, the 'local construction' of scientific facts]. This local context is often anchored in in physical space. I propose to extend the notion of laboratory by taking into account that the joint work in numerous collaborations in theoretical physics is [at least] temporarily detached from a single physical location and 'takes place' in disembedded as well as embedded locales.[17]

[16] Terry Johnson, 'Expertise and the State,' in *Foucault's New Domains* Gane, ed. Mike Gane and Terry Johnsson (Routledge, London, 1993).
[17] Martina Merz, "Nobody Can Force You When You Are across the Ocean': Face to Face and E-mail Exchanges between Theoretical Physicists,' in *Making Space for Science: Territorial Themes in the Shaping of Knowledge*, ed. Crosbie Smith and Jon Agar (London: Palgrave Macmillan, 1998), 320.

The Husén archive changes across his different activities from a series of personal and professional documents into source material for the study of the development of social science research beyond fixed time and space dimensions, that extends science beyond individual ideas, researchers, environments, institutions, and universities. These are practices that create, mobilise, sustain, and challenge relations between actors in innovations, knowledge creation, and various social activities.[18] In other words, the archive represents the socio-material manifestation not only of the intellectual trajectory of a key education actor but of a whole scientific field.[19] The idea of the disembedded laboratory draws attention to spatially oriented histories of scientific thought and practice, symbolised in Husén's wide spaces of work, where knowledge is produced in the interaction of humans, objects and spaces, and in constant practices.[20]

Latour and Woolgar describe the production of scientific facts as a complex fabric of everyday hard work in the laboratory, including reference cultures, scientific prestige, estimates, curriculum vitae, publications, group dynamics, and other processes.[21] Research is, therefore, according to them, to a large extent a social activity. This way of studying the microprocesses of doing research is very pertinent to our work presented in this book. What does a social science 'laboratory' look like, indeed can the term 'laboratory' be applied to the area of educational research? Husén developed a specialist institute in Stockholm at the same time as other European institutes, sometimes with American support, were creating national sites for research. Sweden's role as a neutral and peaceful nation enabled Husén to express his own style of leadership within the new scholarly meetings and institute linkages. On the other hand, Stockholm was a significant place of work in itself and reliable site of objective results and

---

[18] Bruno Latour, *Science in Action: How to Follow Scientists and Engineers Through Society* (Cambridge: Harvard University Press, 1987).

[19] Bruno Latour, *Reassembling the Social: An Introduction to Actor-Network Theory* (Oxford: Oxford University Press, 2005); Pierre Bourdieu, *The Field of Cultural Production: Essays on Art and Literature* (New York: Columbia University Press, 1993).

[20] Wiebe Bijker, Thomas P. Hughes and Trevor Pinch, eds., *The Social Construction of Technological Systems: New Directions in the Sociology and History of Technology* (Cambridge: MIT Press, 1987).

[21] Bruno Latour and Steve Woolgar, *Laboratory Life: The Construction of Scientific Facts* (Princeton: Princeton University Press, 1979/1986).

1 ORGANISING THE FUTURE OF EDUCATIONAL RESEARCH IN POST-WAR... 11

became the centre of a dispersed and moving international network, or in other words, a 'disembedded laboratory.' Using empirical case studies, the mundane and everyday practices through which, eventually, ideas and fact-making are stabilised, and systems are established, will become discernible as shown in the following chapters.

A laboratory implies a place of rational action, and disembedded implies a concern for distance and work over space and time. A brief synopsis, produced by Husén in 1979, reviews some of the problems that a disembedded research network had at that time.[22] They had no internationally valid standards, and instruments had to be developed that were cross-nationally valid, could be applied uniformly over a range of countries with different school systems. Data produced had to be made accessible so that its processing and analyses could be undertaken in one place, which in the early years meant the only place it could be placed on punched cards. In addition, 'lines of authority and responsibility' produced across a new network sometimes produced conflicts. Finally, all these processes, anticipated to be technical, were also political, as they crossed borders of countries and funders, and so different interests. The ways that research and its methods were borrowed, shared, and standardised among a range of heterogeneous institutes, scholars and traditions is a major feature of this internationalisation, and one in which Husén played a major part, from the early days of cross-national work and onto his editing of a global encyclopaedia of education. The embedding of knowledge into transportable forms was crucial to international collaboration and usefulness. Therefore, texts, methods, procedures, and reports are important elements of the study, and while these are often not preserved, they are found in quantity in the Husén archives.

In the sociology of knowledge or history of ideas, knowledge production is viewed in similar, mediating terms: 'the day-to-day actions and processes through which the producers of social knowledge actually go about the on-the-groundwork of making, evaluating, and disseminating

---

[22] Torsten Husén, 'An International Research Venture in Retrospect: The IEA Surveys,' *Comparative Education Review* 23, no. 3 (1979).

the kinds of social knowledge that they are involved in producing.'[23] The different forms of network or relations that Husén worked within began to accumulate major data on national school systems. Husén found in the 1960s and beyond that his advice was sought about international ventures or that he involved himself in others. For example, the formation of another international organisation, the International Institute for Educational Planning, which we return to in some depth in Chap. 4, was linked to UNESCO but was focused on educational planning. It encouraged collaboration worked for affiliation of development organisations. The IIEP worked in a different way to the IEA (Chap. 3), it was more concerned with governance structures and diplomacy during a period of financial stringency. In a series of books, beginning in the mid-1970s, Husén engages with the world of educational research in a new way, that is, not through projects or institutional association, but as a consultant. He is invited to help organise a seminar in Aspen, Colorado, as we describe in Chap. 5, in which several elite American intellectuals and writers wanted to consider the role of the school in future years. Husén's cosmopolitan experience of a data-rich series of projects researching education, in the IEA, combined with his willingness to engage in thought-provoking discussions, had become known more widely. He emerged writing a book on the 'School in Question' and a few years later on the 'Learning Society'; they are more polemical, future-looking, and not bound by project results.[24] In later years, Husén returned to studies of international education, editing the International Encyclopedia of Education (IEE). In this work, Husén and colleagues, a number of academic editors, involved more than 500 authors from over 100 countries to contribute to the 10-volume thick encyclopaedia, consisting of a multilevel subject index with 45,000 entries and 160 overarching entry topics divided into 25 sections. Nearly 1448 larger articles were written. The scale of the project and its success in producing so many national studies, naturally involved many ethnocentric decisions, being biased and at the same time rejecting bias in its editorial processes. His work as an editor-in-chief for the encyclopaedia together with Neville Postlethwaite is described in Chap. 6.

---

[23] Charles Camic, Neil Gross and Michèle Lamont, eds., *Social Knowledge in the Making* (Chicago: University of Chicago Press, 2011), 6.

[24] Torsten Husén, *The Learning Society* (London: Methuen, 1974); Torsten Husén, *The Learning Society Revisited* (Oxford: Pergamon, 1986); Torsten Husén, *The School in Question: A Comparative Study of the School and its Future in Western Societies* (London: Oxford University Press, 1979).

GOVERNING

One of the main influences for the internationalisation of education research was the explicit aim to inform policy. Many parts of Europe had their economies destroyed and their populations displaced. The scale of problems led to a search for solutions and successful models. Academic and technical workers were being mobilised and supported across their economies, and similarly in the field of education. While governments saw them as having a value, they were small and unevenly distributed individual professors, small departments, or little research institutes. Sometimes, they were connected by a shared literature of books on assessment and testing. Governments wanted advice and ideas, and research, on their education systems. Our emphasis here is on the need for governments to acquire knowledge and expertise on education planning and their dependence on these scarce experts. Our focus is on the processes of knowledge construction, produced by post-war actors, their sites and associations, and uses methods and concepts derived from transnational histories. Particular sites or hubs, with particular actors that are mobilised by policy interests as well as their own scholarly interests, play a prominent role in this process. A consequence of the post-war period was an uneven but prevailing association between national institutes and the flourishing post-war statistical and survey expertise: this led to a gradual involvement in national governmental tasks by education experts and the standardisation of educational research and commissions. Overcoming organisational and technical problems allowed the research and its production to become global.

The use of an expert, like Husén, is an interesting phenomenon in relation to the development of the modern state. Experts are bound within their world of technical problems, professional community obligations, urgent tasks and agreements, and funding. They accumulate knowledge about systems, and agreements about the nature and conceptualisation of nations, systems, and schooling. They agree to common and unfolding standards about how the problem can be defined, studied, and what should be excluded. They produce abstract and commensurable units, enabling exchange across borders and places, and producing a newly transparent domain.[25]

---

[25] Martin Lawn, 'Europeanizing Through Expertise: From Scientific Laboratory to the Governing of Education,' in *Uneven Space-Times of Education: Historical Sociologies of Concepts, Methods and Practices (World Yearbook of Education 2018)*, ed. Julie McLeod et al. (London: Routledge, 2017).

14 S. GREK ET AL.

The building of scientific networks seems to rest on circumstances not commonly considered as scientific routines. Through Husén's work, and his close editor colleagues, we can see how international networks work, how social knowledge is produced in these networks, how the relation between societal internationalisation and the internationalisation of social sciences is developed, and finally how educational research functioned as an engine in the modernisation of education systems. The informality of their organisation, the complexity of their knowledge relations and exchanges, the hybridity of their institutional associations, combine with their overall interdependence, to produce a distinctive form of governance in educational research. This form of governance in education cannot be understood as simply instrumental in transmitting policy or in mediating it. Policy is made in this process of governing through knowledge. The sum of this space of flows in education can be portrayed, as a space comprised of organising networks, where territorial proximity has been replaced by network virtual proximity, and its actors exchange information and expertise within trust relations.[26]

International Actors, Networks, and the Modernisation of Education

There is a danger, which we hope to have avoided, that Husén's research career appears as a straightforward narrative of work and engagement, and it represents in its various stages, a clear developmental line of progression, in this case from networks to policy networks and to complex 'disembedded' networks or moving from the national to the European to the global, or from research engagement to research management. Using Husén's career as a tool for exploring the way that national and international research changed and became interleaved, as his actions and interests became synonymous with the subject and the publications he was involved with began to determine or shape subjects of his study. Many of the actors he worked with came and went but in doing so they reveal the embedded nature of growing research communities. What may appear as loosely connected or even coincidental events or relations accumulate and are made serviceable in the act of governing research at a distance, a growing

[26] Lawn, 'Europeanizing.'

practical necessity in the post-war rise of transnational research projects. Conference acquaintances progress into writing partnerships, and onto invitations and joint proposals.

In this work, Torsten Husén appears as a key figure, and the networks he forms and participates in gained some real influence over the modernisation of educational systems throughout the world.

CHAPTER 2

Forming Transnational Networks: The Early 1950s in Europe

An essential element in the formation of networks of researchers, the transferring of knowledge, the creation of joint work, and the construction of a common policy agenda, took place in the conferences and meetings of 1950s educational researchers. Husén used the early post-war years to travel, make useful contacts, and finding common ground with them about the aims of skills of research. An issue which emerges from his travels is that educational research was a weak area and that in itself needed to develop fast. Combined with his anti-provincialism, we can see the problems he reveals and engages with around Europe, mainly through UNESCO meetings, to lead him to new solutions in strengthening this community.

The development of European and American Networks follows the early years of the growth of a national and post-national education research community in Europe. By the late 1940s, the US had become a major force in Western Europe. The problem of modernising and democratising post-war Germany, in the American Zone of Occupation, was the first step in the 1940s to bring into being a commonality of purpose and explanation between disparate groups of academics, many working in war-torn societies. This commonality was produced through a process of selection and recommendation, with an emphasis on the new and meritocratic techniques of testing and selection. This increasingly dominant trend in educational psychology, especially in the US and the UK, was used to shape and unite European researchers, and in so doing, knowingly build a united

© The Author(s), under exclusive license to Springer Nature Switzerland AG 2024
S. Grek et al., *The World as a Laboratory*, Global Histories of Education, https://doi.org/10.1007/978-3-031-68090-8_2

17

Europe (or at least, at its Western edge). In this chapter, we describe the importance of international congresses for the creation and exchange of scientific data between scholars and we will show how actors such as Husén functioned as transnational 'connectors.'

In the early 1950s, Torsten Husén had emerged from the tight constraints of limited cross-border movements and influences of a wartime Sweden. He was still defining himself as a military psychologist, working in education testing. At the end of the decade, he had attended several major psychology congresses, he had been invited to significant research meetings in Germany, the UK, and the USA; he had organised a substantial European conference in Sweden on school reform, and become closely involved with the work of the UNESCO Institute in Hamburg. But by the decade's end, he saw himself as part of a new and important comparative education movement and defined himself as a comparative educationist. The expertise which drew him into international exchanges, mainly in Europe and the US, was to a large extent based upon his interests and work on Swedish school reform, which became part of a pack of skills which he could draw upon, based on this intensive but short career.

This expertise in educational research and testing gradually allows him entry into European and American departments and institutes, which consolidates his position and that of his research institute in Sweden. Throughout this decade, he adapts and transforms his 'position' in Sweden. Chronologically and cumulatively, he is a testing expert, an academic researcher, research manager, national reform expert and he gains a semi-independent work status, becomes a national representative in European forums and develop as a new form of knowledge entrepreneur in education and research. By the early 1960s, Husén has almost lost the identity of the testing expert and become a self-described comparative educationist and crests the wave of this new shift in research. To explain his journey, this chapter will explore the emerging community in post-war European education research, the use of the newly created UNESCO Institute for Education in Hamburg, the first international education research conference, the rise of research institutes and finally, the major UNESCO study group on school evaluation which acts as a foundational stage in the creation of the International Association for the Evaluation of Educational Achievement, the IEA.

In the 1950s, Europe was still emerging from the chaos and destruction of the world war. Reconstructing services and society in most European countries was followed by a concern for the construction of new

2 FORMING TRANSNATIONAL NETWORKS: THE EARLY 1950S IN EUROPE 19

forms of society. Alongside the economy, social services and housing, the education system was a priority, and with the rebuilding of their education systems came the problem of constructing a system fit for an emerging and future society. The shift from a simple mass education system and a limited elite secondary provision, both of which were viewed as imperfect, needed policies for reform, and they needed research and inquiry. Opportunity and social pressure were constrained by inadequate information. Moreover, the national and European context began to transform, and adjustments were required. Europe was divided and turned into adversarial regions. In the West, the United States was influential and provided funding for willing and mutually beneficial actions among its allies. The norms of individual states, protected by borders and interests, were slowly altered by trade and political agreements and most of all, by the growth of regional and international institutions. In the education area, one of the significant new institutions was UNESCO, the United Nations Educational, Scientific and Cultural Organization, which was based in Europe, to act as a United Nations agency for cooperation in education [and science and culture]. Although its headquarters was in Paris, Hamburg was the site of UNESCO's specialist Institute for Education (UIE). With ambitious aims but with very limited staffing, the Hamburg Institute turned towards community building and expert support. It would provide a new scale of work for national specialists in education, and it would, with limited means, provide funding for meetings and travel. This was a radical break with pre-war Europe where European contacts were inadequate and research support was rare.

UNESCO encouraged selected waves of education professionals into focused meetings on educational issues in Hamburg and Paris in the 1950s, including Torsten Husén. Through his work and travel, we can begin to understand the relation between place and space in research, the shift in disciplinary influences, science and policy linkages, and the growth of the international as a significant research effect on the national, and vice versa. This gradual flow of people and ideas across borders has tangible effects. Indeed, while still holding onto the idea of place—of construction, of values, of practices—the idea of space is important in analysing cross-border travel, the movement and impact of ideas and objects, and the way space is imagined (in relation to nation, community, work, or project). These two elements are bound together in our understanding of the flows of ideas, objects, and practices in education sciences. Place [the setting or location] is often the laboratory or institute, widely conceived as the

20   S. GREK ET AL.

practice and discussions of a group or network, from which they communicate and exchange with other places and their actors elsewhere. This is the space they work across—literally—but more often imaginatively, thinking about shared work or projects. Space is not a container but a medium for action, and a taken-for-granted field of action. The new form of international endeavour allows the researcher to stay embedded locally but influenced in work and ideas, by the international settings. There is a new scale of work about its real and imagined arena, its methods and data, and its reconsideration of the nature of the discipline. Consequences in our period include the formation or strengthening of national research institutes to engage in the international, Europe-based expert meetings and projects, and the way that this affects the structuring of work and posts nationally and creates new ones internationally.

A First Major Education Conference

In 1952, Husén was invited, after some pressure from himself, to a meeting in Frankfurt, in which

> scholars from Europe and the USA interacted with about twenty German professors and lectures in a series of seminars. I then continued to keep in touch for many years with several of these German colleagues: we have exchanged publications and visited each other. The aim, I assume, was to infuse new ideas and concepts into German researchers, after their long isolation.[1]

Later, Husen explained further what the Frankfurt meeting represented and its value for him:

> They had the idea that German professors needed an internal injection. A multiplying effect was expected by bringing all of the professors of education together who were full professors (ordinarius). There was only one full professor in each discipline at each university. There were only about 24–25 in all, and then you had some professors of the Pädagogische Hochschulen, the institutions of teacher education. Bringing them together and spending almost two months with colleagues from other countries

---

[1] Torsten Husén, *An Incurable Academic: Memoirs of a Professor* (Oxford: Pergamon Press, 1983), 154.

2 FORMING TRANSNATIONAL NETWORKS: THE EARLY 1950S IN EUROPE   21

would widen their horizons. From abroad there were six colleagues from the United States and six from European countries.[2]

The meeting in Frankfurt was the last of four major workshops in Germany in 1952, but the first one funded by the newly established Allied High Commission (also known as the High Commission for Occupied Germany, HICOG), representing the US, the UK, and France, and the newly established Institute for Educational Research. It was held in their refurbished ex-school building, and it was intended to symbolise the formation of a base for empirical and comparative research in Germany, which was of importance to the US and to Dr. Erich Hylla, the director. The leader of the workshop, Dr. Schultze, had spent May and June visiting 76 West German and Berlin institutes, universities, and individuals to discuss their interests in educational psychology and their possible participation in the workshop. At the same time, US Embassies were aiming to secure from each European country the presence of a leading professor of educational psychology.

In the archive, there is a conference report describing that two weeks were spent among the staff members representing ten countries on planning joint workshops for the final four weeks of the meeting. The topics for the workshop they agreed on were:

1. Problems of selection, admission, differentiation as related to schools and universities
2. Social interaction and social development in schools and universities
3. Human development and the educative process
4. Problems of counselling and guidance as related to schools and education in general
5. Applications of the findings of investigations of learning to the work in schools and universities
6. Teacher training
7. Educational psychology and education for international understanding

Topics 1–5 were the subjects of discussion groups during the first fortnight. At the beginning of the second fortnight, topics 6 and 7 were added at the request of several persons and topic 5 was omitted. Three discussion

---

[2] Arlid Tjeldvoll and Hans G. Lingens, eds., *Torsten Husén: Conversations in Comparative Education* (Bloomington: Phi Delta Kappa Educational Foundation, 2000), 24.

groups met in the morning and three in the afternoon during the second fortnight.[3]

Then the actual workshop took part, involving a larger number of representatives from German psychology and education. The workshop had five overarching objectives:

The following objectives were implicit in the minds of members of the planning committee in developing their proposals for Workshop activities:

1. To promote the exchange among members of the Workshop of scientific information and knowledge within the areas of educational psychology and human development. This exchange of scientific knowledge was to go in all directions, that is between the psychologists of all of the ten nations represented in the workshop. Maximum communication by the non-authoritarian free exchange of ideas was sought.
2. To promote the exchange of ideas about the most effective means of communicating scientific knowledge to prospective teachers and to teachers in service.
3. To promote the exchange of ideas about the implications of scientific knowledge for such problems of educational administrative policy as admission to different types of schools, bases for classifying children, grade level standards and special services for guidance, for clinical work and for remedial teaching.
4. To communicate knowledge of 'workshop' organization, procedure and techniques by securing maximum participation of all Workshop member in the process of this Workshop itself.
5. To build international professional and personal relationships that would facilitate the further exchange od [*sic*] scientific knowledge and of educational ideas.[4]

Evidently, exchange of information and knowledge was central to the participants, and to facilitate long-lasting relations for further collaborations on education.

---

[3] Office of the U.S. High Commission for Germany, Office or Public Affairs, Division of Cultural Affairs, *A cooperative report of the workshop 'Modern psychologies and German education' held at Die Hochschule für International Pädagogische Forschung, Frankfurt am Main, August 4–29, 1952* (The Husén archive, 2.198), 28.

[4] Office of the U.S. High Commission for Germany, *A cooperative report* (The Husén archive, 2.198), 30.

2 FORMING TRANSNATIONAL NETWORKS: THE EARLY 1950S IN EUROPE   23

For the US, the importance of educational psychology, pre-eminently an American subject in their view, would assist the creation of a democratic and equal society in Germany, underpinned by testing. The policies that the American administration encouraged in its Zone reflected American liberal education in its approach. In schools, a free education system and equal educational opportunities was to be offered to 'every German child capable of learning' in order to create and sustain democratic government.[5] Using the US as the model, they pushed hard for democratic practices and accountability in education.[6]

In addition to the six educational psychologists from the United States, 13 came from Austria, Denmark, England, Holland, Italy, Norway, Sweden, and Switzerland. The 38 German participants, coming from all parts of the German Federal Republic, were from leading German universities, teacher education institutions, psychological clinics, and test development institutes. For Husén, in subsequent years, this meeting was one of the most important events in the internationalisation of his work. The archived correspondence witness that he would send his books or articles to those international colleagues he wished to remain in touch with, he would ask for copies of their papers and he would explore ways of visiting them.

The Frankfurt workshop is influential on him in several ways. It involved a direct relation to some important American psychologists in education, who he corresponded with and met again soon after on his first American tour. It was also a chance to discuss with German colleagues, in a language he spoke well, about testing, democracy, and organising schools. He was at the foundation year of the new German Institute of Educational Research Hochschule für Internationale Pädagogische Forschung (HiPF). His own later modelling of a research institute in Stockholm was most probably influenced by his experience in Frankfurt.

The Frankfurt workshop was certainly a useful step in the development of like-minded and useful colleagues in Germany, the US, and elsewhere, but it is possible that it was, unremarked by Husén, a useful introduction to the idea of the research Institute. How much he knew about Teachers College, the very modern model of a research institute, we don't know,

---

[5] Office of Military Government for Germany, US (OMGUS), Education and Cultural Division, Information Bulletin, September 1947 'Education for Democracy', 3 pp.

[6] William D. Wall, 'Research and Educational Action,' *International Review of Education* 16, no. 4 (1970): 488.

24   S. GREK ET AL.

but the Workshop at Frankfurt was an important influence for his ideas of democratic education, educational research, internationalism, and a plan for an Institute. Husén must have thought, when in Sweden, that the events in Germany, involving the US and their German Zone planning, would be helpful transferring this modern research organisation back home. HiPF is just one of the post-war research institutes, on a similar model to Teachers College, although without its foundation funds, formed in European countries, for example, in Belgium, England, Finland, France, Scotland, and Switzerland. They functioned nationally but by networks and institutional links form up international associations.

In the decade after the Second World War, a definite willingness of governments to support and utilise research in education which appeared to be a belief that the studies would be useful to the formulation and conduct of educational policy. Government agencies turned to research workers for 'answers' to what was considered to be basically the 'scientific' problems involved in planning educational reforms. Policy-orientated research increased rapidly.[7] For Husén, the Frankfurt meeting prefigures this new world of educational research and research-based policy in which he played a significant role.

A Post-war Borderless Research Area in Europe

In 1952, the UNESCO Institute for Education in Hamburg was founded. Its role in supporting and organising experts in education across Europe (and increasingly globally) has not been recognised as much as its pioneering work on education, its values and organisation, in the 1950s and 1960s. Following the Second World War, Western Europe had major challenges to manage in its reconstruction. Schooling was a problem. The destruction of schools, a dearth of teachers, and the reorganisation of education systems affected many countries for many years. The importance of collecting and analysing information about state education made a necessity of the formation and shaping of expert seminars and networks, and

[7] The 1967 Plowden Committee in Great Britain, the German Education Commission 1966–75, and the School Commission in Sweden established in 1946 are cases in point. Gilbert de Landsheere, 'IEA and UNESCO: A History of Working Coorperation,' in UNESCO: Fifty Years of Education [CD-ROM] (Paris: UNESCO, 1997); Martin Lawn, 'Governing Through Assessment Data in the UK During the late 20th Century: An Extreme Outlier?,' in Assessment Cultures: Historical Perspectives, ed. Cristiana Alarcón López and Martin Lawn (New York: Peter Lang, 2018).

2 FORMING TRANSNATIONAL NETWORKS: THE EARLY 1950S IN EUROPE 25

which led to the rise of a number of national research institutes in post-war Europe. The first intentions were clearly pacifist. Coming out of war and Nazism, according to the statutes, there was an obligation to create a centre in Germany to allow German educators and those from other countries to compare and exchange ideas and practices, and to undertake research in the sciences of education (comparative, pedagogy, psychology, and sociology).[8] A confluence of problems and opportunities across the war-damaged landscape of Europe, combined with favoured governing interventions, created a series of comparable acts which grew together with strong outcomes in the governing of education, in Europe, and then more globally. The scientific question about what is necessary or what works became interwoven with the governing question about what has to be done and whose expertise is needed. From the insistent necessity of managing an Occupied Germany to the support of national institutes and actors into a European association, the emergence of research agreements and common standards happens over a relatively short time in the late 1940s and the 1950s.

The foundation of the UNESCO Institute aided the formation of networks of national, European education experts who were drawn from their recently established national centres and institutes. In its early period—from the early 1950s to the early 1960s—it was home for expert meetings and planning of research projects, devised by research experts, who, in retrospect, can be seen as providing the basis for what was to become a much more closely woven European research space in the following decade. It was more than a functional response to crisis and policy or a talking shop. In 2004, Neville Postlethwaite (1933–2009), a major collaborator and friend of Torsten Husén, described it as an organised meeting place, a European laboratory, for the post-war generation of national research workers emerging into significance in their national arenas. In various meetings taking place in the mid- to late 1950s, allowed them to discuss and deliberate upon some significant issues in European societies and education.[9] A growing and significant involvement by Torsten Husén by the late 1950s in the Hamburg explorations in curriculum and learning, and its move from seminars into project planning, was a recognition that his skills and interests in empirical research and school

---

[8] Roger Gal, 'L'Institut de l'Unesco pour l'Education à Hambourg. Dix ans d'activité,' *International Review of Education* 8, no. 1 (1962).

[9] T. Neville Postlethwaite, *Monitoring Educational Achievement* (Paris: UNESCO, 2004).

reform could find a home there. And even more so, it would be a useful move into large-scale research organisation. For good reason, this was to be read by Husén as an invitation to join.

A consequence of the post-war period was an uneven but prevailing association between national institutes and the flourishing post-war statistical and survey expertise. A new range of educational research experts was added to the professors of education in place, and their involvement in national governmental tasks. A major consolidation of pre-war work in quantitative research becomes tied into a significant cross-border European governing effect. Educational research is one of the ways in which Europe becomes more governable. It does so because of the growing relation between national scholars and institutes, emerging Cold War and European governing trends, and the creation of common knowledge and standards in educational research. Early scholars' meetings, and their subsequent research together, created standardised subjects and research methods, and put in place a community of experts working across diverse statist jurisdictions, systems, and forms of organisation. The importance of this work in the 1950s and early 1960s is in the relation between the professional expertise and solidarities of senior researchers and the formation of common standards and knowledge. The most powerful transnational area in educational research in 1950 was in the related fields of intelligence testing and factorial studies.

In an early UNESCO study of the training and organisation of psychological services in member states, organised by William D. Wall, at this time Head of Education and Child Development Unit at UNESCO 1951–1956, it was clear that in this dominant area of educational research and of real importance in the reconstruction of education, it had been undertaken by professors of education as part of professional training in the past (p. 78). The group of experts involved in the report contended that there should be strong links between practitioners in the field and a 'laboratory or research team' so that the scientific study was connected to practice.[10] Across a range of suggested subjects included 'difficult and failing children, for educational guidance at entry to school, at transfer to secondary school, and in choice of studies or of employment,'[11] the experts

[10] William D. Wall, *Psychological Services for Schools* (Hamburg: UNESCO Institute for Education Publications, 1956), 131.

[11] Wall, *Psychological Services*, 74.

wanted 'considerably expanded finance' for research,'[12] carefully planned experiments, and 'one controlled pilot project' in each country.[13]

Most research conducted in the decade immediately after the war—although the amount was increasing—was still artisanal and individual in the pre-war sense. Most of it was directed to fairly specific problems, mainly of a practical classroom type, or, like the work of the Geneva school, to the development by empirical means of a broad theory of cognitive development. Its influence was mainly upon teaching method; until the 1950's little of it touched directly upon major issues of educational organization, administration or policy. A striking exception was the immense amount of work carried out by psychologists in England in connection with the allocation procedures used to guide and select children for the different forms of secondary education provided under the 1944 Education Act.[14]

The formation of research capacities at the European level, in transitory or heterogeneous networks, as well as in more settled hubs, was to become important in the gradual formation of a connected European space for educational research. Later, Husén described the context of educational research in this period in this way:

In the development of the intellectual community of educational research and the disciplines that formed the basis for scholarly studies in education, there is a marked break between the period before and the period after the Second World War. In the extra-scientific conditions which affect educational research, mainly, the willingness of governments to support and utilise research in education, the dividing line should perhaps be drawn at least a decade later. Studies in education commissioned and supported by governments in the belief that they would be useful for the making and carrying out of educational policy began to become more frequent in the late 1950s and early 1960s. No doubt, the 1960s were the 'golden years' of educational research on both sides of the Atlantic.[15]

Wall's analysis, in a history of post-war psychology of education, was similar. Post-war Europe attempted wide-ranging 'reforms' emphasising

[12] Wall, *Psychological Services*, 131.
[13] Wall, *Psychological Services*, 132.
[14] Wall, 'Research and Educational Action, 487.
[15] Torsten Husén, 'Educational Research and the Making of Policy in Education: An International Perspective,' *Minerva* 21, no. 1 (1983): 81.

28   S. GREK ET AL.

age, ability, and aptitude, irrespective of social or economic background. A concern about contemporary examination procedures and secondary school selection led into studies of new forms of assessment and suitable curricula.

> This led to classification of objectives for which taxonomies were developed, and a move towards criterion-referenced testing began. Since 1950, worldwide momentum has been gathering to develop educational research.[16]

The immediate post-war period in Europe and elsewhere was marked by attempts at wide-ranging 'reforms' of educational systems. The U.K. Education Act of 1944, to some extent, set a pattern with its emphasis on education according to 'age and ability and aptitude,' its attempts at widening educational opportunity irrespective of social or economic background, and its stress upon secondary education for all. Similar attempts followed in France, Belgium, the Netherlands, and Scandinavia. The American idea of democratic education was associated with the idea of efficiency and pupil testing was a core element in it. Factorial analysis, quantitative data, and large-scale research projects was the means by which UNESCO projects could be envisioned. The first task was to bring together or find surviving post-war key research actors, a task in which the Americans, the British, and the Swedes were crucial.

THE FIRST EDUCATION EXPERT CONFERENCES IN THE 1950S

Central to the argument of this chapter is analysing cross-border travel, that is, the movement and impact of ideas and objects. Here the growing of expert conferences after the World War II played an important part. While the Hamburg UIE was steadily getting down to work with its few resources, the United States, a major financial supporter, was concerned with

> an inherent tension between the internationalism of UNESCO's aims and its practical impact on realms such as national education, which are 'by

---

[16] William D. Wall, 'Psychology of Education,' *International Review of Education* 25, no. 2/3 (1979): 367.

2 FORMING TRANSNATIONAL NETWORKS: THE EARLY 1950S IN EUROPE   29

nature parochial' and are implicated in the forging of national differences rather than internationalism.[17]

This was a misreading of what was happening in the Hamburg IoE early seminars and yet must have placed the activities under pressure. Until the 1950s, few researches touched directly upon major issues of educational organisation, administration, or policy. From 1952, the new Institute in Hamburg had created a series of expert seminars on different aspects of schooling and adult education. These seminars or expert working groups usually took several days, with a leadership responsible for a publication of the findings or a summative report of the discussion. These meetings usually lasted six days and worked through stages; the identification of the issue or common interest; the definition of the problem; assembling material and preparing a discussion paper; discussion in groups; and a printed report, followed by further studies. The first study in 1952, held in Paris, was on the mental health of European children, which led onto meetings on school psychological services and school failure. These meetings were often organised by W. D. Wall.

In early summer 1956, an international study group was created by UNESCO to examine the causes of school dropout and 11 experts from Australia, Austria, Belgium, Egypt, the Federal Republic of Germany, the United Kingdom, Sweden, the United States, and USSR met in Hamburg. These specialists were described as

highly qualified personalities both by their knowledge of child psychology and by their experience of educational problems. Each of them observed attentively the children who did not succeed in school and studied the measures tending to prevent or remedy school failures.[18]

Prior to the meeting, the UNESCO Secretariat had collected important documentation from 16 different countries in the form of national reports, publications, and bibliographic information.

A conference on General Education in 1958, with the same expert structure, was concentrated upon a major reworking of general education for post-war society and reported on by Prof Joseph Lauwerys, Professor

---

[17] S. E. Graham, 'The (Real)politiks of Culture: U.S. Cultural Diplomacy in Unesco, 1946–1954,' *Diplomatic History* 30, no. 2 (2006): 232.

[18] Joseph A. Lauwerys, 'General Education, a Conference of the Unesco Institute for Education, Hamburg, November 1957,' *International Review of Education* 4, no. 3 (1958):

of Comparative Education at the Institute of Education in London and a major figure in UNESCO since 1946.[19] Expert meetings worked in different ways. Twenty-five specialists from fifteen countries came together to discuss school reform in winter 1956 in Hamburg.[20] They were able to create a freeform conversation which was dynamic in form and yet disciplined dialectically, and moved on from positional statements into a sharply defined synthesis of views.

UNESCO called the first general exploratory conference on adult education in 1949 and subsequently realised that the subject could not be contained by single, general meetings. Limited in scope meant a greater intensity of study. The meeting in 1954 had 65 delegates from 30 countries. It was not only the subject that was of continuing and growing interest but also in the value of these discussions. This meeting was different again in its organisation and focused on an exchange of ideas, and proposals to change the methods of instruction in adult education: its emphasis on learning about new ways of communicating in adult education (radio and films). It had an activity focus. This sense of discussion and pedagogical innovation developed in the early 1950s. The new UNESCO journal, the *International Review of Education*, linked theories from comparativists about international education to a coordinated programme of experiments in schools in many countries focused on 'Living in a World Community' to provide a basis for comparison. Again, there was an inquiry into the best methods for changing attitudes. It was described as a landmark in educational history.

A seminar on the Associated Schools Projects was held at the UNESCO Institute for Education from 14 to 22 July 1958 with 19 participants from 19 countries. The Schools Project was an ambitious programme involving many countries and schools and had been running for four years. It had been supported by local UNESCO representatives in each country and by UNESCO materials. The most problematic component of the project was about its evaluation. Tests were not viewed as useful for understanding shifts in attitude. This was an issue which was beginning to generate some attention at the UNESCO Institute in Hamburg, and two expert conferences on the subject in 1957 and 1958 had already been organised and reported on. The question of curriculum led to the formation of an

---

[19] Lauwerys, 'General Education'

[20] Joseph Axelrod, 'International Meeting on School Reform, Hamburg, January 1956,' *International Review of Education* 2, no. 2 (1956).

International Advisory Committee on the School Curriculum for UNESCO, also in 1958. This was only partially about shifts of attitudes, the prevailing concern of the time, but about structural questions. School systems could contain inadequate schools either because countries were just starting out or because developed systems now contained older models of education to meet contemporary problems of work and youth. In all cases, the curriculum would require critical review and improvement.

So, through the 1950s, the ambitions of UNESCO in Hamburg had grown from organising general expert seminars on particular issues and into managing widescale programmes of school innovation. By 1958, the emerging issue, additional to the wider programmes but central to them, was how they could be evaluated and assessed.

THE FIRST INTERNATIONAL CONFERENCE ON EDUCATIONAL RESEARCH 1956

In 1956, UNESCO and the AERA (American Educational Research Association) held a joint meeting in the USA, the First International Conference on Educational Research. At the time, it was said that this meeting had brought together prominent educational researchers in educational research from eleven countries: Australia, Belgium, Brazil, Canada, Chile, France, the German Federal Republic, Japan, the Union of Soviet Socialist Republics, the United Kingdom, and the United States of America. It was small in number, but an equal number of American academics also participated. The report of the meeting signalled the importance of research problems of immediate concern to respective educational systems and suggested that international cooperation would benefit national research.[21] AERA produced the report of the meeting, which UNESCO then published. The initiative came from within UNESCO, and its director-general designated AERA as the lead agency to manage the Conference. In addition to its four main presentations, there were three informal or work sessions which involved the attendees in various ways: these were international cooperation to identify problems beyond national borders, the improvement of communications in educational research, and the training of research workers.

---

[21] American Education Research Association, *Report of the First International Conference on Educational Research Atlantic City, New Jersey, U.S.A. February, 1956* (Paris: UNESCO, 1956).

32   S. GREK ET AL.

The Conference recommended that UNESCO convene an international commission at an early date to study the possibility of developing common methods and techniques, international scales and measuring instruments, and essential terminology in educational research. Such a commission would probably require considerable time and financial support for its work since the nature of the task is one requiring inter-national cooperation and agreement in the highest degree. The dictionary referred to above could well be one of the responsibilities of such a commission if an international research project would be administratively possible and meaningful.[22]

As Wall reflected later:

The very fact that international scientific co-operation in educational research can be effectively organized implies the existence of powerful and highly developed research institutions in the member countries and a much more widespread technical and scientific competence than might have been expected ten years ago.[23]

Following the Conference, AERA decided to begin publishing reviews of educational research, in its journal, the *Review of Educational Research*, drawn from some 18 countries, to improve communications between educational researchers. It was assumed early on that this meeting would herald a period of international collaboration in educational research.[24] Victor Noll, who was an organiser for the New Jersey conference, wrote in the UNESCO journal an account of it, and reported that

Educational research is the most substantial and important factor in educational progress. It should be encouraged and supported, both materially and in spirit. Nations can improve their own educational programs and can help one another through research. They, like individuals, are dependent on each other and learn from each other. International cooperation in educational research has become a reality.[25]

---

[22] T. Neville Postlethwaite, 'International Project for the Evaluation of Educational Achievement (I.E.A.),' *International Review of Education* 12, no. 3 (1966): 358.

[23] Wall, 'Research and Educational Action,' 497.

[24] American Education Research Association, *Report of the First International Conference.*

[25] Victor H. Noll, 'International Cooperation in Educational Research,' *International Review of Education* 4, no. 1 (1958): 84.

2 FORMING TRANSNATIONAL NETWORKS: THE EARLY 1950S IN EUROPE   33

The discussions in the working groups of the meeting, which UNESCO would use as its expert advice in the future, are interesting on several counts. They involved some leading researchers who were involved in the Hamburg UNESCO experts' groups and special study meetings, with Wall, and they also outlined, in effect, the programme for establishing international projects, of which the IEA was probably the first.

The Western world, represented in these conversations within UNESCO and AERA, began to recognise that the tasks facing them in the reconstruction of European education went beyond the renewal of damaged material structures. It went beyond the need for lone professors of education in small departments, the mid-century model of work in education research, sparse though it was.[26]

In the 1940s and 1950s, a number of countries (UK, Denmark, Norway, Sweden, Belgium, Finland, German Federal Republic) had set up commissions and organisations of varying degrees of independence concerned with the conduct and fostering of educational research directly concerned with policymaking. in addition, whether through governmental or private initiative, new university institutes of educational research were founded and the staffs of existing ones increased.[27]

There was a distinct willingness of governments to support and utilise research in education appeared in the belief that the studies would be useful to the formulation and conduct of educational policy. Government agencies turned to research workers for 'answers' to what was considered to be basically the 'scientific' problems involved in planning educational reforms. Policy-orientated research increased rapidly (e.g., the 1967 'Plowden Committee' in Great Britain, the German Education Commission 1966–1975, and the 'School Commission' in Sweden established in 1946, are cases in point).[28] What was no more than fragmented national initiatives became joined into early networks of expert comparativists, statisticians, and collators of translated data.

In total, they were providing for UNESCO a manual, a vade mecum, for its work, and one which must have coloured the thinking and planning for the earliest IEA meetings. The Report concluded with a

---

[26] American Education Research Association, *Report of the First International Conference.*
[27] Wall, 'Research and Educational Action,', 488.
[28] Gilbert de Landsheere, 'IEA and UNESCO: A History of Working Cooperation,' Retrieved 20 January 2014 from: www.unesco.org/education/pdf/LANDSHEE.pdf, (1997), 8.

34   S. GREK ET AL.

recommendation that UNESCO acted as a catalyst to aid and support cooperation in research, but also that it needed member states and their institutions to take responsibility. The American influence, clearly present here, is that UNESCO should start producing common methods and measurement scales for researchers.

NEW RESEARCH INSTITUTES AND THEIR NETWORKING

In effect, in the 1950s, the 'first post-war wave' of international collaboration in educational research began and its contribution to the foundational intelligence testing community, their assumptions and techniques, and the actors and partners it linked together or created. It coalesced around the early UNESCO planning meetings and meetings held at the UNESCO Institute for Education. As well as psychometricians, these meetings involved some leading professors who began to act as comparativists, and embryo national research institutes in education, and it helped the formation of others. Diverse centres of education research moved to a new level of regional and international organisation in the early post-war years.[29]

An accelerant in this process was the demand from European Ministries of Education for research data for planning and policy purposes from within their departments or by commissions from universities.

Since 1945, and with gathering momentum since 1950, country after country has established either National Councils for Research in Education or powerful and well-equipped university research institutes; many have done both. Governments and benevolent foundations, in the United States and in Europe, have increasingly turned their attention and their finances to highly complex problems arising in the day-to-day life of the schools. This has been part of a general expansion of finance for research on all kinds of social problems but, from a relatively slow start, and with some hesitations, education has emerged as a major field of scientific study. Germany, Sweden and to some extent Belgium, France and Switzerland have taken part in this expansion; and in a somewhat different way a similar growth has taken place in the USSR and the other countries of the Eastern Bloc.[30]

[29]Wall, 'Research and Educational Action.'
[30]Wall, 'Psychology of Education,' 377.

2 FORMING TRANSNATIONAL NETWORKS: THE EARLY 1950S IN EUROPE   35

Examples of these kinds of institutes, often bringing together a generation of mental testers or statisticians, and new scholars, include the following: the Scottish Council for Research in Education [SCRE), established in 1928 with a strong track record in empirical research and large-scale projects; the National Foundation for Education Research, in England, formed in 1946, as a self-governing and representational body, using a foundation grant from the pre-war International Examinations Inquiry. West Germany had established the German Institute for International Educational Research (HiPF) in Frankfurt in the early 1950s as a research institute. In Finland, Martti Takala, a professor of Psychology at the University of Jyväskylä was a senior researcher who acted as a specialist link until the National Centre for Research in Education was established in 1965. Fernand Hotyat in Belgium had a similar role. With a gathering momentum, country after country established either National Councils for Research in Education or powerful and well-equipped university research institutes; many had done both. According to Wall, there was also an expansion of educational research in UK universities, some of which now have 'specialised departments for the purpose.'[31]
In Sweden,

> The new institution at the Stockholm School of Education, which became operational in the autumn of 1956, was almost immediately entrusted with a series of large—scale research projects that were initiated by the 1957 Governmental School Committee or by the institution itself. ... A considerable portion of the department's resources was accordingly spent on survey research, which amounted to administering achievement and attitude tests to randomly sampled pupils in both types of school.[32]

The consequences of this national shift towards a focused and 'scientific' research organisation were several. Firstly, a number of national large-scale research on school organisation, streaming and failure began. Secondly, a shift in the nature of comparative education as an international dimension in education research came into view:

> The entry of the psychologists, the scientific curriculum designers and the subject specialists who look at their disciplines from a developmental viewpoint, into the comparative study of school systems in different cultural

[31] Wall, 'Psychology of Education,' 377.
[32] Torsten Husén, 'Two Decades of Educational Research,' *Interchange* 1 (1970): 86.

36 S. GREK ET AL.

settings has added a dimension of investigatory science to what has been a rather descriptive discipline, with little in the way of a hard core.[33]

For Torsten Husén, this shift reflected the contemporary nature of his work and, in particular, how national experience began to connect with European events, and specifically with the developments at the Institute of Education in Hamburg. Swedish policy and UNESCO initiatives seem to come together. Husén felt, at the end of the decade, that evaluation and its tools had become an important issue for educational researchers for the first time.

SCHOOL EVALUATION 1957/1958

On 14 November 1956, Husén had been invited to an expert meeting in Hamburg by Alv Storheid Langeland, the head of the Hamburg institute, on methods and instruments of school evaluation, to take place in February 1957. The meeting was connected to the Associated Schools Project, consisting of 100 secondary schools in 30 countries, which was searching for a method of evaluation which could aid its purpose of a shift in attitude to learning and school organisation. Participating schools in this large project had used a variety of assessment methods, and UNESCO needed to find 'substantial information on the relative effectiveness of the various approaches, methods and materials' and it needed an 'expert assessment' of the validity and instruments to continue development. By December, Husén had invited Alv Storheid Langeland to lecture in Stockholm, and mentioned invitations to Philip Vernon (a leading psychologist and friend to Husén), W. D. Wall, Roger Gal (on the UNESCO Steering group), and Dr. Schultze (professor at HiPf in Frankfurt and a friend).

In January 1958, Husén wrote to Langeland thanking him for the invitation to participate at the conference on 17–21 March ('the theme of the conference seems very much enticing') and referred to again on 1 March to this meeting. Hardi Fischer in his report about the meeting of experts on evaluation, chaired by Wall, said it focused on the interaction between the assessment of academic or educational performance, on the one hand, and teaching methods, on the other. The two aspects of education were seen as inseparable. Thus, the criteria for measurement or evaluation

---

[33] Wall, 'Research and Educational Action,' 378.

implicitly or explicitly depend on educational goals.[34] Experts from many countries were engaged in this work. It was decided to carry out a pilot study to discover if an international research project would be administratively possible and meaningful.

But discussions led to a further complexity. The experts, mostly from Europe and the USA, had decided that it was essential to have some information on what pupils in schools actually knew at various points in the school system. Economists had used the proportion of the school age group continuing to the final year (grade 12) as an indicator for quality in education. It was felt to be insufficient. This meeting was a perfect fit for Husen's interests and experiences. He was at the centre of Swedish school reform through his responsibility for curriculum assessment and evaluation, and he was beginning to develop close links with UNESCO as one of their advisers. In fact, the field of discussion and inquiry expanded as the experts worked through questions about the shifts in education towards skilled technical work and away from manual work, and consequently, onto the growth of secondary education and its different systems.[35] Thus, the wide purposes of evaluation in education came to the fore, ranging from school quality, teacher quality, selection of pupils, diagnosis, failure rates, and so on. What is the purpose of evaluation, for which pupils, which age and which problem? Examinations, tests, questionnaires, interviews, and observation-based study were reviewed and analysed, as were school records.

The experts gathered in Hamburg thus reviewed several evaluation techniques in use: intuitive or systematic observation, structured interview or not structured (oral test), the questionnaire, the scales of marks, the school exams and the standardized tests of various types, as well as the school file.[36]

The tension in school assessment which the 1958 meeting intended to explore was the relation between examinations and tests, each of which had flaws, and relied upon single methods of assessment. Their innovative idea was that the teacher must be able to accumulate a material of

---

[34] Hardi Fischer, 'Réunion d'experts sur l'évaluation en éducation, Hambourg, Mars 1958,' *International Review of Education* 4, no. 4 (1958).

[35] Fernand Hotyat, *Evaluation in Education: Report on an International Meeting of Experts, held at the UNESCO Institute for Education, Hamburg 17–22 March 1958* (Hamburg: UNESCO Institute for Education, 1958), 66.

[36] Fischer, 'Réunion d'experts,' 492.

38 S. GREK ET AL.

objective observations which could be used as a basis for his interviews with the parents, for educational guidance, and development or new study plans. In the light of what was to happen in the following decades, the Report of the meeting concluded with some cautionary notes. A system of evaluation could only provide a picture of part of the system and methods of evaluation are established to serve the system. A further point is concerned with the new phenomenon of 'teaching to the test.' The meeting acted as a specialist forum in Europe to unpick and analyse the various forms of assessment in operation nationally and their consequences for the child and the school authorities.

HUSÉN AT THE END OF THE 1950S

The key idea which seemed to draw Husén forward, and which serves as a metaphor for the research networking which he was involved with and promoted throughout the 1950s, was his anti-provincialism. One of the key skills Husén brought to his work as it developed in complexity from its national to its European setting was his absolute resolve in the importance of research in opposition to its provincial and normative nature. He disliked an attitude among researchers of contemporary period in which 'provincialism,' a closed, national attitude to ideas and questions, prevailed. He mentions this in an account of his work.[37] The world cannot survive with this attitude, he said. Repeatedly, he stressed his opposition to provincial attitudes in research. This produced a restlessness and dissatisfaction with his situation and a search for new possibilities.

> It is in the very nature of education as a field of practice to be provincial in character. It is after all moulded by the cultural and historical tradition of the particular country it serves.[38]

In this context, it appears to mean Sweden, but it is repeated later in the different context, of the domain of research. He cannot stress the point enough. It appears at different time and places in his work. He detested

---

[37] Husén states: 'too many educators suffer from provincialism. ... I was eager to widen the horizon'. Torsten Husén, 'The International Context of Educational Research,' *Oxford Review of Education* 9, no. 1 (1983): 33. He writes about his again in Torsten Husén, *The Learning Society* (London: Methuen, 1974); Torsten Husén, *The Learning Society Revisited* (Oxford: Pergamon, 1986).

[38] Husén, 'International Context,' 23.

2 FORMING TRANSNATIONAL NETWORKS: THE EARLY 1950S IN EUROPE   39

provincialism in research. When Eva Malmquist and Hans U. Grundin reviewed research cooperation in the 1970s, they cautioned against the high degree of provincialism in education which should be carefully watched by comparative educators.[39] Husén's attitude to the importance of research without borders is critical to an appreciation of his success. His travelling can be seen as a blow against his locale and its norms, and his sense of confinement in Sweden for many years. In later years, travel seems to define his identity as a researcher and writer. He travelled to international meetings of the IEA, the IIEP and the early OECD, and for long stays at US universities. The seminars at Hamburg or Paris for the UNESCO Institute of Education, which he attended from 1955, were the key pivot in his breakout into his transnational work. Husén was impressed by Langeland, its director, and his intention to make the Institute 'a meeting place where leading researchers on education could come together and exchange experiences.'[40]

He began to attend the annual seminars on curriculum and schooling but the advent of a new subject, that of evaluation in 1957, followed by a meeting on comparative education were formative in materialising a way forward for him. His new colleagues, including C. Arnold Anderson, had the same approach to research, verified 'knowledge and facts by measuring.'[41] The new idea of a major project on evaluation, a cross-national study, proposed by Anderson became his way forward, 'a next step.' His antagonism to provincialism and his sense of a collegial and scientific 'home' came together then. For example, 'an extensive international network was built up which later turned out to be highly beneficial to me' and 'nothing can be more rewarding for an academic than to work with colleagues all over the world engaged in the same pursuits as himself.'[42] Attributes that Husén brought to his work or created, which were noted in the recollections of working in the IEA by his colleagues, were several in number. He was viewed as an optimistic but incredibly productive researcher. His optimism was vital, as it produced a 'refusal to acknowledge seemingly insurmountable obstacles including finding the funding, securing the right institutional arrangements, getting political

---

[39] Eva Malmqvist and Hans U. Grundin, 'International Co-Operation in Educational Research,' *International Review of Education* 22, no. 3 (1976).

[40] Tjeldvoll and Lingens, *Conversations*, 44.

[41] Tjeldvoll and Lingens, *Conversations*, 95.

[42] Tjeldvoll and Lingens, *Conversations*, vii.

40   S. GREK ET AL.

support, and ensuring the willing compliance of many teachers. His optimism was always remarked upon. His research experience was vital to assist in the technical standards needed for international comparison.[43]

In his transnational work, Torsten Husén was the diplomat, and his ability to encourage people to cooperate, to smooth ruffled feelings, and to deal with various funding agencies complemented Neville Postlethwaite's ability to manage the details of the overall project, to press everyone to a high standard of care with an optimum of speed, and to oversee the technicalities of a project so that all went smoothly. These two, perhaps better than other combinations, were able to affect the cooperative nature of the IEA, to make each worker in each national centre feel a part of the project. For Alan Purves, 'he was the diplomat, and his ability to encourage people to cooperate, to smooth ruffled feelings, and to deal with various funding agencies,' while Postlethwaite dealt with the technicalities of the project.[44] He was significant in the creation of a collegial research relation with a 'spirit of cooperation' and 'friendly atmosphere,' which we also see in the following chapters. Among this group of research directors and professors, all undertaking their activities voluntarily, a 'keen sense of something exciting was beginning to emerge ... among like-minded people working on a common problem that engaged their intellectual interest.'[45] So, his most substantial attribute judged against the ambition of the task, its complexity and the various researchers enrolled in its tasks, was his ability to motivate, lead, and stimulate a spirit of close cooperation, over time and space.

A New Form of Comparative Research

The older comparativist language, rooted in close observation and concern for contexts and cultures, was superseded, in their view, by this approach. The language of this group of professors used new terms such as 'probability,' 'reliability,' 'diagnostic tests,' and 'standardisation,' and the new tools of sampling, test construction, questionnaire items, timetables, and costing.[46] This approach had several advantages in Europe at this

---

[43] Alan C. Purves, 'The Evolution of the IEA: A Memoir,' *Comparative Education Review* 31, no. 1 (1987): 13.

[44] Purves, 'Evolution of the IEA,' 13.

[45] Purves, 'Evolution of the IEA,' 16.

[46] Purves, 'Evolution of the IEA.'

2 FORMING TRANSNATIONAL NETWORKS: THE EARLY 1950S IN EUROPE   41

time. Firstly, the few researchers in each country who worked in this way were also internationally minded. They shared the same literature, training, and attitudes. Secondly, this was the language of America, its policy-makers and scientists, and America was a driving force in European affairs in the 1960s and 1970s. Support from that quarter would depend on the determination of like-minded people to make transparent, and to open up and 'modernise' European education systems, and to aid the West in the conflicts with the East. Husén's dislike of provincialism was a persistent attitude. He searched for colleagues who wanted to work across borders; the borders of the subject, of method and of country. It was an intellectual response that went beyond efficiency of operation and organisation. It was an approach that was willing to depend upon what was known or familiar, and then push it on. He recognised that they were inventing a new stage of comparative education, in creating a scholarship based upon data, which was drawn from several sources.

But as Noll observed, his tasks were large. Noll was concerned about the philosophical or even polemic nature of the European research he read in 1957. But allowing for these considerations, there remained, taken altogether, a substantial body of apparently solid research material in the reports. Noll's concerns about European research in education, and one that Husén would be dealing with, in a disciplined and focused project, were ....

> ... articles presenting conclusions based largely or solely on the opinions or judgments of the author do not fall within the purview of this issue.' In spite of these suggestions many reports were cited which obviously violate this restriction. In some cases this may have been the result of a natural desire to make a good showing. It seems, also, to reveal a wide variation in concept of what constitutes research. In this country it is generally recognized that greatest progress in education and psychology resulted when they separated from philosophy, and applied scientific rather than philosophical methods to their problem.[47]

He pointed out the problems of translation and loss of meaning. Further misunderstandings must be openly examined and discussed, he said.[48] In sum, the IEA will have to face problems of translation, the issue

[47] Victor H. Noll, 'Introduction: Educational Research in Countries Other than the U.S.A.,' *Review of Educational Research* 27, no. 1 (1957): 5.
[48] Noll, 'introduction,' 6.

of common standards, the importance of scientific method, the dominance of the philosophical approach, and national authorities defining research problems and solutions. So, the progress of Husén and others must be judged against these weaknesses in their planning for a large-scale project. Interestingly, it is possible to see this new joint direction not as one in which like-minded researchers, often isolated in their own countries sought each other out, supported by the US, but a more direct form of 'scientific colonisation,' and an 'intellectual domination of an existing culture by a foreign, more powerful culture.'[49] Peter van Strien saw this as a hegemony achieved by voluntary submission, a recognition of cultural dominance, in which key members of the colonised culture travel towards it, learn its language, and represent its ideas on return. Husén had seen this close at hand. Husén never revealed any sense of colonisation in his writing. Instead, for him this new internationalism meant using the best empirical research methods and attitudes, usually but not only emanating from the US (and sometimes the UK). The view from the US State Department that

> scientific expertise and public education could advance the international interests of the United States, even against totalitarian societies, whilst safeguarding the nation's traditions of liberty and individualism[50]

was not his view, many of his new colleagues also. They did not oppose their new ally, the USA, as its purposes, policies, and methods in educational research were homologous with their own. They were willing participants and even missionaries.

A TRANSNATIONAL CONNECTOR OF RESEARCH

The work of Torsten Husén in the 1950s is one in which, while taking a significant role in research in Stockholm, he begins to work across borders. Travelling to congresses, and special conferences and seminars in other countries, he creates links with other academics. They become regular correspondents, friends, family friends, colleagues, and prospective

---

[49] Peter J. van Strien, 'The American 'Colonization' of Northwest European Social Psychology after World War II,' *Journal of the History of the Behavioural Sciences*, 33, no. 4 (1997): 349.

[50] Ellen Condliffe Lagemann. *An Elusive Science: The Troubling History of Educational Research* (Chicago: University of Chicago Press, 2000), 30.

partners. He gives papers, sends books and pamphlets overseas, and discusses research in work and social circles. He has a determination to build partnerships on the modern ideas and practices of psychology. Friendships appear readily given and he corresponds with those making inquiries or asking for material. He travels across significant distances at a time when this is still difficult. He appears to feel released from wartime restrictions and to be determined to make up time and space.

Over the decade he shifts from a position of the outsider trying to enter academic places into an organiser of significant spaces. In doing so, he connects Swedish knowledge in education research and reform to wider audiences, from Germany to the United States, the United Kingdom, and into European meetings. He had begun his career as a military psychologist, working on personality and aptitudes, and then used his psychology of education proficiency to work with a wider group of scholars. He maintains links with other researchers although it appears that he invested effort on American scholars; he was offered opportunities for funding and academic posts through their support. Most of all, he acts as a go-between the US and Sweden as he works in major reform-linked education research, and takes this knowledge into other settings. As a transnational connector of research, he assembles a growing set of contacts in which meetings, publication, and translation produce a circulation of ideas in which he is a major energiser. Following his movements, a fixedness of purpose and solid bonds appear, but is also clear that on the way, many are broken or appear temporary.

As he travels and joins groups together, he shares what later appears to be a 'standard narrative,' one formed in the strict classifications and standards of the international testing community, which was his first research experience and one which gained him entry into a post-war community in educational research, disciplined by the experience and methodology.

This community was widely spread but it shared the same concepts, methods, and procedures, and most of all, texts. As the decade moves along, his identity appears to shift. While it is built on solid experience and a presence in psychology and testing, the context of Swedish education, school reform, comes to dominate his thinking. In doing so, his interest and contacts transfer into comparison, and comparative education. This is partly an intellectual curiosity, a motivation for innovation, material opportunities, and scholarly ambition. So, while he moves, he also changes, leaving the decades with skills in place but his goals and experiences altered. The complexities of his tasks, its intricacies and scale, had only just begun.

Soon the focus of their work, as they assemble, was no longer just policy ideas and common interests, but on methods. Their shared research technology, their background in experimental educational psychology (in most cases), transferred onto developing statistics about education and planning.

CHAPTER 3

Collecting International Data: Husén and the International Association for the Evaluation of Educational Achievement

In 1962, Husén was elected chairman of what is today known as the International Association for the Evaluation of Educational Achievement (IEA). At the time, it was not defined as an 'association'; instead, it had the word 'project' in its title, indicating the temporary nature of the endeavour. However, the IEA proved to be long-lasting, and so did Husén's role in it: he remained a chairman for 17 years, until 1978 when he was succeeded by his protégé Neville Postlethwaite. The long period of his chairmanship indicates that it was an important part of Husén's professional life, a period in which he became deeply involved with an association that in many ways came to shape a particular strand of educational research. In essence, the IEA was the organisation that pioneered the use of international standardised tests. With their surveys of educational performance in different countries, they were trying to do something that had not been tried before, but which has become very common in today's

© The Author(s), under exclusive license to Springer Nature Switzerland AG 2024
S. Grek et al., *The World as a Laboratory*, Global Histories of Education, https://doi.org/10.1007/978-3-031-68090-8_3

45

46   S. GREK ET AL.

society, not least through PISA, but also through tests like TIMSS and PIRLS that the IEA conducts.[1]

Husén had been involved with the IEA from the beginning, though not as a central figure at first. His entry into the field of international testing was a new experience for him, as it was for other scholars, but he also had some relevant expertise to draw on. In particular, he had extensive experience working with large-scale data. As mentioned in the preceding chapters, he worked during the 1940s in the army with large-scale tests of conscripts. In the 1950s, he entered the world of teacher education and pedagogy, and among other things was involved in developing new standardised tests for schools. In other words, Husén had knowledge of large-scale data, but only on a national scale. He could not possibly fathom all the complexities involved in creating, interpreting, and disseminating scientific knowledge on an international scale. This chapter will describe some of the challenges that Husén and his colleagues faced as they developed the first international tests on educational achievement.[2]

---

[1] This chapter is based on work that is further developed in a forthcoming book on the early history of the IEA (Landahl, forthcoming). For previous publications, see Joakim Landahl, "The Punched Cards Were Sent Yesterday, We Hope They Arrive Undamaged': Computers and International Large-Scale Assessments During the 1960s and 1970s,' *Learning, Media and Technology* 49, no. 1 (2023); Joakim Landahl, 'Data Friction and Precarious Knowledge: IEA and the Movement of Data in the 1960s and 1970s,' *On Education: Journal for Research and Debate* 6, no. 18 (2023); Joakim Landahl, 'The Pisa Calendar: Temporal Governance and International Large-scale Assessments,' *Educational Philosophy and Theory* 52, no. 6 (2020); Joakim Landahl, 'De-scandalisation and International Assessments: The Reception of IEA Surveys in Sweden during the 1970s,' *Globalisation, Societies and Education* 16, no. 5 (2018). See also Constantinos Papanastasiou, Tjeerd Plomp & Elena C. Papanastasiou, eds. *IEA 1958–2008. 50 Years of Experiences and Memories* (Nicosia: Cultural Center of Kykkos Monastery, 2011); Oren Pizmony-Levy, Testing for All: The Emergence and Development of International Assessment of Student Achievement, 1958–2012 (PhD diss., Indiana University, 2013).

[2] The sources used here come primarily from three archives: the archive of the IEA available at the Hoover Institution, Stanford University; a smaller archive of the IEA available at Stockholm University, and the personal archive of Torsten Husén. In these archives there are many traces of the actual work of designing international large-scale tests. Useful sources include correspondence, test manuals, memoranda, and minutes of meetings. In addition, among the printed sources there are the actual reports of the studies, as well as journal articles reporting on or reviewing the work. Among these sources, correspondence has proven to be particularly useful. Correspondence between IEA staff, including programmers, subject matter experts, and project managers, provides valuable insights into how an international organisation attempted to communicate about data issues. From here on, the archive located at the Hoover Institution (the International Association for the Evaluation of Educational Achievement records) is referred to as 'The IEA archive.'

STATISTICS: NATIONAL AND INTERNATIONAL DATA

The history of statistics has often been studied in relation to the state. As the word suggests, statistics has been an important part of how different nation-states have governed and monitored themselves, whether in the form of censuses or other kinds of surveys. Knowing its population by collecting statistics on crime, education, the economy, and so on, has been an important part of the modern nation-state. The historiography of statistics has reflected this fact: it has often been a history of the relationship between a particular, relatively limited territory and a particular way of producing knowledge.[3]

However, as recent research suggests, there is also a long-standing international dimension to statistics that deserves to be highlighted. Early attempts to develop international cooperation date back to the 1850s. A major figure in the history of statistics, Adolphe Quetelet, took the initiative for the first international congress on statistics, held in Brussels in 1853. Several congresses followed in the following decades. However, these cosmopolitan beliefs clashed with a reality that prioritised the nation-state, and the nineteenth-century vision of statistics as an international science can be said to have failed.[4] But the dream of collecting standardised data across national territories lived on, and during the twentieth century a number of international organisations entered the arena, with the United Nations, the League of Nations, and the OECD as major players, creating new conditions for collecting global data.[5]

The ambition to make statistics international and the failure to do so are both understandable. Both tendencies can be seen as part of what statistics is. The ambition to move across borders can partly be seen as a reflection of the kind of knowledge that numbers can produce. Theodore

---

[3] Examples of fine scholarship in this tradition include Christina von Oertzen, 'Paper Knowledge and Statistical Precision,' *Isis* 114, no. 2 (2023); Arunabh Ghosh, *Making It Count: Statistics and Statecraft in the Early People's Republic of China* (Princeton/Oxford: Princeton University Press, 2020).

[4] Catherine Michalopoulou, 'Statistical Internationalism: From Quetelet's Census Uniformity to Kish's Cross-National Sample Survey Comparability,' *Statistical Journal of the IAOS* 32, no. 4 (2016).

[5] On the internationalisation of statistics, see for example Nico Randeraad, *States and Statistics in the Nineteenth Century: Europe by Numbers* (Manchester: Manchester University Press, 2010); Daniel Speich Chassé, 'How the Global Became a Framework for Numerical Communication: A Comment,' *European Review of History: Revue européenne d'histoire* 30, no. 1 (2023).

48 S. GREK ET AL.

Porter has discussed quantification as a technique of distance. 'Since the rules for collecting and manipulating numbers are widely shared, they can easily be transported across oceans and continents and used to co-ordinate activities or settle disputes.' Moreover, and most importantly, reliance on numbers 'minimizes the need for intimate knowledge and personal trust. Quantification is well suited for communication that goes beyond the boundaries of locality and community.'[6] The complexities of extending the statistical gaze to foreign territories can at the same time be understood in relation to all the local ways of counting, standardising and comparing. There is a local dimension to the production and understanding of statistics that historically have made international standardisation problematic. These national idiosyncrasies of data collecting were once described by Ian Hacking in the following way: 'Every state, happy or unhappy, was statistical in its own way.'[7]

In the history of educational research, this tension between universal ambitions and local particularities was played out early. Perhaps the first examples might be the strive to collect international data by Marc-Antoine Jullien, often regarded as the father of comparative education. His *Esquisse d'un Ouvrage sur l'Éducation Comparée* (Plan for a Work on Comparative Education) appeared in 1816–1817 and encompassed a large number of questions. Jullien's work was divided into six parts, but only two were published. It would take many years thereafter for substantial quantitative data about education to emerge. The field of comparative education, some argued, had no use of quantitative methods. In his book *Comparative Education*, the leading comparativist Nicholas Hans wrote that he had tried to collect some statistical data, but concluded that the existing data were currently not comparable. One reason was that statistics were originally collected at the national level, with different standards and ideas about what and how to count, making them incomparable. 'Each country has its own terminology, based on national history, its own classification, and its own method of collecting and compiling statistical tables. In some cases, these statistics are only conjectures and serve the purposes of propaganda.'[8]

---

[6] Theodore M. Porter, *Trust in Numbers: The Pursuit of Objectivity in Science and Public Life* (Princeton: Princeton University Press, 1995), ix.

[7] Ian Hacking, *The Taming of Chance* (Cambridge: Cambridge University Press, 1990), 16.

[8] Nicholas Hans, *Comparative Education*, 3rd ed. (London: Routledge, 1958), 7–8.

3 COLLECTING INTERNATIONAL DATA: HUSÉN AND THE INTERNATIONAL... 49

When the IEA embarked on the production of international statistics, with the first publications coming out in the 1960s, it was in part an attempt to overcome the limitations of previous statistical studies. Since the data collection was designed by an international organisation instead of by national agents, there was from the outset a higher degree of international standardisation. This was an ambition that received both scepticism and enthusiasm. Among the supporters were Wilfred Douglas Halls who in a review called it 'epoch-making' and Edmund King who described it as 'a breakthrough in comparative studies in education,' and claimed that it beyond doubt would 'go down in history as a revolutionary example of the application of science to education.'[9]

Introducing IEA

The IEA, as described in the previous chapter, grew out of meetings at the UNESCO Institute for Education in Hamburg in the 1950s. The fundamental problem for the Association was the lack of quantitative data on school performance. Stimulated by developments in comparative education, Cold War rivalries, and educational reforms, scholars from mostly Western countries decided to undertake a study of educational achievement in 12 countries. The first studies were published in the 1960s. A pilot study covering several subjects was followed by a 12-country study of mathematics achievement. In the 1970s, several reports were published covering six different school subjects. These reports were part of a larger project called the Six Subject Survey, which involved some 258,000 students and 50,000 teachers from 9700 schools in some 20 countries.[10] The scale of the project was spectacular for its time. 'The IEA project represents the biggest, costliest and technically most ambitious study ever

---

[9] W. D. Halls, 'Review of International Study of Achievement in Mathematics,' *Comparative Education Review* 12, no. 1 (1968): 87; Edmund King, 'Review of International Study of Achievement in Mathematics. Phase I. A Comparison of Twelve Countries by Torsten Husén,' *International Review of Education* 13, no. 3 (1967), 359, 362.

[10] The countries involved in the Six Subject Survey were Australia, Belgium, Chile, England, West Germany, Finland, France, Hungary, India, Iran, Ireland, Israel, Italy, Japan, the Netherlands, New Zealand, Scotland, Sweden, Thailand, Rumania, and the United States. The subject areas covered were civic education, reading comprehension, literature education, French as a foreign language, English as a foreign language, and science.

50 S. GREK ET AL.

undertaken in the social sciences,' wrote Patricia Broadfoot, in a 1978 review of IEA reports.[11]

The IEA sought to produce international knowledge about school performance, and this required a network of scholars and institutions in different countries working together to collect, analyse, disseminate, and ultimately store knowledge. All countries involved, whether developing countries like Thailand and Iran or developed countries like the US and France, were part of the network and all had to produce data that could be analysed. As a network, it had no clear centre, although Western countries dominated in terms of influential positions in the organisation. A small secretariat was initially based in Hamburg, but key people in the organisation worked in other locations, including Stockholm, Chicago, New York, London, and Edinburgh. Much of the collaboration took place over great distances, making correspondence, telephone calls, and telegrams important means of communication.

Relocating the Headquarters

International organisations are always faced with the question of where to locate their work. Should they organise their work in a decentralised way or should they try to concentrate their work in one place? As a transnational organisation consisting of research institutes in different countries, the IEA was not an entity with a fixed connection to a specific place. In this sense it has clearly been a 'disembedded laboratory.' If there was one city that was originally more important than others, it was perhaps Hamburg, where the whole project originated and was formally located, but the relationship with the UNESCO Institute was ambiguous and full of tensions. Key figures in the organisation did not live in Hamburg, and the chairman from 1958 was English (W. D. Wall) and the chairman from 1962 was Swedish (Torsten Husén). In this sense, the IEA lacked a clear centre, a place where key people were physically gathered. But over time there were attempts to strengthen the role of some locations, not least Stockholm, where the Secretariat was moved in 1969.

It is most likely that the IEA would never have existed without the Hamburg institute. It was partly at this site that the idea emerged,

---

[11] Patricia Broadfoot, 'Review of The IEA Studies in Evaluation: Some Views on the Six Subject Surveys,' *Prospects* 8 no. 1 (1978): 121.

3 COLLECTING INTERNATIONAL DATA: HUSÉN AND THE INTERNATIONAL... 51

networks were formed and it was a place that provided the IEA with initial financial and administrative assistance. But the fact that IEA had the institute to thank for its life does not mean that the relationship was altogether harmonious. Instead, the relationship was rather complicated, and eventually the IEA and the institute went separate ways.

One point of contention was who was in charge. Was the IEA essentially a UNESCO project, or was it a project in collaboration with UNESCO? Correspondence points to a critical period in 1962 when the UNESCO Institute wanted to take the lead, while the IEA wanted to be more of an autonomous organisation. In June 1962, the director of the UNESCO Institute, Saul B. Robinsohn, wrote a memorandum on how to develop the relationship between the IEA and the Institute. He explained that the IEA had been conceived as a loose federation of research institutions and individuals, with the UNESCO Institute providing administrative and technical co-ordination, effectively acting as an international centre for the IEA. Now Robinsohn wanted to strengthen this position. Instead of seeing the IEA as a loose federation without a definite centre, he wanted the UNESCO Institute to be 'recognized as the centre for the I.E.A. project so as to give the project continuity and a stable framework.' He argued that the project needed a centre capable of more than administrative and technical coordination. The project needed 'a research centre which [...] provides day-to-day direction, takes initiative and can act responsibly to promote the project.' He further argued that the Institute had already been acting as such a centre for the past 18 months, and he wanted to have this position confirmed by the IEA Council. In line with this proposal, he argued that the name of the IEA should be changed to reflect its affiliation with the UNESCO Institute (see Fig. 3.1). He also stressed that the UNESCO Institute should have an influence on the work of the IEA and be represented in its publications.[12]

Robinsohn's efforts to maintain control over the IEA seem to have been somewhat frustrating for some of those involved, and energy and time were spent trying to regulate the exact relationship between the two bodies. Husén complained in a letter that he had been forced to spend several hours discussing a phrase in one of their bulletins that resulted in

---

[12] Memorandum by the Director of the UNESCO Institute concerning the position of the Institute in the I.E.A. Project. 5/61962 (The Husén archive, 2.237).

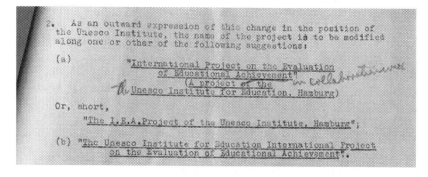

Fig. 3.1 Document showing proposals for a new name of the IEA that would strengthen the role of the UNESCO Institute for Education. The pencil notes indicate that the reader of the document disagrees with the proposal. (The Husén archive, 2.237)

the IEA being described as 'under the auspices of the UNESCO Institute for Education, Hamburg.'[13] Robinsohn's willingness to get involved in the details of applying for American funding from the US Office of Education was another issue that irritated the American scholars involved in the IEA. C. Arnold Anderson wrote to Robinsohn saying, 'I repeat, you are wasting your time scrutinizing these internal papers we send to the Office.'[14]

In 1964, Robinsohn resigned from the Institute to take up a post at the Institute for Educational Research at the Max Planck Institute. He was replaced by the Swede Gustaf Ögren, who served from 1964 to 1967. The change in leadership raised hopes that relations would improve. But the new leadership did not entirely solve the problem of how the two bodies should relate to each other. In 1966, Neville Postlethwaite wrote that his relationship with the staff of the UNESCO Institute had been 'deteriorating rapidly.' The main reason was that he thought they were 'utterly incompetent' and had 'put up unnecessary bureaucratic walls against new ideas.' In his letter to the chairman of the IEA, he made what could be seen as a radical proposal, namely that the IEA should move its centre

---

[13] Torsten Husén to C. Arnold Anderson, April 4, 1963 (The Husén archive, 1.21).

[14] C. Arnold Anderson to Saul B. Robinsohn, January 16, 1963 (The Husén archive, 1.21). For a letter where Robinsohn expressed his complaints, see Saul B. Robinsohn to Torsten Husén, January 4, 1963 (The Husén archive, 1.23).

3 COLLECTING INTERNATIONAL DATA: HUSÉN AND THE INTERNATIONAL... 53

from Hamburg to England, and the National Foundation for Educational Research in England and Wales (NFER). Postlethwaite was aware that it was a quite controversial suggestion:

> I know that both you and Ben [Benjamin Bloom] have fought to keep I.E.A. at the Unesco Institute. This has been in the hope that the Institute would do work in the future which was complementary to I.E.A. and also that the calibre of work at the Unesco Institute would improve. We have waited for three years now for both of the above to happen; they haven't! As you know I have been offered good jobs in England, but because I like the I.E.A. work very much and the people in I.E.A. with whom I work I would prefer to remain with I.E.A. On the other hand the frustrations at the Institute are surpassing the level of tolerance of any reasonable man (me). I hope you will have some ideas as to how to solve these problems.[15]

Instead of moving to England, however, the organisation relocated to Stockholm in 1969, the hometown of Torsten Husén. The departure from Hamburg can be seen as a symbolic move, emphasising a change that had already taken place in 1967, when the IEA was formally incorporated under Belgian law and thus became independent of the UNESCO institute in Hamburg. Leaving Hamburg for Sweden further emphasised this declaration of independence. The move from Germany to Sweden also symbolised a change in the power dynamics of the organisation. By creating an organisation in the country where the chairperson was already active, there was a greater sense that the previously decentralised organisation was getting a stronger centre. The move was soon accompanied by other developments that strengthened the Swedish position in comparative education. These developments were the creation of a new professorship for Husén dedicated to international and comparative education, the establishment of an institute for international education, the creation of Spencer fellowships for international scholars to come to Stockholm, and a database of IEA data. Another example of how Stockholm established itself as an international centre is the fact that many doctoral theses were written on IEA material with Husén as supervisor. Twelve PhD students at Stockholm University submitted a thesis that was developed within the

---

[15] Neville Postlethwaite to Torsten Husén, January 28, 1966 (The IEA archive, 299).

54   S. GREK ET AL.

IEA framework between 1967 and 1981.[16] Eight of them came from abroad: Australia, the UK, the USA, and Canada. Some of them were or became long-term members of the inner core of the IEA, notably Neville Postlethwaite and Douglas Pidgeon, both from the UK, as well as John P. Keeves (Australia) and Richard Noonan (USA).

Given the consolidation of comparative research in Stockholm, with Spencer Fellows, a database, a new research institute and a professorship, it might seem that the choice of Sweden as the location for the IEA was more or less self-evident. But after less than a year in Stockholm, as a confidential document shows, there were in fact serious discussions among some staff about moving headquarters again, this time to London. The document is undated and unsigned, but correspondence shows that it was written in early 1970 by Neville Postlethwaite and Richard Noonan. The document, entitled 'Personnel Problems and Location of IEA Office,' discusses the pros and cons of moving to England. The advantages of moving to England included better secretaries at a lower cost, lower international travel costs, lower telephone costs, lower cost of hiring office equipment, that professional staff would be paid less, and that communication with the technical director and certain key people would be easier. Finally, Postlethwaite and Noonan mentioned a more personal view: they felt that 'they would be more satisfied with a London environment than a

[16] Scholars from the UK, US, Canada and Australia were: Neville Postlethwaite, *School Organization and School Achievement* (1967); Douglas Pidgeon, *Expectation and Pupil Performance* (1970); John P Keeves, *Educational Environment and Student Achievement* (1972); Richard Noonan, *School Resources, Social Class and Student Achievement* (1976); Alison Kelly, *Girls and Science: An International Study of Sex Differences in School Science Achievements* (1978); Dean Nielsen, *Tolerating Political Dissent: The Impact of High School Social Climates in the United States and West Germany* (1977); Malcolm Rosier, *Early School Leavers in Australia* (1978); Rodney A. Clifton, *Socio-Economic Status Attitudes and Educational Performance: A Comparison of Students in England and New Zeeland* (1978). Then there were also a number of Swedes. Ian Dunlop (not technically a Swede but had been living there for many years) published *The Teaching o English in Swedish School: Studies in Methods of Instruction and Outcomes* (1975); Ingrid Munch, *Model Building in Comparative Education: Applications of the LISREL Method to Cross-National Survey Data* (1979); Lars Mählck, *Choice of Post-Secondary Studies in a Stratified System of Education* (1980); Kurt Bergling, who wrote two dissertations within the framework of IEA research: *The Development of the Hypothetic-Deductive Thinking in Children: A Cross-Cultural Study of the Validity of Piaget's Model of the Development of Logical Thinking* (1974) and *Moral Development: The Validity of Kohlberg's Theory* (1981).
The most important contact was of course with Postlethwaite, see Torsten Husén, 'Thomas Neville Postlethwaite: A Doctorfather's Subjective Portrait,' in *Reflections on Educational Achievement: Papers in Honour of T. Neville Postlethwaite to Mark the Occasion of his Retirement from His Chair in Comparative Education at the University of Hamburg*, eds. Wilfried Bos and Rainer H. Lehmann (New York: Waxmann Münster, 1995).

3 COLLECTING INTERNATIONAL DATA: HUSÉN AND THE INTERNATIONAL... 55

Stockholm one.' In sum, a move to London would bring financial benefits and make collaboration and communication easier, in addition to London being a pleasant city. At the same time, there were a number of disadvantages to choosing England over Stockholm. In Stockholm, office space was free, free computer time was offered by the computer centre, and there was an IEA data processing unit in Stockholm. In addition, the IEA was only funded for three more years and it might not be a good idea to move with only three years left. Other arguments in favour of staying in Sweden included good relations with an international aid organisation (SIDA) and a donor (the Bank of Sweden Tercentenary Foundation). Furthermore, there was the fact that the IEA's statues stated that the headquarters were in Stockholm, and the possible prospect of tax relief. Finally, an argument was about the role of Torsten Husén, the Swedish chairman. 'It would be an embarrassment both to various members of the Swedish Civil Service (who have helped get free office space and $ 125,000 worth of computer time) and Professor Husén for IEA to move out.'[17] It is likely that the last argument was a strong one, given that Husén was the chairman of the IEA and also had used the organization to strengthen his overall position in the field of comparative education. These discussions reflect a decision that every international organization faces at least once— where to locate its headquarters. Decisions on such issues can be useful because they affect the power dynamics of the organization. When a particular location becomes headquarters, it tends to privilege certain individuals and certain networks.

DATA PROCESSING

A related issue was where to locate data processing. In the 1960s and 1970s, powerful computers were rare, exclusive, and expensive. Computing was centralized, with computing centres first in the US and later in Stockholm—places to which data were sent in the form of punched cards, answer sheets, or answer cards. In a transnational research project like the IEA, where different countries were involved, expertise was naturally scattered across different locations, but the computer work had to be concentrated somewhere. Inevitably, there was a geographical dimension which

---

[17] 'Confidential: Personnel problems and location of IEA office (First draft).' Undated and unsigned document but written by Richard Noonan and Neville Postlethwaite in 1970 (The IEA archive, 403).

included a power dimension where some sites became more important than others.[18] When the mathematics survey was conducted, the computer centre was located in Chicago. It was chosen on the basis that key figures in the IEA (Benjamin Bloom, C. Arnold Anderson) were based in Chicago, but also because the university had its Computation Centre, which had 'both the facilities and personnel available to undertake the huge processing job that was required for the IEA study.'[19]

Chicago's position as the obvious location for data processing was soon challenged. As the organization was about to embark on a new project, the Six Subject Survey, new locations were proposed. An undated document, probably from 1967 or early 1968, discusses the question of where the data centre should be located in the future. The pros and cons of locating the centre in Chicago, New York, Stockholm, and London were considered. The IBM 360, the computer system chosen for the forthcoming study, was available in each of the cities. All of the alternatives were considered reasonable, although each had potential drawbacks. In the case of London, it was unclear whether enough computer time could be made available, and it would also be difficult to find people in England with sufficient knowledge to use the machine well. New York, on the other hand, was seen as a place well placed to work with Europeans, although it lacked experience in conducting IEA surveys.[20]

In May 1968, Torsten Husén met with Benjamin Bloom in Chicago to discuss where to locate the data processing unit. Husén, who had close links with several American scholars, was at the time a visiting professor in Honolulu, Hawaii, a long way from Europe. Bloom argued strongly that the computing should be done in the US, but this time at Columbia.[21] Husén fully endorsed Bloom's view on the preferable location.[22]

In contrast, some European staff at the IEA argued that at least some of the data processing should be done in Europe. Douglas Pidgeon, technical director of the IEA and employed by the National Foundation for

---

[18] See Thomas F. Gieryn, *Truth-Spots: How Places Make People Believe* (Chicago and London: University of Chicago Press, 2018).

[19] Torsten Husén, ed., *International Study of Achievement in Mathematics: A Comparison of Twelve Countries* vol. 1 (Stockholm: Almqvist & Wiksell and New York: John Wiley & Sons, 1967), 208–7.

[20] 'Arrangements for data processing', undated, ca. 1967 (The IEA archive, 243), 1.

[21] Torsten Husén, 'Notes taken at a meeting in Chicago on May 20, 1968, with Professor Benjamin S. Bloom on IEA business' (The IEA archive, 357).

[22] Torsten Husén to Neville Postlethwaite, May 21, 1968 (The IEA archive, 357).

Educational Research in England and Wales, wrote in a letter to Husén that a better alternative would be to do the initial work in London and then move to Teachers College, Columbia, at the end of 1969. The reasons for this were to do with the development of the computer programmes needed to process the IEA data. Pidgeon felt that close contact with the IEA Secretariat, then based in Hamburg, was essential to the development of the computer programmes. Many of the problems that had arisen during the previous study were probably due to the great physical distance between the data processing centre (Chicago) and the coordinating centre (Hamburg). Decisions had been made in Chicago without being checked against administrative decisions in Hamburg. Pidgeon conceded that locating data processing in London was still not an ideal solution (an optimal solution would be to have the data centre in the same building as the secretariat), but the move to Europe would anyway facilitate communication and meetings since it was 'fairly easy to phone Hamburg or London or vice versa' and it was also easier to meet on a fairly regular basis.[23]

The American Richard M. Wolf, who had been in charge of the data processing for the mathematics survey, disagreed strongly. Not only would it be costly and ineffective to divide the task between two different locations, it would also be dangerous: 'it would mean that one half of the data processing team will be in London & the other half in N.Y. & all sorts of problems can arise.' For example, letting people from IBM in London develop programmes for future use in the US made it complicated to control the quality of the programs: 'The IBM London people who develop the programs would not be at Columbia to tend to their own creations.'[24]

As this correspondence shows, there were tensions within the organization as different sites competed to host the data centre. In part it was a power struggle, with Wolf accusing one of the advocates of the London solution of being an 'empire builder.'[25]

The time factor played a crucial role in the discussion. Embarking on a major study with huge amounts of data without knowing in which country the computer analyses would be carried out was problematic. In July 1968, Bruce Choppin pointed out that programmes had to be written

---

[23] Douglas Pidgeon to Torsten Husén, May 27, 1968 (The IEA archive, 357).
[24] Dick [Richard M. Wolf] to Neville Postlethwaite, undated (The IEA archive, 357).
[25] Wolf to Postlethwaite, undated (The IEA archive, 357).

58   S. GREK ET AL.

before computer processing could begin. In the mathematics survey, this had taken a year. Choppin was in the process of writing such programmes, but he needed one or two assistants to do the job, and it was difficult to recruit someone before it had been decided where that person would work. So the whole project was in danger of being delayed.[26]

In addition, the task of relocating a computer centre was not easy at a time when computers were scarce, and their compatibility could be limited. The IEA had chosen a new computer system in 1967. The IBM 360 system computer had been selected because it was becoming the standard research computer at major universities around the world, and because it was compatible with different data stores and programming techniques, which meant that the analysis of IEA data could be 'done in many different places with different sized computers with little extra effort.'[27] However, it was not used everywhere. In 1968, Bruce Choppin investigated the possibilities of using London as a data processing location. One alternative was the IBM data centre in London. Another was the University College Computer Centre. After a meeting with the centre's director, Choppin was told that the IBM 360/65 computer was only available for University of London projects and was advised to contact the Newcastle University Computing Centre instead, which had the right computer, as well as the time and space for its computer. New to the business, they still needed customers.[28] Choppin went to see the Newcastle centre, and was rather enthusiastic. 'Briefly, Newcastle has adequate equipment to do our job and is eager to provide facilities to encourage us to come there. They need customers!' The price would be £40,000 for about 250 hours of computing time. While this was a substantial sum, there was a generous quality to the offer that probably set it apart from many other computer centres: it would not count the hours exactly:

> for this sum of money they would not want to account very carefully for the time we use and would, within reason, allow us to run and re-run our data

---

[26] Bruce Choppin to Torsten Husén, July 3, 1968 (The IEA archive, 399).

[27] Anonymous, 'Arrangements for data processing,' 1. The introduction of the system 360 was a watershed moment in the history of IBM and the computer industry, and the system has been described as one of the most important products of the twentieth century, comparable to the light bulb and Ford's Model T car. James W. Cortada, *IBM. The Rise and Fall and Reinvention of a Global Icon* (Cambridge, Massachusetts: MIT Press, 2019), chapter 8.

[28] Bruce Choppin to Douglas Pidgeon, February 29, 1968 (The IEA archive, 399).

until it was correct, even if it took us over the 250-hour estimate. Such a freedom is to me rather attractive.[29]

The offer is a reminder of the special conditions for data-driven research at the time. The cost of hiring computers was considerable, and under normal circumstances every hour counted, even if the computers counted wrongly, or if the analyses proved misleading or irrelevant.

In the end, neither London nor Newcastle was chosen; instead, a third alternative emerged. In 1969, it was decided that computer processing would take place in two places: New York and Stockholm. By setting up a computer terminal in Stockholm, it would be possible to carry out more advanced statistical analyses, closer to the team that were busy writing up the results of the Six Subject Survey. The solution had its drawbacks that had to be dealt with, an example is that computer tapes were more expensive in Stockholm, so the tapes would be purchased in New York and shipped to Sweden.[30] But there were other factors that made Stockholm and Sweden attractive. The organization moved its headquarters from Hamburg to Stockholm in 1969, where the chairman, Torsten Husén, was also based. Having a data centre in Stockholm was, therefore, part of a larger transformation of the organization, where expertise was increasingly being moved to Stockholm.

ELECTING A CHAIRMAN

The early years of the IEA are dominated by two figures who were close to each other, Torsten Husén and Neville Postlethwaite. Both chaired the organization for long periods, Husén from 1962 to 1978 and Postlethwaite from 1978 to 1986.

But before Husén became a chairman in 1962, there was a more short-lived chairman whose dramatic departure from the IEA is interesting to follow: W. D. Wall. He had a background in UNESCO, Paris, and was since 1956 director of the National Foundation for Educational Research in England and Wales. He has been described as the person who first brought together the group of scholars at the UNESCO Institute in 1955

---

[29] Bruce Choppin to Neville Postlethwaite, March 18, 1968 (The IEA archive, 399).

[30] T. Neville Postlethwaite, 'IEA major decisions reached at the New York meeting', June 17, 1969 (The IEA archive, 14).

60 S. GREK ET AL.

who eventually formed the IEA.[31] As a person, Wall was, according to Husén's recollections, 'a dynamic person, so efficient that other people sometimes felt offended.'[32]

In 1962, he dramatically decided to resign as chairman, apparently in protest at Saul Robinsohn, the director of UNESCO Institute for Education. Wall's resignation has been described as a surprising, almost scandalous act, leading to a situation where an international organization found itself without a leader. As Alan C. Purves later put it:

> Robinsohn was cool toward the type of work that the IEA was thinking of doing and was none too happy to have this quite different groups of researchers forming an independent unit within his fiefdom. Conditions became so difficult that, at the beginning of the next meeting, in June 1962, Wall had a stormy meeting with Robinsohn about the place of the institute in the new mathematics study, and, as a result, Wall went back to England. Here was a new, large-scale, cooperative venture—suddenly without a chairman.[33]

What happened at the meeting? One of the participants, Torsten Husén, arrived late to the meeting, a day after the others, and by then Wall had already resigned. In his recollections of the meeting, Husén chooses not to comment on the reasons, only noting that the organization was now in a kind of crisis and, therefore, asked him to take over the chairmanship.[34]

However, the tensions that led to Wall's resignation were not new. Correspondence shows that as early as 1961, there was a sense that the organization might soon be without a chairman. In a remarkable letter, Benjamin Bloom, one of the IEA's leading figures, urged Wall to stay on and not let personal conflicts interfere with the work:

> We are attempting to embark on a venture so large and complex that personalities and irritations must not be permitted to block our efforts. As

---

[31] Alan C. Purves, 'The Evolution of the IEA: A Memoir,' *Comparative Education Review* 31, no. 1 (1987): 532; see also Maren Elfert, 'Six Decades of Educational Multilateralism in a Globalising World: The History of the UNESCO Institute in Hamburg', *International Review of Education* 59 (2013): especially 271.

[32] Arlid Tjeldvoll and Hans G. Lingens, eds., *Torsten Husén: Conversations in Comparative Education* (Bloomington: Phi Delta Kappa Educational Foundation, 2000), 44.

[33] Purves, 'Evolution of the IEA,' 12.

[34] Tjeldvoll and Lingens, *Conversations*, 49.

3 COLLECTING INTERNATIONAL DATA: HUSÉN AND THE INTERNATIONAL...   61

between you and Robinsohn there is no question. If anyone is to be dropped—it must not be you. Please be assured of my confidence in you and my willingness to drop Robinsohn and the Unesco Institute if this must be done.[35]

This way of putting things is interesting, as it suggests that although the IEA was formally working under the auspices of the UNESCO Institute, it was already by this time possible to envisage the IEA developing into an autonomous institution, which it subsequently became. Equally interesting is that while Bloom could imagine the IEA separating from the UNESCO Institute, he could not imagine an organization without the leadership of W. D. Wall: 'You are necessary to the international study. Each of us has a contribution to make but we can be easily replaced. You can not. Neither Husén nor Bloom could possibly manage this venture—you can.'[36]

A factor that made the issue of leadership more urgent was the fact that the IEA was applying for funding from the US Office of Education at the time. Bloom, who was heavily involved in the application process, felt that it was vital that the organization could hold together, at least until funding was secured. He, therefore, advised Wall on how to proceed. 'Our small venture may in the long run speak directly to the central problems or our time. Let's not miss this opportunity because of the friction created by one incompetent sick man.'[37]

Husén also wrote to Wall to express his support for him as chairman. Unlike Bloom, he didn't express any anger at Robinsohn, but focused entirely on Wall and his positive qualities:

Among all uncertainty of our huge undertaking there is one axiomatic feature of our Committee. I have seen enough of you in that capacity to feel 100% convinced that the only chance of getting our venture into the final harbor is to have you as the skipper.[38]

This belief in the influence of one single person is in a sense a paradox. Wall does not appear to have had a very strong role as a scientific leader. IEA's first study, released in 1962, was headed by an American researcher, Arthur W. Foshay, and sources are unclear about what Wall actually

[35] Benjamin Bloom to W.D. Wall, August 25, 1961 (The Husén archive, 1.20).
[36] Bloom to Wall, August 25, 1961.
[37] Bloom to Wall, August 25, 1961.
[38] Torsten Husén to W. D. Wall, October 9, 1961 (The Husén archive, 1.20).

62 S. GREK ET AL.

contributed with. He didn't write anything in the report and his name appears only once in the text, in a list of some 20 people who had contributed to the study. The person who wrote the foreword to the report was Wall's antagonist, Saul Robinsohn, and he didn't mention Wall with a word. The fact that Robinsohn wrote the foreword illustrates that the project was still associated with the UNESCO Institute, and that the IEA still had to find a status as an autonomous organisation.

A few weeks after his resignation, Wall wrote a letter to Husén. They also spoke on the phone, but what was said is not known. The letter was about whether the research institute where Wall was director, the National Foundation for Educational Research in England and Wales, would continue to be involved in the IEA. Wall confirmed that they would, but on one condition: that the IEA would remain a collaborative project and not be dominated by the UNESCO Institute for Education.[39] Husén replied that he agreed with Wall's position and that he saw UNESCO's role as merely one of co-ordination.[40]

Becoming chairman in the midst of an organizational crisis was probably a challenge for Husén, although there is little comment on this in the sources. In a letter to his predecessor, written after the Hamburg meeting at which Husén surprisingly became the new chairman, he described how unusual the new role felt for him. He said that he 'had a hard time in Hamburg trying to perform some of the functions you so skilfully carried out at our previous meetings.' He also referred to 'linguistic shortcomings' and 'tensions in the meeting atmosphere.'[41] In the coming years he would get many possibilities to try adapting to the role as chairman, gradually becoming more or less synonymous with the organisation itself.

The election of Torsten Husén as chairman in the summer of 1962 meant that the IEA got a chairman who was more academically visible than Wall. As chairman, Husén was dependent on a large number of staff, and much of the practical work was done by his colleagues, but he was still involved in many decisions and was highly visible in publications. The first major publication, the two-volume study of mathematics in 1967, has Torsten Husén's name on the cover, as he was the editor of the volumes. The following reports from the six subject survey had forewords by Husén.

---

[39] W. D. Wall to Torsten Husén, June 29, 1962 (The Husén archive, 1.24).
[40] Torsten Husén to W.D. Wall, August 27, 1962 (Husén archive, 1.24).
[41] Husén to Wall, 27 August, 1962.

RECRUITING COUNTRIES

The discussion above has directed attention to the location of specific centres of calculation, specific places where expertise has been concentrated. But international large-scale assessments are fundamentally about collecting data from a broad range of countries, and in that sense the project is by its very nature distributed in space. To understand what the IEA was, it is important to consider which countries were involved, as this says a lot about the nature of the studies conducted, as well as the power asymmetries within the organization. The organization had a clear base in European countries and the US, but it was never an exclusively European organization, and over time there was a change in which countries were involved. The particular countries that choose and are chosen to participate play a crucial role in determining the character of the comparative endeavour. A small-scale study with a few, relatively homogeneous countries is quite different from a large-scale study with countries with different social and political systems and with different levels of competence in educational research. Over time, the number of countries participating in international assessments has steadily increased. During the two last decades, more than 90 countries and economies have participated in PISA. The first two studies conducted by the IEA, the pilot study in 1962 and the mathematics study in 1967, involved 12 countries, mainly from Europe.[42] But already in the 1960s, when the Six Subject Survey was planned there was a process of expansion, as several new countries joined the organization.

As an international organization, the IEA presupposed the existence of national research on education. The IEA described itself as an international, non-profit-making scientific association. As such, the criteria for membership were clear. Only institutions that conducted research in education were eligible for membership.[43] Thus, it was not countries that were members, but research centres that represented the country.

---

[42] The countries that participated in the 1962 pilot study were Belgium, England, Finland, France, Federal Republic of Germany, Israel, Poland, Scotland, Sweden, Switzerland, USA, and Yugoslavia. In the mathematics study, the countries were Australia, Belgium, England, Finland, France, Federal Republic of Germany, Israel, Japan, The Netherlands, Scotland, Sweden, and the United States.

[43] International Association for the Evaluation of Educational Achievement, *Information on the International Association for the Evaluation of Educational Achievement (IEA) 1968* (Hamburg: UNESCO Institute for Education, 1968), 3.

64   S. GREK ET AL.

Such an international organization would have been difficult, if not impossible, just a few decades earlier, when there were few national centres for educational research. Early steps towards the establishment of a national educational research organization were taken in the late 1920s with the establishment of the Scottish Council for Research in Education in 1928, followed by similar organizations in Australia and New Zealand, and then in the 1940s with the establishment of a National Foundation for Educational Research in England and Wales.[44] In Sweden SPPI was formed in 1944.[45] In other countries this happened later, and that establishment was a prerequisite for membership in the organisation.

National centres from some 20 countries participated in the Six Subject Survey published in the 1970s. The participating countries were Australia, Belgium (Flemish-speaking), Belgium (French-speaking), Chile, England, West Germany, Finland, France, Hungary, India, Iran, Ireland, Israel, Italy, Japan, the Netherlands, New Zealand, Romania, Scotland, Sweden, Thailand, and the United States. In other words, the IEA was not a clear example of a Europeanization of educational research. It extended well beyond the borders of Europe, and important financial and intellectual influences were American. This created a research space that was arguably more diverse and thereby prone to tensions over issues such as translation and comparability. In a sense, the IEA stood on the shoulders of all these institutes around the world. In January 1969, the IEA's full-time staff was limited to just three people, whereas the national institutes with which it collaborated were considerably larger (around 30 people per institute was a common figure).

The process of enlargement can be traced in the sources. In November 1966, the Standing Committee of the IEA discussed the question of admitting new countries to the organization. As the IEA was about to embark on a new study, the Six Subject Survey, it was felt that there was room for more countries. Attitudes towards enlargement were somewhat ambivalent: On the one hand, it was stressed that the IEA should not expand at any cost; the machinery was complicated and the number of countries should not exceed 18 or 20 in the next phase of the project. On

[44] Martin Lawn, 'The Institute as Network: The Scottish Council for Research in Education as a Local and International Phenomena in the 1930s,' *Paedagogica Historica* 40, no. 5/6 (2004): 726.

[45] Christian Lundahl, *Viljan att veta vad andra vet: Kunskapsbedömning i tidigmodern, modern och senmodern skola* (Stockholm: Arbetslivsinstitutet, 2006).

the other hand, the inclusion of developing, semi-developing, or socialist countries could be beneficial to the organization, as it would include a wider range of education systems, which would make for more interesting cross-country comparisons. Two types of countries were suggested as being of particular interest: socialist countries (USSR, Hungary, Poland, Yugoslavia) and Asian countries (Thailand, India, Korea, Taiwan). Nigeria was also mentioned as a possible collaborator.[46] In the following, one aspect of the expansion will be highlighted: the efforts to include socialist countries.

Given that the IEA was born during the Cold War, in the aftermath of the Sputnik crisis, it was a flaw in the project that so few socialist countries were represented. The pilot study published in 1962 included two socialist countries (Yugoslavia and Poland), but not the mathematics study published in 1967. As the project expanded in the second half of the 1960s, with new countries, new populations, and new subjects, it was felt important to include a greater variety of countries. The USSR and Poland were two countries that the organization tried unsuccessfully to recruit, while Hungary participated in several studies and Romania in one (French).[47]

Among socialist countries, the USSR was the top priority country. The first documented attempt to recruit the USSR to the IEA dates back to 1961, when Saul B. Robinsohn, the director of the UNESCO Institute for Education, contacted Aleksei Leontiev on at least three occasions. Two of the letters have been found in the archive, and they give the impression that the initiative to collaborate came from the people at the IEA rather than from the Soviet scholars. The latter seem to have been slow at best in replying. In the first of the two remaining letters, Robinsohn refers to an earlier letter he had written and asks whether Leontiev had been able to take any steps to secure Soviet participation in the IEA project. In the letter he mentions that he had already sent a pamphlet on the project, but as Leontiev had not replied, he was now sending two more copies. A month later, Robinsohn sent another letter, enclosing—for the third time in a row—the information folder on the project.[48]

---

[46] 'Criteria for National Centres Participating in the IEA Study (Extract from Minutes of Standing Committee Meeting, Nov 21, 1966)' (The IEA archive, 357).

[47] In fact, Poland did participate in the Six Subject Survey, but decided not to release data to the IEA.

[48] Saul B. Robinson to Aleksei Leontiev, May 19, 1961 (The IEA archive, 299); Saul B. Robinson to Aleksei Leontiev June 20, 1961 (The IEA archive, 299).

The 1961 attempts were unsuccessful, but more ambitious contacts soon followed. In 1965, Neville Postlethwaite, Torsten Husén, and Benjamin Bloom travelled to the USSR to meet with the Academy of Pedagogical Sciences and discuss their participation in the IEA studies. Postlethwaite has described the meeting in an account written some decades later. He writes that the meeting went well, but there were two surprises. First, that the Soviet researchers had very little experience of sample surveys in education, and second, that they did not have lunch. Instead, the guests were offered a remarkable dinner in the evening. They were driven in state cars to a Georgian restaurant, where the tables were 'overflowing with the very finest culinary delights.' In contrast to the low-quality food at the hotel or nearby restaurants, this was exceptional food that made them feel like 'high-level dignitaries.' It was an evening that seemed to promise future collaboration.

> The evening was filled with innumerable vodka toasts to all sorts of good causes and ended with hearty hugs. Despite the many promises made and goodwill shared, however, it would be more than twenty years before the USSR joined the IEA effort.[49]

In the summer of 1967, Neville Postlethwaite and Torsten Husén made another trip to the USSR, trying once again to recruit the country to the IEA. The attempt failed, even if it for a while looked as if they had succeeded. In December 1967, an IEA Council meeting was held in Stockholm. A person from the Soviet Union was invited to attend as an observer. At the last minute he cancelled, sending a telegram blaming a sudden illness.[50] Nevertheless, the IEA decided at the meeting to formally accept the USSR as a new member of the organization. Whether the USSR accepted this admission is unclear. Later documentation from the following years shows that the country did not become a member at this stage. In fact, it was only after the collapse of the Soviet Union that Russia finally participated in IEA surveys.[51]

---

[49] T. Neville Postlethwaite, 'A Man of Principle', in *Benjamin S. Bloom: Portraits of an Educator*, ed. Thomas R. Guskey (Lanham: Rowman & Littlefield Education, 2012): 72.

[50] Telegram quoted in a speech by Torsten Husén at the IEA Council meeting in Stockholm 1967 (The IEA archive, 357).

[51] For a short historical background on testing in the Soviet Union and Russia, see Nelli Piattoeva and Galina Gurova, 'Domesticating International Assessments in Russia: Historical Grievances, National Values, Scientific Rationality and Education Modernisation', in *Assessment Cultures. Historical Perspectives*, eds. Cristina Alarcón and Martin Lawn (Berlin: Peter Lang, 2018).

In the absence of the USSR, Hungary became an attractive alternative. According to a letter written by Postlethwaite in 1966, Hungarian actors expressed great interest in taking part. He had been approached by the Hungarian professor György Ágoston, probably at a meeting at the UNESCO Institute for Education in Hamburg. Ágoston, who was to join the board of the UNESCO Institute the following year, urged Postlethwaite to come to Hungary to study its methods. In a letter Postlethwaite described that Ágoston was 'very keen for me to go to Hungary, and speak to the research workers there, and for me to look at some of the work which they are doing.' Postlethwaite thought that it would be good to have a socialist country join the IEA, and Hungary was a good alternative 'since it seems to be unlikely that the USSR will come in.'[52] However, the inclusion of Hungary was a politically sensitive issue. Dependence on the Soviet Union was still palpable. In 1967 there were proposals to organize a small IEA meeting in Hungary. Professor Ágoston agreed to organize the meeting, but on two conditions: (a) that the IEA could promise funding from sources other than the US government, (b) that the Moscow authorities would still have a positive attitude towards the IEA after the trip that Postlethwaite and Husén were planning in the summer of 1967. If these conditions were met, he would be able not only to arrange the meeting but also to invite observers from the USSR, Czechoslovakia, and Poland.[53] In sum, the IEA was an organization that wanted to grow, and the logic of growth was shaped by the current relationships between countries, where it was deemed attractive, yet not unproblematic, to recruit socialist countries.

THE DREAM OF GLOBAL KNOWLEDGE

The idea of international statistics stretches back to the nineteenth century but has ever since been fraught with difficulties. While statistics has an inherent ability to work at a distance, there are a number of challenges that occur when data is collected on an international level. When the IEA embarked on their first studies published in the 1960s and 1970s, they had to decide on a number of questions. How many countries should be included? Where should it be managed? Who should lead (chair) the project? As this chapter has shown, such issues were not resolved once and for all, but became subjects of potential negotiation. Collaborating across

---

[52] Neville Postlethwaite to Torsten Husén, April 22, 1966 (The IEA archive, 299).
[53] Neville Postlethwaite to Torsten Husén, March 22, 1966 (The IEA archive, 357).

borders was a complex issue that involved how work should be distributed across space and whether certain sites should have a privileged status as centres of collaboration. Over time we can see both stability and flux when it comes to how the organisation was governed. Some sites held a privileged position for a while, such as the Chicago computer centre or the headquarters in Hamburg and later Stockholm, but none of the sites had a permanent status. One of the stabilising factors in this volatile situation was actually Torsten Husén, who stayed as a chairman for 17 years, providing the group with a continuity that made it possible to continue with its overarching strive to collect more and more information of the educational world.

Put in other words, that ambition was part of what Hewson calls 'informational globalism,' a tendency that he argues has been reinforced by international organizations and global governance. He emphasizes that while the mobilization of information is undoubtedly ancient, it was not until the nineteenth century that we began to see information networks that were global in scale.[54]

The rise of this informational globalism has been supported by beliefs as much as by techniques of data collection. In his study *World projects*, Krajewski discusses various attempts to collect global information around the year 1900. He notices that at the time there was a thorough enthusiasm for different kinds of global projects. From today's perspective, they appear, as he says, 'as naïve as they are megalomaniacal.'[55] International statistics might be included in this story of global projects. It shared the view of scientific progress and the possibility to change the world by collecting data on it, but it often proved difficult to implement it in practice. It is possible to describe a similar story when it comes to international assessments in education. The scholars involved needed to feel a sense of enthusiasm in order to engage in the projects that were poorly funded and required a lot of complicated work that was only partly paid in terms of money and time. The enthusiasm was, however, not shared unanimously by the people who took part of the studies. Nevertheless, what the IEA did in the 1960s and 1970s in the long run turned out to be highly influential.

---

[54] Martin Hewson, 'Did Global Governance Create Informational Globalism?,' in *Approaches to Global Governance Theory,* ed. Martin Hewson and Timothy J. Sinclair (Albany, NY: State University of New York Press, 1999).

[55] Markus Krajewski, *World Projects: Global Information Before World War I* (Minneapolis: University of Minnesota Press, 2014), x.

CHAPTER 4

The Rise of a Global Expert Network: The International Institute for Educational Planning, 1963–1973

The history of educational planning represents an important, yet severely neglected theme in the global history of the production of educational knowledge. During the 1960s, educational planning emerged as a swiftly expanding field of knowledge with global outreach. It was within this context that the International Institute for Educational Planning (IIEP) was founded, with the main purpose of supporting educational planning capacities in developing countries. Located in Paris from 1963 onwards, but with staff from all over the world, the Institute exemplified a new way of collaborating internationally, focused on the newly emergent agenda of educational planning. Similar to the IEA, the IIEP represents an excellent example of a dis-embedded laboratory, producing educational knowledge for policymaking, not only within Europe, but having global aspirations and with a particular focus on linking education with development, especially of countries in the Global South (what was then called 'the third world'). In some respects, and as often implied in the IIEP documents, the work of education planning of the middle of the twentieth century came as a response to the fast wave of decolonisation of countries in the 'developing' world, which were now seen as needing the support of—primarily Western European and American—experts in order to develop their fast-expanding education systems.

The original version of the chapter has been revised. The year [1963] was misspelled in the initially published version of this chapter and has been corrected. The correction to this chapter can be found at https://doi.org/10.1007/978-3-031-68090-8_8

© The Author(s), under exclusive license to Springer Nature Switzerland AG 2024, corrected publication 2024
S. Grek et al., *The World as a Laboratory*, Global Histories of Education, https://doi.org/10.1007/978-3-031-68090-8_4

69

Nonetheless, the IIEP was not merely a research organisation. It stood on two legs: research *and* training. This dual role, how it came about, how it worked out and its implications for the rise of expert education knowledge for policymaking, will be the focus of this chapter. In other words, not only was IIEP an organisation that funded studies about the relatively new field of education planning, but a very significant aspect of this work was to disseminate this knowledge in order to teach others. Therefore, the IIEP represents one of the earliest examples of what much later (from the 1980s onwards) would become a standard feature of the work of many international organisations in education; that is, the translation of education research into specific policy recommendations. By conducting studies in a variety of countries, and especially in the Global South, as well as training researchers and practitioners working in these countries (often as part of these studies), the Institute represented one of the first attempts at merging policy and research on a global scale.

As we have seen in the discussion of the work of the IEA, specific circumstances and conditions shaped the emergence of the IIEP as a disembedded laboratory. IIEP represents an early example of the ways that international organisations, tied to state power, also emerged as powerful bureaucracies in themselves. The Institute, which has been surprisingly neglected in the research about international organisations, also warrants attention as a focal point and norm-setter of the role of education in post-war foreign policy in the context of the Cold War and decolonisation. Its double remit is particularly significant in showing the effort not only to establish an international field of comparison and commensuration, but also promote and expand it through communicating its practices and ideals to others.

Thus, this chapter begins by exploring the historical circumstances and specific conditions that enabled the creation of the IIEP; it then moves on to explore Husén's archival material in order to document the history of the IIEP in the decade 1963–1973, in an effort to examine the emergence and evolution of the field of educational planning and development discourse and travelling knowledge; although Husén served as a chairman between 1970 and 1980, his archive is rich in relation to that early period in the history of the IIEP that is mostly of interest here. The chapter focuses specifically first on revealing the emergent *interdependencies* of government, universities, international organisations and philanthropic foundations in the systematic production and stabilization of a new field of education research and practice: that is, the field of educational planning. Second, the chapter examines the significance of *narrative-making*, especially in relation to the construction of the discourse around the need for educational planning, as well as the links of education with economic development. Finally, the chapter focused on the importance of IIEP's influence in terms of teaching others, especially developing countries. This latter function of the IIEP heralds another novel function of the organization; that is, the close linking of education in facilitating development in countries of the Global South, through teaching courses, offering intensive training and other processes of socialization through the governing board meetings.

A Brief History of the IIEP

According to the IIEP's own website, the Institute was created 'in July 1963 amid unprecedented educational expansion and change. Science, technology, economic development, politics, and culture were also undergoing major changes—which would all impact education in various ways' (IIEP 2023). At the same time, the period after the post-war European reconstruction was characterised by major political and social change: a wave of decolonization was sweeping African nations, 17 of which gained independence in the 1960s. This major development led to the need to create an organization that would guide the planning of education in the Global South and beyond: the IIEP, founded at the initiative of UNESCO and with the collaboration and support of the World Bank, the French Government and the Ford Foundation, was

> From the outset, ... conceived as an autonomous, multidisciplinary organization, designed to support educational planning capacities in developing nations, to build bridges between international actors, and offer expertise on strategic educational issues.[1]

The official foundations of the IIEP lay in UNESCO's adoption of the 'Convention Against Discrimination in Education,' signed on 14 December 1960 and entering into force two years later, on 22 May 1962. The Convention was a major milestone in UNESCO work, as it was the UNESCO's first major international instrument that had binding force in international law. At the same time, the links between education and the economic prosperity of nations were becoming stronger and stronger, especially after the organization of the Washington Conference on

[1] IIEP, *40th Anniversary of the IIEP* (Paris: UNESCO, 2003), not paginated in original.

Economic Growth and Investment in Education, convened by the OECD, in October 1961. UNESCO continued its international mission by organizing conferences in multiple cities of the South, such as Addis Ababa, Karachi and Santiago de Chile, as well as receiving 'requests for technical assistance' (IIEP 2003) by developing nations. According to Clarence Edward Beeby, the mission was clear: although multidisciplinarity was described as the core of the IIEP's independent research agenda,

> I know of no human activity that is much more important at this moment in the world's history than research and teaching in educational planning, and I know none that is more difficult. For it involves the marriage of two social sciences, economics and education, each, we must admit, a bit uncertain in itself, and each traditionally somewhat suspicious—or at least neglectful—of the other. To make a love-match between that pair is not going to be simple.[2]

Similarly, such direct linkages between education and the economy of nations were made by IIEP director, Philip H. Coombs, in his first report to the Governing Board in July 1963:

> In a broad sense the Institute's establishment at this time expresses the growing recognition by economists, educators, general planners and national leaders that more emphasis must be placed on the human factor in economic and social development. Shortages of competent manpower, reflecting educational inadequacies, have become in many countries a serious handicap not only to economic growth, but to the strengthening of crucial social institutions and advancement generally.[3]

Following this direction in terms of linking education with increasing 'manpower' and economic prosperity, a consultative committee met at UNESCO in June 1962, comprised of representatives from Brazil, France, Germany, Italy, Nigeria, Sweden, the UK, USA and USSR, as well as actors from IOs, such as the Food and Agriculture Organisation, the International Labour Organisation, the World Bank, the World Health Organisation and the UN. The committee agreed on developing a new institution, the IIEP, with the aim for it to be 'multidisciplinary,'

---

[2] IIEP, *40th* Anniversary, 4, quoting Clarence E. Beeby.
[3] IIEP, *40th Anniversary*, 6, quoting Philip H. Coombs.

4 THE RISE OF A GLOBAL EXPERT NETWORK: THE INTERNATIONAL... 73

'autonomous' as well as 'a place for practitioners and potential practitioners in educational planning to take courses and gather useful experience.'[4]

Although the French government had originally offered a villa for hosting the IIEP in Rue Eugène Delacroix in Paris' 16th arrondissement, the space was too small to cater for the needs of the growing institute and especially for hosting trainees from all over the world; a new building was constructed in the same site and was ready in 1973, the same building that still hosts IIEP today. The IIEP's autonomy was an issue of debate at the time, as the committee wanted to ensure the intellectual independence of the institute, so as to attract the best education expertise available. In the end, UNESCO created the Institute as a quasi-autonomous body—within UNESCO's legal framework, yet outside the UNESCO Secretariat. The Institute was given its own Statutes and a Governing Board with authority over the Institute's policies, programmes and budget. In addition, a set of rules was prepared to address the IIEP's specific needs and circumstances. The Institute was given the authority to receive financial support from any appropriate source, and space to manage its own administrative affairs.

IIEP, therefore, became one of the first international organisations in the field of education where its governing board consisted entirely of eight acclaimed education experts and economists, four of whom *had* to come from Latin America, Asia, Africa and the Arab States, as well as four members of IOs, specifically from the UN, the World Bank, a UN agency and the UN Economic Commission. From the start, the IIEP would emphasise the need for the production of 'applied' research: for example, in 1964, Coombs organised the first gathering of whom were called 'producers' and 'consumers' of education research in Bellagio, Italy, with the aim to create an *Inventory of Research Needs*.[5] Priorities for the rising field of educational planning were a focus on the performance of education systems; the 'mutual adaptation of educational and economic systems'; and the 'internal effectiveness' of educational systems.[6]

At the same time, right from the start, the IIEP blended its research and studies with the offer of training and 'technical assistance' to those that requested it, and particularly countries of—what was then seen as—the developing world. Launched in 1965, the Advanced Training

[4] IIEP, *40th Anniversary*, 7.
[5] Philip H. Coombs, *Educational Planning: An Inventory of Major Research Needs* (Paris: UNESCO, 1965).
[6] Coombs, *Educational Planning*.

74   S. GREK ET AL.

Programme in Educational planning and management allowed education professionals (mostly civil servants and statisticians) to stay in Paris for nine months in order to learn concepts, tools and techniques that relate to the field of educational planning, alongside mixing with peers from a number of countries and learning from best practice in Europe. Other trainee programmes were instigated in early 1970s, including visiting trainees (for those that could only stay in Paris for limited amount of time), as well as intensive training courses on specific matters, either in Paris or other locations.

From the start, it was obvious to IIEP members that producing applied research in combination with the offer of training programmes

> represents not only contributions to the study of various aspects of the educational field and educational planning, but also an original form of assistance in *building up the capabilities for research and action* of those countries that request the Institute's co-operation.[7]

However, apart from the interest in capacity-building the IIEP was key in shaping some of the dominant narratives of the time in relation to education planning, which for decades would become the 'bread-and-butter' of quantitative education research: these were, first, issues around education financing (specifically how to finance the massive education expansion that was taking place in 1960s, with a focus on studying different finance mechanisms and costs); second, school mapping and microplanning (the study of administrative, economic, demographic, and social factors that would determine student access); and, last but not least, the issue of raising quality in education, as a way of building 'a broader vision of educational planning.'[8]

Two specific landmark events started the discussion around raising the quality of education systems: the first was the 1966 IIEP international seminar on 'The qualitative aspects of educational planning' (attended by the economist and Nobel Prize winner Arthur Lewis) with the intention to work on a philosophical analysis of the concept of 'quality in education';[9] and second, Coombs' book *The World Crisis in Education* which

---

[7] International Institute for Educational Planning, *IIEP Medium-Term Plan 1979–1983* (Paris: UNESCO, 1980), 3 (our emphasis).

[8] IIEP, *40th Anniversary*, 25.

[9] Clarence E. Beeby, ed., *Qualitative Aspects of Educational Planning* (Paris: UNESCO, 1969).

'challenged the field of educational planning to adopt new planning techniques that would examine the impact that schooling structures, curriculum content, and teaching methods had on the success of educational plans.'[10] This continued interest in issues of quality would be the engine that would motor IIEP's pivot to the measurement of outputs, rather than inputs in education, which would come later on, from the 1980s onwards, when the science/policy nexus in education would reach maturity and look for new challenges, new fields of enquiry and new ways to closely connect education with the changing economic markets.

However, this examination is beyond the scope of this chapter. Instead, the focus is on IIEP's early development as a disembedded laboratory of the social construction of post-war international education research. Before doing so, however, we will briefly examine the Husén archive in terms of sources for studying the IIEP, since it covers a lot of interesting materials which will help guide our analysis later on.

THE HUSÉN ARCHIVE ON THE IIEP

Amidst the 32 IIEP-related archival boxes that the Husén archive hold,[11] we examined the first five in depth: these cover the organisation's institutional procedures and work carried out by its members spanning from 1966 to 1980. The folders are separated in chronological periods and/or topic. Within the folders, three major categories of documents can be distinguished; letters, reports and studies, while statutes, brochures, newspaper articles and evaluation forms are also present. These documents illustrate the operation of IIEP and allow a first understanding of the inner-organisational collaborations, relations between its members, the aims and focus as well as the challenges the organisation was facing. Cross-organisational collaborations within UNESCO and outwith international institutions and government bodies are also presented through reports, letters, memoranda, and studies.

The first category of documents provides an insight into the above through the formal communication between different actors and highlights both fruitful collaborations and inter-personal or organisational

---

[10] Philip H. Coombs, *The World Educational Crisis: A Systems Analysis* (London: Oxford University Press, 1968); IIEP, *40th Anniversary*, 26.

[11] The Husén archive, 2.53, 2.54, 2.55, 2.56, 2.65, 2.66, 2.70, 2.71, 2.72, 2.73, 2.74, 2.75, 2.76, 2.77, 2.78: 2.79: 2.80, 2.81, 2.82, 2.83, 2.156, 2.225–2.235.

conflicts. By paying attention to the context and pre-context of the letters, three key characteristics of IIEP are emerging. Firstly, the diversity of the nationalities of its members, which reflects the internationalised character of the organisation and the post-war sentiment of international collaboration. Secondly, the diversity of positions and backgrounds of its members, who are not only based on academic, teaching or solely educational-related roles but also in organisations affiliated to development more widely (the ILO, WHO and SIDA are some examples), which also illustrates the perspective of education being inextricably connected with economic and labour affairs. Thirdly, as probably expected for this period, despite its diversity in nationalities, backgrounds and roles of its members, the vast majority of participants are men.

The second category, of thematic documents, presents a detailed view on the operation and collaborations of IIEP, its priorities and negotiations, challenges and opportunities that emerge. Given that the programme of the Institute was being reviewed by the IIEP's board and staff members annually at the sessions of the governing board, the archive contains reports by the director that shed light onto the projects, governance and decision-making processes of the organisation. Documents related to Board meetings also provide detailed analysis and elaboration on the operation of the IIEP, often resulting in medium-term plans, as the immediate outcomes of such processes.

The locations of meetings and the sessions of the Governing Board were rotated in different countries and continents, although an evident disproportion of meetings held in Europe is evident. Apart from aiming to make these as accessible as possible to all members, moving locations of the meetings was also creating the opportunity to hold parallel meetings with educational and other officials during the days of the proceedings and discuss wider/specific issues to each country region. For example, there is communication during the preparations for the 10th session of the Governing Board which took place in Chile about the possibility of holding a meeting with President Allende and including an official from Cuba in the proceedings. Therefore, governing board meetings were fertile ground not only for the inner workings and governance of the IIEP, but also a way to promote its work and make connections with local and national actors in different world regions. Indeed, the letter exchanges between members of the IIEP show clearly how meetings, either formal or informal—during dinners, for example—were scheduled as part of the visits, alongside lectures, bilateral meetings, and conferences that created additional opportunities to discuss issues (or socialise). Thus, we need to examine governing board meetings not only as a way for the members of the IIEP to meet but also as spaces of exchanges, diplomacy and creating new connections, networks, and interdependencies. We will return to the role of governing board meetings in the empirical sections below.

Thirdly, in terms of IIEP research projects, the archive folders are rich with studies, papers, and research proposals, alongside lists of publications, that illustrate the immense body of work that was produced through the years. Like the reports, these show the priorities of the organisation as well as the various needs for educational development and planning in different parts of the world, from rural education to adult learning, and from the connection of the university with labour markets to new information technology that could be utilised in the classroom. As already discussed, the IIEP research in the decade 1963–1973 is significant not only for the studies in themselves, but also for the emergent focus on linking education with international development. Apart from the emergent and increasing focus on planning and its application for 'developing' those systems deemed underdeveloped (usually in the Global South), new interlinkages between organisations, particularly between IIEP, and universities and ministries are emerging through these studies; these connections underline a wide network of actors and resources, showing that collaborations were not only horizontal with other IOs, but also with national actors. In this respect, governing board meetings and associated events link up closely with new IIEP research which is usually presented at these spaces, embodying IIEP's values and aims, but also the challenges that large scale, national or international studies face. These collaborations and interdependencies are a focal point of the analysis below.

In addition, the folder materials document significant changes in the governance, structure, and infrastructure of the organisation during the first decade of the IIEP. Transitions in the governing board are the most common, with nominating procedures and elections taking place after members have reached the end of their term, or if they resigned. Although nominating committees and the Governing Board were holding meetings related to new appointments on the board or other positions, such as the council of consultants, a large trace of letter communication shows the backdrop of such procedures and discussions on preferences and concerns about specific candidates among members of the board and IIEP's management. Beyond the frequent changes that were inevitably taking place on the Governing Board, the change of the Directorship initiated in early

1973 resulted in a challenging procedure that caused frictions among members of the IIEP and showed vulnerabilities with the IIEP's governance. Several letters in the archive document how John Vaizey, initially elected as IIEP's director in 1973, had to resign after a medical diagnosis that he received. This event led the organisation to consider either extending the term of the previous director or appoint a new standing director. A controversy arose around this issue between Vaizey, secretary to the Governing Board Charles Berkowitch, and other members. At the same time, Hans Weiler who was invited to an interview for the directorship, highlighted his disappointment with the process and criticised UNESCO in writing. This move resulted in René Maheu, director general of UNESCO, attempting to discredit him. Beyond such inter-personal conflicts and the effects they had on the governance of the organisation, this incident clearly illustrated the only partial autonomy that IIEP had and the power asymmetries between IIEP and UNESCO.

Finally, in relation to the infrastructure of the IIEP, a major change in its history was the completion and inauguration of the new headquarters of IIEP in Paris. This was anticipated for several years as it was seen as a way to, on the one hand, create the capacity to host the organisation under one roof, and on the other have extra capacity to expand its programmes through the recruitment of new and more interns; IIEP internships became during this period a major part of IIEP's workforce, with the interns having a profound role in the expansion of its research agenda. Nevertheless, as the folders show, the completion of the new building did not fulfil these promises for the IIEP. The relocation coincided with a financially challenging time for UN, which disseminated restricted funds to UNESCO for all its programmes. This reduction in resources meant that IIEP had to operate with a budget that wasn't allowing for the anticipated expansion of its operations, and necessitated attempts to raise funds from members in order to keep up with its agenda and targets.

As we saw from the above, at an earlier stage, this was achieved through the travelling of IIEP Governing Board meetings to different locations around the globe and accompanying proceedings with a lot other formal and informal events, such as conferences, other bilateral meetings with national actors (from universities to governments) and of course, dinners! On the other hand, from 1973 onwards, with the new premises in Paris, the IIEP could significantly expand its training programme by accepting large number of interns from around the world, a practice that continues to present day. Internships was another way to influence national education systems, while projecting IIEP's role as a global actor in education. The next section will empirically examine some of these governing board meetings, and explain their significance in constructing a global network of expertise in education, linking it much closer not only to economic and developmental discourses, but also to new regions and global actors.

THE IIEP GOVERNING BOARD MEETINGS: RESEARCH AND INTERNATIONALISATION

Torsten Husén was the chairman of the governing board between 1970 and 1980, during the directorship of IIEP by Raymond Poignant (from 1969, taking the lead after Coombs until 1974), Hans Weiler (Professor of Education at Stanford, director of IIEP from 1974 to 1977) and finally, Michel Debeauvais (director of IIEP between 1977 and 1982), who worked intensely on quantitative indicators and forecasting in education. This section will examine some of the key issues that the Governing Board (GB) discussed in its meetings in various locations, as a way to give an inside perspective to the workings and issues that dominated the GB's discussions during this time. We will start with the 9th session of the GB in Paris, (1–2 December 1970), and move to the 10th session in Santiago (22–23 November 1971), the 11th session in Paris (28–29 November 1972), ending with the 12th session that took place in IIEP's new headquarters in Paris (26–29 November 1973).

The 9th session of the IIEP's GB meeting was the one during which Husén was elected as the chairman (alongside notable other new additions as members of the council, such as Pierre Bourdieu and the re-election of John Vaizey). The meeting began by a discussion on training matters, and the heterogeneity of the composition of the 20 participants was debated, alongside the need to increase numbers once the new site was built. Issues of technology were discussed, with many stressing the need for the institute to 'develop some programmed instruction types of materials that could be used by planners on a correspondence basis,' for example, 'cassette combinations of audio and visual materials.'[12] However, the director, while acknowledging the need to 'relieve the institute's teaching staff burden and to assist specialists in the field,' he suggested that at this instance,

[12] International Institute for Educational Planning, '9th Session of the Governing Board,' December 1–2, 1970, Paris (The Husén archive, 2.53), 48.

80   S. GREK ET AL.

'it was not possible to launch a programme of correspondence courses.' Some of the research studies discussed were in relation to 'the most important demographic factors in the growth of educational costs,' with case studies taking place in 'Ceylon, Colombia, Tanzania and Tunisia, based on a model which had been devised in the Institute'; on 'planning the development of universities,' including case studies carried out at the Universities of Sussex and Leningrad, with the view to construct a questionnaire, enquiring on issues such as planning teaching, training of teaching staff and access; a study on 'techniques for the evaluation of educational output'; and ' a retrospective and prospective study aiming at assessing how sizeable the problems of financing the development of education would become during the forthcoming decade.' The latter study was planned to conduct

> 8 to 10 national case studies and approximately 10 specific studies. It would then be possible to sum up the results of all these studies, and to offer Member States a comprehensive picture of the problems of educational financing as they now arise and as they will emerge in the future, while offering them a choice of alternative solutions to these problems.[13]

Thus, it is clear how IIEP's work related not only to the training of education professionals but also put emphasis on informing policymaking and shaping the knowledge base available for governance. Similar projects, intending to inform not only school managers but also policy professionals, too, was the project on 'rationalisation of school location' which had an international character, too, including a number of countries from around the world.

Beyond training and research, the GB approved the budget, elected several new members (including Husén), as well as discussed the need to increase the geographical representation among staff, however without imposing 'a fixed geographical quota system,' but rather make the selection of members 'primarily on the basis of their qualifications,' noting that,

> The director accepted these indications but felt that in a number of cases, it would be extremely difficult to recruit qualified specialists from developing countries as such as this policy might deprive these countries of the services of the only key-men in the field of educational planning.[14]

[13] IIEP, '9th Session.'
[14] IIEP, '9th Session.'

The 10th GB meeting took place in Santiago de Chile, following the board's decision to have the meeting taking place in a location away from Europe every second year. The Board discussed the increasing numbers of full-time interns and expert fellows (from 23 in previous year to 26 in 1971); however, the director noted that due to the lack of an appropriate headquarters, 'the level of activity, particularly on the training side, does not correspond to that foreseen in 1968 when the five-year plan was drawn up (Fig. 4.1).'[15]

Alongside the discussion on training of the different types of fellows and the discussion of new or continuing studies, the GB discussed the production of new instructional materials, new publications and new changes to the training programme, both in relation to courses, as well as study visits: this included the introduction of three new courses on 'financing of education,' 'out of school training' and 'evaluation of educational systems,' as well as,

> In 1972 the interns will, in addition to the traditional visits to Geneva and Rome, visit a new French academy to study planning problems: the Institute will also try to organise a study visit to the Federal Republic of Germany. Fresh contacts with Italian education will be made during the Rome visit.[16]

Apart from organising such travels and field trips, the expansion of the work of certain projects is notable, too, since the project on education financing expanded to include eight new cases studies (including Iran, Pakistan, Thailand, Morocco, Senegal, Ivory Coast, Ghana and the People's Republic of Congo), with plans to expand further, including a number of countries in Latin America, namely Colombia, Chile, Peru, Ecuador and Brazil, as well as increase the sample through the inclusion of Cameroon, Nepal, Ethiopia, Philippines, Turkey, Afghanistan and Yugoslavia. Such projects show not only the internationalisation of education research expertise, but in fact its global character and the ways that the IIEP, through both the research and the training services, created a truly global network of education expertise.

Finally, in terms of funding, the IIEP relied primarily on the support of UNESCO, the voluntary contributions of different countries and the Ford Foundation, which supported the IIEP for at least the first decade of

---

[15] IIEP, '9th Session.'
[16] IIEP, '10th session.'

35. TABLE 5 – STATISTICAL SUMMARY OF IIEP TRAINING PROGRAMMES DURING THE LAST FOUR ACADEMIC YEARS	1967-68	1968-69	1969-70	1970-71
INTERNS (1 October–31 July)[1]				
Number	21	17	20	20
Participant weeks	765	706	828	820
EXPERT FELLOWS (1 October–31 July)[1]				
Number	–	6	3	1
Participant weeks	–	252	126	41
VISITING FELLOWS (1 September–31 August)				
Number	10	20	19	15
Participant weeks	89	105	102	172
UNESCO EXPERTS (1 September–31 August)				
Number	13	13	5	19
Participant weeks	31	36	12	41
SEMINARS AND SPECIAL WORKSHOPS (1 September–31 August)				
Number	23	53	96[2]	66[3]
Participant weeks	23	77	122	92
TOTAL PARTICIPANTS	67	109	143	121
TOTAL PARTICIPANT WEEKS	888	1 178	1 190	1 166

Fig. 4.1 Table showing the 'Statistical Summary of IIEP Training Programmes during the Last Four Academic Years' (International Institute for Educational Planning, '10th Session of the Governing Board,' November 22–24, 1971, Santiago de Chile (The Husén archive, 2.53), 30)

its existence. The table below, from the 11th GB meeting in 1972 is indicative of the sources of funding available (Fig. 4.2):

In 1973, although the IIEP was given its shiny and new headquarters in Paris, funding cuts hit the work of the Institute, due to 'exceptional rises in costs due simultaneously to the devaluation of the dollar and to inflation' with consequences both to the growth of the training programme, as well as the delay of the completion of research projects. Although the funding situation presented IIEP with difficulties, its members did not stop travelling and internationalising their expertise: notable

4 THE RISE OF A GLOBAL EXPERT NETWORK: THE INTERNATIONAL... 83

94. TABLE 7 - FINANCIAL RESOURCES AVAILABLE IN 1972 AND 1973 (in U.S. $)		
Source	1972	1973
1. Basic Funds[1]		
(a) Unesco	500 000	654 100[4]
(b) Voluntary contributions		
Denmark	30 000	30 000
Ireland	12 000	12 000
Italy	17 152	-
Spain	3 247	-
(c) Carry-over from previous year	147 733	64 843
(d) Miscellaneous revenue[2]	20 000	20 000
Total basic funds	730 162	780 943
2. Other voluntary contributions[3]		
(a) Member States		
Canada: Carry-over - 15 328		6 387
New allocation - 99 010		98 000
	114 338	104 387
Norway: Carry-over - 3 200		
New allocation - 30 000		30 000
	33 200	30 000
Sweden: Carry-over - 117		
New allocation - 200 000		
	200 117	200 000
United Kingdom	57 894	67 609
(b) Ford Foundation	40 000	-
Total other voluntary contributions	445 549	401 996
3. Contracts		
(a) European Cultural Foundation	9 411	9 411[5]
(b) Ford (Africa)	6 661	-
(c) Population Council	23 860	3 839[5]
(d) UNFPA	35 000	30 161[5]
Total contracts	74 932	43 401[5]
TOTAL FINANCIAL RESOURCES AVAILABLE	1 250 643	1 226 340
of which Carry-over - 182 450		114 631
New funds - 1 068 193		1 111 709

Fig. 4.2 Table showing the IIEP's 'Financial Resources Available in 1972 and 1973' (International Institute for Educational Planning, '11th Session of the Governing Board,' November 28–30, November, Paris (The Husén archive, 2.56), 24)

meetings included papers presented at the OECD Scientific Affairs Committee (November 1972); the annual assembly of the AERA (New Orleans, February 1973); and the conference on Educational Achievement organised at the Graduate School of Education, Harvard University (November 1973). There was collaboration with the World Bank, too, with T. N. Postlethwaite heading a project that would evaluate the methodologies that the WB was employing for evaluating certain aspects of its projects in the education field.

THE IIEP INTERNSHIP SCHEME: EDUCATING THE EDUCATORS

This section focuses specifically on the IIEP's internship programme, as the flagship project designed to further enhance the institute's research reputation through the training of education managers and professionals more generally, in order to enhance their knowledge and application of education planning. The reach and influence of the programme is evident in the following map which shows the countries that interns in the period 1965–1972 came from (Fig. 4.3):

Interns (between the ages of 20 and 25, at least in the period 1965–1972) had to attend training for ten months in Paris, which included

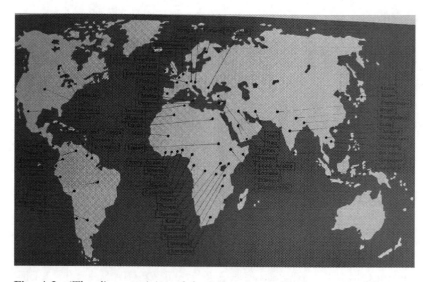

Fig. 4.3 'The diverse origins of the 131 trainees who have successfully completed courses of six months or longer at the Institute since 1965 are geographically illustrated in the map ... which shows the 68 countries from which they have come' (International Institute for Educational Planning, *IIEP 1972* (Paris: UNESCO, 1972), 6–7)

4 THE RISE OF A GLOBAL EXPERT NETWORK: THE INTERNATIONAL... 85

daily lectures and seminars, practical exercises, field trips and culminated in a paper written by the intern on a topic selected by them and their instructors. The link with of the IIEP and its remit to link education more closely with development is evident through the additional fellowship programme with the UNDP, the United Nations Development Programme: this special, additional programme was intended for UNESCO international experts and was organised for the first time in 1968/1969 (due to lack of financial support, it was subsequently offered to other young researchers that were expected to either return to work to the member state they came from, or work for an international organisation). In addition, on offer was also a Visiting Fellowship scheme which enabled highly qualified people to spend from one to six months at IIEP in Paris, in order to further their expertise and knowledge of a specific area of educational planning.

The IIEP, a hothouse of research on education planning, did not limit its training to the internship and fellowships programmes: it also offered series of special seminars and workshops for UNESCO experts serving in member states, directors and professors of UNESCO regional offices and other specialists. In addition, specialised training courses were offered, which lasted for three months and covered topics such as the 'rationalisation of the school map,' the financing of education systems, the planning and management of education reforms and innovations and many others. IIEP publications were also produced, 'written by a distinguished authority in the field of in clear non-technical language, easily understood even by a reader unfamiliar with the topic concerned.'[17] In 1970, IIEP staff prepared an outline of the ways a concrete education 'plan' would need to become integrated in a government's economic administration; this was produced for the 'theoretical and practical training of interns (Fig. 4.4).'

The IIEP, being quasi-autonomous from UNESCO, offered training to UNESCO experts and regional directors in the form of additional support for their projects. For example, in 1971, more than 40 experts were trained at the IIEP prior to taking up assignments in the field. The Institute cooperated closely with the UNESCO regional offices in Beirut, Dakar, Bangkok, and Santiago by offering specialised training courses, as well as through regularly sending instructional materials.

It is important to mention that it was not only the trainees that were diverse and global; the IIEP experts themselves were not all IIEP staff.

[17] IIEP, *IIEP 1972*, 20.

Fig. 4.4 'The discussion is usually lively when educational planning experts come to an IIEP seminar to exchange experiences and to catch up on new developments in research and methodology' (IIEP, *IIEP 1972*, 13)

The Institute worked closely with a very high number of consultants from across the world, who were selected on the basis of their expertise and specialisation. In addition, national commissions were also offering such services or guided the choice of consultants and the selected trainees: for example, the French Commission was active organising study visits in France for many of the IIEP's interns and fellows. The IIEP worked closely with other IOs too and not only those that worked exclusively in the field of education: given the interest in linking education to economic development, multiple visits were arranged for IIEP interns to the International Labour Organisation (ILO), the World Health Organisation (WHO) and the Food and Agriculture Organisation (FAO). Finally, training was not offered only through courses and in the field: the IIEP's Library and Documentation Centre was a place of gathering and socialisation of many of the interns and other experts who spent their time in Paris. The library was established by an initial donation of books and reports by the World Bank and grew to include more than 17,000 titles, some of which were rare. The IIEP Library became a place of meeting and working and brought together not only young interns but also experienced experts from around the world.

The Epistemic Power of Socialisation

This brief overview of the IIEP's first decade of work offered a unique window in understanding processes of expert formation and networking. Above all, the case of the IIEP shows how the production of expert knowledge is both guided and guides the emergence of new dominant discourses and paradigms. As discussed, these paradigms involved on the one hand the glossing over of personal and political differences in favour of a consensus over what constitutes authoritative knowledge, as well as the processes of rebranding educational research as planning, especially for those countries perceived in need of such. In particular, the case of the IIEP, a relatively less well-known IO in the field of education governance, shows how the emergence of education planning, combined with the organisation of relevant training of new experts and policymakers from across the world, gave rise to a new conceptualisation of education research as not merely a scientific field in itself but as one is 'disembedded' (i.e. can travel) and that can and should guide education policymaking.

Applying a retrospective analytical lens on the IIEP case, little of the above is surprising. Indeed, expertise needs to 'de-politicise,' in order to claim its legitimacy and authority; this is the main reason 'why International Organisations hate politics,' according to the recent book by Louis and Maertens.[18] There have been plenty of detailed accounts of the processes of technicisation that social problems often undergo, in order for experts to render them technical, and thus factual and neutral, and distinct from obstructive political struggles and ideologies.[19] Similarly, Diane Stone uses the term 'scientization' to describe the processes of transforming social issues into problems amenable to the scientific cause-effect relationship; the latter is seen as authoritative enough to control or even reduce uncertainty and risk.[20] Of course, there is nothing a-political in such processes of rendering social problems as technical issues; on the contrary, the rise and role of new expert elites is deeply political work that involves decisions

---

[18] Marieke Louis and Lucile Maertens, *Why International Organisations Hate Politics: Depoliticising the World* (London: Routledge, 2021).

[19] Matt Wood and Matthew V. Flinders, 'Rethinking Depoliticisation: Beyond the Governmental,' *Policy & Politics* 42, no. 2 (2014).

[20] Diane Stone, 'Understanding the Transfer of Policy Failure: Bricolage, Experimentalism and Translation,' *Policy & Politics* 45, no. 1 (2017); André Broome, Alexandra Homolar and Matthias Kranke, 'Bad Science: International Organizations and the Indirect Power of Global Benchmarking,' *European Journal of International Relations* 24, no. 3 (2017).

about what to know and what to ignore, and, as we saw from the analysis above, whom to train and whom not to.

This chapter discussed the political work of constructing a disembedded laboratory of education research as a project that does not 'land' into policy contexts as a top-down agenda, sent from some unknown 'centre of calculation,' but one that is open to contestation and negotiation with a wide variety of actors, from IOs to universities, participant countries and other organisations. One of the underpinning assumptions of the epistemic power of expertise and its influence has been the separation of the spheres of science and politics.[21] Thus, through the discussion of the empirical cases of the rise of the IIEP as a 'disembedded laboratory' of education planning and of training policy practitioners, we showed how expert work is not merely the technically and scientifically robust process experts promise, but that it came to deliver a function that politically was even more significant and necessary if a global education policy field were to be achieved: this is the work of socialisation, interdependence, and brokerage that many of the IIEP experts, including Husén, experienced as they were involved in the IIEP's projects, field trips, courses or even at the library's cafeteria.

Through the IIEP's processes of collective puzzling and social learning, experts brought forward new modes of researching and new narratives of what the main issues dominating the education policy agenda should be. Policy and education practitioners would travel to Paris, stay for shorter or longer periods of work; they would socialise, work and learn and then return home in order to communicate their newly acquired knowledge to others, before they themselves had the opportunity to do the same. This is how international reform agendas entered national policy spaces and shaped them through the slow, continuous, and consensual build-up of the new, common *esprit de corps* in education—the inescapable 'right thing to do.'[22] It is these processes of learning and socialisation that embedded

---

[21] Bård Lahn and Göran Sundqvist, 'Science as a 'Fixed point'? Quantification and Boundary Objects in International Climate Politics,' *Environmental Science & Policy* 67 (2017).

[22] Christoph O. Meyer 'Convergence Towards a European Strategic Culture? A Constructivist Framework for Explaining Changing Norms,' *European Journal of International Relations* 11, no.4 (2005).

the international much deeper into the national consciousness, and in many ways continued the colonisation of the Global South, through the shaping of education policy in very specific ways. Crucially, as we showed, socialisation and the learning that it produces, did not merely entail the learning of facts. It became constitutive, generating or strengthening trust, commitments, identifications, and loyalties—it embodied, as Shona Hunter has fittingly described, 'the connective tissue of governing itself.'[23]

[23] Shona Hunter quoted in Janet Newman, 'Beyond the Deliberative Subject? Problems of Theory, Method and Critique in the Turn to Emotion and Affect,' *Critical Policy Studies* 6, no. 4 (2013).

CHAPTER 5

Education Futuramas: Torsten Husén and Futurological Thinking in Education

Come tour the future with General Motors! A transcontinental flight over America in 1960. What will we see? What changes will transpire? This magic Aladdin-like flight through time and space is Norman Bel Geddes's conception of the many wonders that may develop in the not-too-distant future ...
... *this world of tomorrow is a world of beauty.*[1]

This chapter examines the processes, practices and politics of numbers and expertise in the discursive construction of crises and anticipation. As we saw in the previous chapter, contextual pressures, such as economic crisis and the political change of decolonisation, created the need to reconceptualise education research as education planning; the latter was not meant to develop in some remote 'centre of calculation' but was envisaged as disembedded, that is, constructed to travel through training and the socialisation of actors. However, laboratories are not only operating through set procedures and the planning of the present; they are also key in creating work that anticipates the future and produces knowledge that can counter uncertainty and risk. Thus, Torsten Husén's work is central in this examination, not only because of his place in establishing the central role of statistical analysis in education, but also, as we will see in this

---

[1] Excerpt from the souvenir booklet of the 'Futurama' ride, 1939, in the 1939/40 New York World's Fair. See Arthur Morella, 'This Is Futurama!', American History, January 5, 2011, https://americanhistory.si.edu/explore/stories/futurama.

© The Author(s), under exclusive license to Springer Nature Switzerland AG 2024
S. Grek et al., *The World as a Laboratory*, Global Histories of Education, https://doi.org/10.1007/978-3-031-68090-8_5

91

92   S. GREK ET AL.

chapter, his specific focus and interest in 'futurology,' that is, the systematic consideration, analysis, and forecasting of what the future holds. Despite arguments that the study of the future can and should be analysed through the mathematical science of probability, the analysis of futurological debates in the 1970s—the period that Torsten Husén works in—shows that most of the expert analysis and debate was at the level of discursive and narrative production of desirable future education worlds—what this chapter terms 'education futuramas.' What are these narratives about? What spurs their construction? How are they developed? Who are the experts that put them forward? What are the qualities of these actors and what are the processes they go through to achieve the legitimacy and stage to communicate these future world visions?

In order to answer these questions, the chapter focuses on two separate sources: first, this is the Aspen/Berlin seminars, organised by Torsten Husén, on the 'Future of Education,' and, second, his key work of that period that summarised these seminars, *The School in Question*.[2] Both Husén's book and the seminars took place in the economic recession of the 1970s and the crisis in education it ensued; this is a crucial context since, as we will see, crises lend themselves productively to the thinking and planning of alternative future scenarios. In this specific case, as the chapter discusses, some of the central questions that experts were asked to grapple with concerned the connection of education with society, and particularly the connection of education with the labour market. The chapter applies a frame that draws on and combines the sociology of risk and anticipation with theoretical perspectives on the production of expertise, in order to examine how 'futuramas' are built, what their essential elements are and the reasons for their construction.

THE POLITICS OF PREDICTION

There is nothing new in human ambition to predict and tame the future. From ancient oracles and medieval wizards to fortune tellers and statistical modellers, governing societies has always entailed the act of trying to forecast the future and best prepare for what it holds. According to Ewald,

---

[2] Torsten Husén, *The School in Question: A Comparative Study of the School and its Future in Western Societies* (London: Oxford University Press, 1979).

anticipating the future is a key function of the apparatus of government.[3] Indeed, the knowledge produced by predictive tools and practices steers governmental interventions and is seen as crucial in innovation and risk management. Indeed, major crises are often understood as failures to predict correctly; the examples of the global financial crisis of the 1970s, as well as the recent global pandemic, have been considered as major failures of nations to predict, prepare, and protect their people. As a result, they trigger even greater and more urgent efforts to improve forecasting and thus global preparedness for such crises.

As we will see, the point of the forecasting exercise is essentially different from achieving mere prediction and 'readiness'; rather than offering the reading of a crystal ball, narrating the future involves establishing a discursive agenda of the values of the present, and the ideas and ambitions of how future generations will live. In bringing together these futuristic stories, narrating the future becomes essentially a governing manifesto of contemporary considerations, uncertainties and potentialities.

Of course, none of these exercises is disassociated from the practice of measurement. The discursive construction of desirable futures works because it is predicated on the existence of a well-oiled and effective machinery of numerical calculation. However, we know by now that measurement is not only descriptive but also *prescriptive*, as it always invokes a desired course of action.[4] Thus, numbers are performative as they implicitly construct, rather than simply measure political phenomena.[5] On the other hand, the literature has also—at least recently—examined the power of numbers to enhance democracy by giving political voice and power to those that did not have it before.[6] In this chapter, we move beyond the performative versus emancipatory logics of quantification,[7] in order to

---

[3] Francois Ewald, 'The Return of Descartes' Malicious Demon: An Outline of a Philosophy of Precaution,' in *Embracing Risk: The Changing Culture of Insurance and Responsibility*, ed. Tom Baker and Jonathan Simon (Chicago: University of Chicago Press, 2002).

[4] Benedict Kingsbury, Sally Engle Merry and Kevin E. Davis, 'Indicators as a Technology of Global Governance,' *Law & Society Review* 46, no. 1 (2012).

[5] Donald MacKenzie, *An Engine, Not a Camera: How Financial Models Shape Markets* (Cambridge: MIT Press, 2008); Afshin Mehrpouya and Rita Samiolo, 'Performance Measurement in Global Governance: Ranking and the Politics of Variability,' *Accounting, Organisations and Society* 55 (2016).

[6] Andrea Mennicken and Robert Salais, eds., *The New Politics of Numbers: Utopia, Evidence and Democracy.* (Cham: Springer, 2022).

[7] Wendy Nelson Espeland and Mitchell Stevens,' Commensuration as a Social Process,' *Annual Review of Sociology* 24 (1998).

examine the ways that the materiality of number-making is necessitated by narrative future-making: more specifically, the chapter focuses on the ways that quantification facilitates governing the present, through the making of educational futures.

Therefore, through a focus on the futurological work of Torsten Husén, the chapter examines the early organisation of education number-making as a mode of imagining a political future—not the future that is probable but also (or perhaps predominantly), a future that is desired.[8] Our focus is on the paradox of, on the one hand, a utopian aspiration of an education for all and, on the other hand, a dystopian vision of inaction (which, at the time of the analysis, would have schools as unable to contribute to economic prosperity of societies and thus question—at least for some—one of education's perceived core functions). Here, paradoxically, quantification is not simply a technical exercise: rather than just seen as facilitating depoliticisation or, on the contrary, assisting collective action, the Aspen/Berlin seminars created a material space of interaction, driven by utopian thinking and the hope of a better tomorrow. It is the materiality and procedural character of anticipatory governance that is the focal point of analysis in this chapter.

Before we move on to the empirical analysis, we will briefly turn to the concept of anticipatory governance, as the primary field that has so far dealt with futures making in policy terms. Roberto Poli, first UNESCO Chair in Anticipatory Systems and editor of the 1735-page long *Handbook of Anticipation*, distinguishes among 'forecasting, foresight and anticipation' as the primary three levels of futures study. According to him, forecasting is 'the properly predictive component of futures study'; it can be found in either short-term modelling of the future (e.g., econometric modelling) or longer models, such as climate change ones. Such forecasting is primarily quantitative and tends to assume continuity, or what Poli calls 'past-based' futures—an extrapolation that the laws governing the phenomena under question will remain the same.

Second, foresight is characterised differently, as it includes 'most traditional' futures studies. Foresight studies are mostly qualitative and they are not meant to predict but construct 'a variety of possible futures.' According to Poli, 'foresight exercises are primarily used to challenge the mindset of

---

[8] See Ali Aslan Gümüsay and Juliane Reinecke, 'Researching for Desirable Futures: From Real Utopias to Imagining Alternatives,' *Journal of Management Studies* 59, no. 1 (2022).

decision makers by exploring possible futures.[9] Finally, anticipation is 'grounded on the outcomes resulting from forecast and foresight models and aims at implementing them into decisions and actions.' Riel Miller, another key UNESCO figure through his 'Futures Literacy' project comments: 'The future does not exist in the present but anticipation does. The form the future takes in the present is anticipation.'[10] Interestingly, Miller also noted that anticipatory governance is the knowledge and skill of how to 'use-the-future.' However, as he suggests, to 'use the future is strictly speaking, not possible since the future does not exist as an object or tool to be used. *The future as anticipation however, is continuously instrumentalised.*'[11]

It is the instrumentalisation of future imaginings that this chapter is interested in; in other words, who, how and with what effects future versions of education worlds are put together and projected. The chapter aims to explore these questions with the politics of expertise in mind: what role does expert knowledge have? What kinds or expert qualities dominate in organising the future? Through an analysis of archival material on the Aspen/Berlin seminars, as well as a discourse analysis of the Husén's *The School in Question*,[12] this chapter sheds light on these questions.

Torsten Husén's 'Future Think': The Aspen/Berlin Seminars and *The School in Question* (1979)

As discussed earlier, 'futurology' and 'futurological thinking' became a core aspect of Husén's work from at least the end of 1960s onwards.[13] This book has so far evidenced the multifaceted-ness of Husén's activities and interests: his decade-long engagement with the IIEP, a core function of which was research into planning and forecasting, meant that futurological perspectives in education was at the forefront of his expert work. In addition, Husen was particularly good at discussing futurological think-

---

[9] Roberto Poli ed., *Handbook of Anticipation: Theoretical and Applied Aspects of the Use of Future in Decision Making* (Cham: Springer, 2019), 7.

[10] Riel Miller, *Transforming the Future: Anticipation in the 21st Century* (London: Routledge, 2018), 2.

[11] Miller, *Transforming the Future*, 59 (our emphasis).

[12] Husén, *School in Question*.

[13] See for example Torsten Husén, *Skola för 80-talet: Framtidsperspektiv på utbildningssamhället* (Stockholm: Almqvist & Wiksell, 1968); Torsten Husén, *Utbildning år 2000: En framtidsstudie* (Bonnier: Stockholm, 1971).

ing in education presents with additional benefits: this was his engagement with international education leaders, who, even if ignorant of developments in education statistics, were keen to share their views on how education could and should be shaped in future terms.

Similar to education planning, futurology becomes a new field of research and debate in the 1970s. It is significant not only because it encapsulates the idea that a science of education can exist, but also because it builds on Husén's core idea that educational research should inform policymaking, and that, according to Husén, the school is part of a much broader 'ecology' of society, and therefore education debates need to take place alongside broader considerations about the economy and other policy fields.

Thus, and similar to the workings of the IIEP, Husén uses expert knowledge, as well as informal processes of socialisation and collective learning, in order to create quite an abstract, high-level discussion by key academic and professional figures on building broader norms and understandings about 'the learning society.' It is precisely this combination of 'Husén/the researcher' and 'Husén/the cosmopolitan' that makes him the well-established, trusted scholar that he is, seen by many of his peers not merely as a technocrat expert, but also as an education visionary.

ASPEN/BERLIN SEMINARS: A TIMELINE

The Aspen Institute was founded by the Chicago businessman Walter Paepcke (1896–1960) in the town of Aspen, Colorado, in 1949 with the intention to celebrate the 200th birthday of the German poet and philosopher Johann Wolfgang von Goethe. The intention of the institute was to celebrate the arts and humanities and educate future leaders with ideas that otherwise would not be accessible to them:

> The Executive Seminar was not intended to make a corporate treasurer a more skilled corporate treasurer, but to help a leader gain access to his or her own humanity by becoming more self-aware, more self-correcting, and more self-fulfilling.[14]

---

[14] Walter Paepke quoted in Aspen Institute, 'A Brief History of the Aspen Institute,' Aspen Institute, February 22, 2024, https://www.aspeninstitute.org/about/heritage/.

During the 1960s and 1970s, the range of the activities of the Aspen Institute grew and involved seminars in education, communications, justice, Asian thought and other subjects.[15] Thus, the idea for organising the Aspen/Berlin seminars came about in 1975, when Husén was asked by Lord Alan Bullock, Aspen Trustee, and Dr. Francis Keppel, director of the Aspen Educational Policy Programme, to create a series of seminars on the future of schooling. The idea involved organising seminars that would take place in both sides of the Atlantic, that is, both in Aspen, Colorado, and in the Aspen Institute in Berlin; the latter was founded in 1974, in order to promote the creation of a transatlantic expert community.[16] Notable is the fact that although numerous Aspen Institutes exist around the world, the Berlin one was the very first one to be founded amongst them. According to Husén, the seminars were ambitious and had the comparative dimension at their core:

> In my view, the first step should be an attempt to *identify cross-nationally the salient trends* in ... formal education ... A review of *relevant literature, systematic fact-finding*, and *international seminar sessions and workshops* were to be instruments for clarifying issues and for discussing means of reshaping the school system in order to make it better fulfil its role in the society of today and tomorrow.[17]

The series of seminars that brought together a distinguished group of discussants posed this broad question for analysis: 'What is an educated person in the last quarter of the twentieth century?' According to Bullock, Husén was chosen as the expert that would organise the seminars, since he brought together a set of rare qualities at the time; first, he had experience as principal researcher of a cross-country study, a study that gave him access to data from countries such as Canada, Japan, US and Sweden; secondly, through his travels he developed the personal acquaintances and experience of seeing these systems from close by and getting to know them first hand (Bullock in Husén, 1979).[18] Thus, Bullock, in his

---

[15] Aspen Institute, 'Brief History.'

[16] Aspen Institute Germany, 'Aspen History,' Aspen Institute, February 22, 2024, https://www.aspeninstitute.de/aspen-history/.

[17] Husén, *School in Question*, 1.

[18] Alan Bullock, 'Foreword,' in *The School in Question: A Comparative Study of the School and its Future in Western Societies* by Torsten Husén (London: Oxford University Press: 1979).

98   S. GREK ET AL.

justification for his selection, he offers an in-depth perspective of the kinds of expert qualities that were valued at the time: first, Husén was an expert in comparative analysis, what was back then a relatively new science. Such comparative analysis would allow the study not only of individual systems, but also their 'horizontal,' comparative examination and thus bring up issues of education performance and learning from best practice. Second, as Husén himself suggests, the systematic examination of 'facts' was of pertinence. Third, and perhaps most importantly in the case of the Aspen/ Berlin seminars was Husén's socialisation in the field: he was unique in knowing not only education systems themselves, but crucially having contacts, and in some cases, contacts that were powerful enough to be able to debate and take decisions that would shape not only education research but education governance itself.

The first seminar in 1976, bringing together more than 20 participants from 13 countries, many of whom were education ministers and senior civil servants, took place in Aspen, Colorado. The seminar in Colorado lasted for a fortnight and was devoted to the broad question 'What is an educated person in the last quarter of the 20th century?' Some of the participants that attended that first seminar were Alan Bullock (British historian) and Stephen Graubard (American historian), Lionel and Diana Trilling (American literary critics), Daniel Bell (American sociologist and professor at Harvard), Daniel Boorstin (American historian at the University of Chicago), William Bouwsma (Sather professor of history at Berkeley), Steve Weinberg (American Nobel laurate in Physics), Carl Schorske (American cultural historian and professor at Princeton), Martin Meyerson (American city planner and president of the University of Pennsylvania), Fred Dainton (British academic chemist), Asa Briggs (British historian), Francis Keppel (former US Commissioner of Education), Mortimer Adler (American philosopher) and Eric Weil (French/German philosopher). The seminar focused on identifying 'crisis symptoms': After the optimistic view of the 1960s, the economic crisis of the 1970s revealed an education in crisis, and especially a crisis of secondary schooling and how it corresponded to the needs for economic development. As we will see, the discourse of crisis was a key instrument in facilitating the debate at Aspen/Berlin and in persuading high-profile actors to take part in the discussions, with the prospect to bring education a lot closer to the needs of the economy and society.

A few months later, another seminar took place, this time in Aspen/ Berlin and was attended by quite a different group, such as Hellmut

5 EDUCATION FUTURAMAS: TORSTEN HUSÉN AND FUTUROLOGICAL... 99

Becker (German education academic), Max Kohnstamm (Dutch historian, diplomat and one of the founding fathers of the European Union), Jan Szcepański (Polish sociologist) and many others, predominantly European scholars and policy actors. According to Bullock, 'there were a number of striking differences between the two (seminars), reflecting the best different ways in which a predominantly American and a predominantly European group approached the question.'[19] However, it is also evident that the expertise of Torsten Husén in comparative education was the key ingredient of the success of the seminars. According to Bullock,

> Torsten Husén, a scholar with the rare, if not unique, qualifications to look at the question in the context not of one or two but of the whole group of advanced industrial countries belonging to the OECD to which he has been educational consultant for many years. He has also been able to draw upon his experiences as a leader of the research team which conducted an evaluation study of some twenty national systems of education. Thanks to his background he has had access to—has indeed largely collected—data reflecting the experience of countries as widely different in their historical development as Canada and Japan, the USA and Sweden.[20]

A report was written after the seminar and was distributed to all participants, in addition to conducting more research and new mini-studies that would inform the organisation of the smaller workshop, which took place in July 1977, this time in Aspen, Colorado; the workshop focused specifically on education and youth unemployment.

Finally, the third international seminar of the series took place in Berlin in September 1977 and the discussion had three broad aims:

1. Interaction between school and society, with particular reference to working life;
2. Decision-making and governance in school education;
3. The 'inner life' of the school.

According to Husén,

> The task has been set as three-fold: 1) to identify the '*crisis*' symptoms; 2) to diagnose the '*disease*' that accounts for the mismatch between school and

[19] Bullock, 'Foreword,' ix.
[20] Bullock, 'Foreword,' x.

100   S. GREK ET AL.

society, and 3) to reassess the school as an institution. *The ultimate purpose of the exercise is to arrive at a plausible scenario for the school of the future.*[21]

Although Husén admitted that the task is 'indeed audacious, not to say an overambitious one,' it appears that his efforts to identify the problems and create the conditions for dialogue that will explore possible scenarios for the future were seen as an achievement. A series of interrelated questions were posed to the seminar series participants. These were the following: 'What major problems are besetting school education?' 'How do we account for them?' 'What should be done with the youth/school by way of reshaping the institution in order to come to grips with its problems?'[22]

Similar to the first seminar, there were some heated discussions in the event which lasted a number of days and brought together not only education ministers and civil servants but journalists, too. It is not possible to know what the effects of the seminars were, however, in terms of their role in helping us understand the role of future-making in the 1970s in education, Aspen/Berlin further explains not only the production of expertise in education, but also the ways that crisis narratives helped shape very specific understandings about the role and contribution of education in society.

Summarising, thanks to funding from the Stifterverband fur die Deutsche Wissenschaft (based in Essen, Germany), there was a series of meetings and discussions, which always began from Husén's analysis and contributions:

> Whenever we met, it was Torsten Husén's draft which provided the focus of our discussions; but no author was less concerned with defending his point of view or more open-minded in listening and drawing from the contributions of others.[23]

Aspen/Berlin shows how the production of futures was *in need of* a crisis discourse in order to be effective and justify the high-level character that it adopted. Although it required technical knowledge and evidence in order to be considered a-political and thus robust, it also involved blue-skies thinking, and the effort to consolidate values and principles; in that

---

[21] Husén, *School in Question*, 3.
[22] Husén, *School in Question*, 4.
[23] Bullock, 'Foreword,' xi.

sense, it did not fall in the trap of creating policy 'recommendations' that would have caused dissensus and confrontation. Rather, it produced common ideas and norms, and thus had a far longer-lasting impression than any other seminar would. The focus on 'futures' was a smart way to invite powerful (primarily academic) actors in, engage them in interesting discussions and in fact, keep them engaged. The Aspen/Berlin seminars were not a one-off event, but they took place over space and time: they developed slowly, and they took a lot of material, day-to-day work (travels, interviews, invitations, writing, drafting, applying for funds etc.). Lastly, they did not evaporate; rather, they were meticulously transcribed and discussed in the publication that the next section discusses, the 'School in Question.'

The focus of the following section on one of Husén's key publications is double: first, it has the aim to show the *materiality* of his work, in that all his work has been made known to us through his inscriptions, detailed notes and archival material; there is perhaps no other expert that was so obsessed with collecting documentation of every travel, meeting and discussion he had. Second, the focus on 'The School in Question' aims to discuss how the futurological discussions of Aspen/Berlin were not just speculative, blue-skies discussions of a privileged expert elite, but in fact became the material of one of Husén's most significant works, which influenced a high number of academics and policymakers at the time. In other words, the 'School in Question' gave *validity, solidity,* and *endurance* to debates that would last for decades to come, as well as allowed these ideas to travel far and wide and to a much larger audience than the participants of the meetings. These are the reasons that the materiality of expert work matters: through its inscription, it not only becomes 'true' but also travels through space and time, shaping academic and policy agendas far and wide.

TORSTEN HUSÉN'S *THE SCHOOL IN QUESTION: A COMPARATIVE STUDY OF THE SCHOOL AND ITS FUTURE IN WESTERN SOCIETIES* (1979)

Having worked with planners and policy makers at both national and institutional levels, I am keenly aware of how meaningless it is to try to come up with sweeping recommendations compiled in the laundry-list fashion. Such recommendations are particularly useless if they are not consistently related to the diagnosis conducted and to each other. They are, if they are taken

102   S. GREK ET AL.

seriously, dangerous, since piecemeal and short-term panaceas tend to be attractive to politicians given the conditions of office under which they operate. ... Educational reforms cannot substitute for social reforms. The former must be part of the latter if they are going to have a lasting impact.[24]

The School in Question is a combination of 'future-centred' blue skies thinking ('My main concern is how the school as an institution relates to society at large'),[25] but without trying to be too radical ('the present chapter does not pretend to advance a blueprint for school reform').[26] Key topics in the analysis relate to the establishment of connections between school and work and the governance and administration of schooling. The book is clearly focused on advancing 'big' ideas, as it perceives the multiple crises hitting societies and education in particular, as important precursors and the springboard onto which to develop new ideas about education. Husén suggests from the foreword that the book has a clear ideological orientation:

> What is the 'ideological' basis of the present study? Over some twenty years I have been involved in research related to Swedish school reforms. In recent years I have been conducting international surveys focusing on policy problems of cross national relevance. Since 1945 social scientists in many countries, not least in Sweden, have increasingly been called upon to put their competencies at the disposal of government commissions and agencies in studying social problems empirically. Studies of the quantitative, 'political-arithmetic' type gained momentum in the 1950s and early 1960s and were to provide policy makers and planners with an extended knowledge based for their decisions. This research on both sides of the Atlantic often took place in an atmosphere of an undogmatic political radicalism of the liberal brand, which, to quote Karabel and Halsey (1977, p. 27) had 'it commitments ... towards making a reality of the idea of the Welfare State.'[27]

Some of the key issues that emerge from an overall analysis of the book, therefore, are, first, its commitment to liberal education and to the post-war Western values of comprehensive schooling and the significance of education for the improvement of societies. Second, having a comparative, bird's eye view perspective on analysing common problems and

[24] Husén, *School in Question*, 3.
[25] Husén, *School in Question*, 149.
[26] Husén, *School in Question*, 149.
[27] Husén, *School in Question*, 4.

5 EDUCATION FUTURAMAS: TORSTEN HUSÉN AND FUTUROLOGICAL... 103

phenomena is not only the starting point of the analysis, but also the key reason that the project was led by Husén's expertise and contacts in the field; if the IIEP was a collective exercise to which Husén contributed, the Aspen/Berlin has his signature and would have never come to fruition without him. Third, the book finds legitimation since it is the outcome of the dialogue of a number of key figures that participated in the Aspen/Berlin seminars in 1976; after these seminars, Husén emerges as the trusted professor who not only has the expertise but also the personal acquaintances and experience to produce such blue skies, new thinking about how to resolve education problems.

In terms of the separate chapters of Husén's analysis, the book starts with an introduction to 'Crisis' and its symptoms, suggesting that after the euphoria of the upsurge of access to secondary education, there came the disenchantment of several issues besetting education, culminating in 1967 and the Williamsburg meeting of 150 leading educators from around the world, organised on the initiative of President Johnson and having as the main theme the 'world crisis in education,' which was also to become the title of one of Coombs' most famous publications (produced by the IIEP). Some of the symptoms that Husén identifies are the fact that there was a recognition that education is not only a matter of pedagogical concern, but it operates as part and parcel of far wider socio-economic realities. Husén saw education and inequalities, as well as 'negativism in the class-room' as key symptoms of the crisis, and he thought that 'there are clear indications that education policy has slipped down the political priority scale.'[28] Interestingly, Husén presents a high degree of reflexivity when he concludes the chapter with questioning the 'crisis' rhetoric:

> In view of experiences gained during the last decade we do not need further evidence to support the assertion that the school as an institution is in trouble—some say in deep trouble. To talk about 'crisis' is perhaps to overdramatise, but it is significant that term has frequently appeared in book titles and speeches by leading public figures on issues in education. At the Aspen/Berlin seminar in 1976 some participants took exception to the use of the term which they regarded as rhetoric that tended to obscure the concrete problems. This is one reason 'crisis' has been put within quotation marks.[29]

---

[28] Husén, *School in Question*, 15.
[29] Husén, *School in Question*, 19.

104   S. GREK ET AL.

Chapter 2 deals with 'Criticisms of the school as an institution,' outlining critiques by both conservative and progressive commentators who, respectively, complain either that standards are slipping and that there was not enough differentiation, or that the school is the main driver of social inequality and class oppression. Chapter 3 offers a historical overview of 'Institutional Schooling: Historical Roots and Evolution,' whereas Chap. 4 turns to the provision of evidence and systematic, comparative analyses through the examination of 'Recent trends and changes': Husén here offers comprehensive overviews of quantitative comparative data on different aspects (such as 'differences in instructional time,' 'public expenditure on education,' 'enrolments and growth indices') across more than 20 countries, while also offering case studies, such as the one on 'cost development in the city of Stockholm.'[30] Chapter 5 considers broad issues of education and the equality/meritocracy dilemma, whereas Chap. 6 returns to more quantitative comparative analysis, asking the question 'Have 'Standards' declined?' Chapter 7 focuses on 'bureaucratisation' in education and the effects of 'overbureaucratisation,' while Chap. 8 asks broader questions in relation to secondary education and 'preparation for life':

> The social role of the teenager in highly industrialised societies has over a few decades undergone a profound alteration. The most striking change is that the great majority of teenagers today are found in the schools and not at work places.[31]

The final chapter of the book 'Reshaping the School for the Next Decades' summarises the discussions held at the Berlin seminar in 1977: it focuses on the relationship of school and work; the governance and administration of the school in the 'learning society'; and, the 'inner life' of the school, both inside and outside the classroom.[32] According to Husén, it was also informed by interviews he took with faculty at the Universities of Stanford and Chicago. The concluding chapter finishes off with a set of questions, rather than recommendations that ask broad questions such as 'what changes are required to cope with the dwindling financing of education?'; 'how do we equip the educational system for self-evaluation and self-renewal?'; 'how do we reshape governance and administration of the

[30] Husén, *School in Question*, 66.
[31] Husén, *School in Question*, 145.
[32] Husén, *School in Question*, 151.

education system in order to better achieve the genuinely educational goals?' Husén suggests that instead of arriving at a list of recipes for the future, 'what we have in mind here, however, is a systems and long-range approach which, within the given societal setting, aims at reshaping the school as an institution in its entirety.'[33]

FUTURES THINKING AND UTOPIA AS A NEW MODE OF POLITICAL IMAGINATION IN EDUCATION

This chapter discussed Torsten Husén's futurological thinking, as exemplified through his work in bringing together powerful actors in discussions in Aspen/Berlin, as well as his publication that followed the seminar, *The School in Question*. Both empirical examples show that futurology became an important aspect of expert work, because it fuelled idealistic ideas in relation to what education planning, forecasting and comparison could achieve for improving education and hence the prospects of societies to live better and more prosperous lives. Faced with a financial crisis that threatened world economies, and, as a result, the financing of expert organisations themselves (like the IIEP, as we saw in the previous chapter), futurological thinking gave the impetus to participants to think transformatively and hence attempt to add a utopian impulse to the in-depth, systematic work of scientific research.

The imbrication of the production of knowledge in governing the future can be traced historically; it is especially common in the rise and formation of contemporary governance, which relies largely in quantitative measures and modelling tools to construct reliable evidence of what the future holds. According to Aradau and Blanke,

> Rather than a shift from the predictable to the unpredictable, as diagnosed by Ulrich Beck (2009), from regimes of truth to regimes of anticipation (Adams et al., 2009), from topological to temporal governance (Rouvroy, 2010), or from risk to new techniques of governing uncertainty (O'Malley, 2004; Aradau and van Munster, 2011; Samimian-Darash and Rabinow, 2015), prediction has not vanished today. Big data has revitalized the promise of prediction across social, political and economic worlds.[34]

---

[33] Husén, *School in Question*, 180–1.
[34] Claudia Aradau and Tobias Blanke, 'Politics of Prediction: Security and the Time/Space of Governmentality in the Age of Big Data,' *European Journal of Social Theory* 20, no. 3 (2017): 374.

106   S. GREK ET AL.

Indeed, in earlier work, Aradau and Munster argued that efforts to predict future catastrophic events, from terrorism to climate change, have significantly stretched the imaginative capacities of governments, whilst simultaneously allowing the development of practices at present which become part of the 'preparedness' and 'resilience' for the future.[35]

Although these phenomena and their management are of high significance in the analysis of governance practices, this chapter questions the extent to which quantifiable predictions of worlds-to-come dominate the production of future-making. Although, as we discussed, statistical data remains a key building block in these future forecasts, Husen's futurological endeavours foreground the collective and discursive construction of narratives of desired futures; such futures might still feel distant yet become palpable through the narrative production of idealised versions of a time not yet lived.

Therefore, we examine futurology as a mode of utopian thinking—a way of seeing, constructing, and performing the 'desired possible worlds' of the future.[36] The vast body of literature on 'governing by numbers' has shown how, although numbers are inherently political, their politics is hidden behind—and legitimised by—the veil of technocracy.[37] Similarly, expertise is not only descriptive, but also prescriptive as it always invokes a desired course of action.[38] Thus, the expert production of knowledge (and especially blue-skies events, like Aspen/Berlin) is performative, as it implicitly—sometimes even explicitly, as we have seen—constructs rather than simply measures political phenomena.[39] In this chapter, we examined the ways that forecasting, anticipation and measurement (all essential aspects of futurological thinking) facilitate the governing of the present through the making of utopian futures.

Second, as we saw, Aspen/Berlin was attended primarily by academic experts from the US and Europe. As we showed, the rise of internationalisation of education research and the expert networks that brought it to existence quickly became an ever-expansive exercise, because of the need

[35] Claudia Aradau and Rens van Munster, *Politics of Catastrophe: Genealogies of the Unknown* (London: Routledge, 2011).

[36] Ruth Levitas, *Utopia as Method: The Imaginary Reconstitution of Society* (London: Palgrave Macmillan, 2013).

[37] Theodore M. Porter, *Trust in Numbers: The Pursuit of Objectivity in Science and Public Life* (Princeton: Princeton University Press, 1995).

[38] Kingsbury, Engle Merry and Davis, 'Indicators.'

[39] MacKenzi, *Engine*; Mehrpouya and Samiolo, 'Performance Measurement.'

to establish an infrastructure that would link national education decision-makers with the global structures and interests of the newly established international organisations; notable in the Aspen/Berlin case is the exclusion of participants from countries of the developing world (and in contrast to the IIEP). The participation of national policymakers and experts was not only a matter of equity but also a matter of political buy-in into the growing infrastructure of measurement in education. Alongside policymakers (and particular previous and current commissioners of education in the US), It is also important to note the particular positioning of academic professors in these discussions, coming to them from a variety of disciplines (not only education); the following decade would be the one of the slow demises of academic expertise as they were quickly replaced by IO experts and consultants. Above all, as we saw in Aspen/Berlin, the production of expert knowledge was not a purely technocratic exercise but—through the focus on education futures—it also became the main forum of deliberation: The debate on the making of ideal education vistas turned the development and validation of education research into a process of creating a socio-technical imaginary of a utopian common future. Although *The School in Question* concludes with questions rather than statements, it is these questions that aim to shape the education debate in national systems in decades to come.

Thirdly, using the cases of Aspen/Berlin and 'The School in Question,' we discussed the role of crisis narratives in the construction of dystopian narratives that necessitate radical action and change. We argue that education crises must be understood as a key component of number-making and are essential for constructing ideal futures.

Fourth, this chapter discussed the ways the rise of the internationalisation of education expertise represents the political endeavour not only to rationalise and 'technicise' the process of education planning, but also—and perhaps primarily—the ways data as utopia became the new mode of political imagination of an education that would be closely aligned with economic development and prosperity. Thus, Aspen/Berlin, alongside the numerous other international seminars and workshops organised in the 1970s, captured the imagination of a wide set of actors in the field, since they purposefully allowed multiple 'entry points' in their world: on the one hand, they promoted the use of technocratic and management principles to create an objectified and comparable field,[40] and thus appear acceptable, accountable and in line with the novel (at the time) scientific approaches to policymaking, whilst also proclaiming to be developmental and transformative, distinct from older Western ideas and schooling practices that appeared to be behind their times. The open framing of the futurological debates allowed them to adapt to contemporary concerns of the time and become influential, no doubt partly due to the malleability and idealism of the narratives they developed.

As the chapter shows, building such quantified education futures lends itself well to their analysis through a focus on the structures and interlinkages between data, actors, and politics. Thus, our chapter focused analytically on the materiality of data, actors' expert work, and numerical narratives in the making of education futures. The 'opening out' of education elites not only to new actors but also more experimental and even (and often) quite provisional 'futures-think' led to a sense of idealism, provisionality and inclusion. As Star says, because 'nobody is really in charge of the infrastructure' (1999, p. 382),[41] it lends itself easily to the making of a narrative of a common, collective, utopian future, built on both democratic and inclusive governing ideals, as well as technical know-how, statistical robustness and the advent of comparative education; the latter was slowly creating a commensurate field, one in which every system became visible and accountable.

To conclude, through the case of the Aspen/Berlin and 'The School in Question' that concretised the discussions and disseminated them, we can observe a nuanced process of creating material spaces of exchange, where numbers and actors interact. Thus, futurological thinking represents a clear case of the politics of expertise emerging not only behind the veil of technicisation, but also through the process of creating education futures which allow for imagining—and consequently acting towards—education futuramas; in other words, worlds of tomorrow being shaped today.

---

[40] See e.g. Maria Kaika, "Don't Call Me Resilient Again!': The new Urban Agenda as Immunology ... Or ... What Happens When Communities Refuse to be Vaccinated With 'Smart Cities' and Indicators,' *Envirionment and Urbanization* 29, no. 1 (2017).

[41] Susan Leigh Star, 'The Ethnography of Infrastructure,' *American Behavioral Scientist* 43, no. 3 (1999): 382.

CHAPTER 6

Editing the *International Encyclopedia of Education*, 1980–1994

This chapter explores the International Encyclopaedia of Education, which serves as a significant statement of international and comparative education research as a primary source for global educational development. Encyclopaedias are collections of facts, and facts are typically perceived as unconstructed by anyone.[1] However, producing an encyclopaedia is not a straightforward or simple editorial process. The structure of thematic articles is subject to constant change due to new insights and uncontrollable circumstances. To improve the framing of knowledge in an encyclopaedia, it is suggested to view it as a product of a specific epistemic culture or as a 'disembedded laboratory.'[2] As demonstrated in this chapter, it is important to consider the processes, decisions, problems, and relationships involved in the production of an encyclopaedia.

Between 1980 and 1994, Torsten Husén, by then in his retirement age, worked on a very ambitious project: to edit *The International Encyclopedia of Education—research and studies* (IEE) together with Neville Postlethwaite (first edition 1985, with two supplement volumes, and a second edition in 1994, also available on CD-ROM). The IEE had as its ambition to be the first true *international* encyclopaedia of education

---

[1] Bruno Latour and Steve Woolgar, *Laboratory Life: The Construction of Scientific Facts* (Princeton: Princeton University Press, 1979/1986).
[2] Karin Knorr-Cetina, *Epistemic Cultures. How the Sciences Make Knowledge* (Cambridge: Harvard University Press, 1999).

© The Author(s), under exclusive license to Springer Nature Switzerland AG 2024
S. Grek et al., *The World as a Laboratory*, Global Histories of Education, https://doi.org/10.1007/978-3-031-68090-8_6

109

110   S. GREK ET AL.

solidifying knowledge that was otherwise dispersed. This meant trying to break with the ethnocentrism the editors thought had characterised earlier encyclopaedias of education—especially the one produced by the American Educational Research Association (AERA) in 1969[3]—as well as reaching out to educational systems in the Third World. The editors clearly wanted to show how education researchers could contribute to public education and curriculum development around the world. On the need of an international encyclopaedia of education the preface of the first edition states:

> Since the Second World War there has been an unprecedented expansion in the number of people engaged in education, in expenditures on schooling and on nonformal programs in education, and in efforts to make learning a lifelong pursuit. The number and complexity of problems to be solved have also increased. The expansion has been paralleled by what has been commonly called 'the knowledge explosion'—the vast and rapid increase in books, journals, microfilms, and electronically stored information—far outreaching educators' abilities to remain well-informed on a broader scale about educational matters. Recent decades have also witnessed increased global interdependence which has prompted education to become more internationalized. The exchange of research results and experiences among scholars and practitioners has become much more frequent, making comparative education an important field of scholarship in education.
>
> In view of these conditions, it is convenient for educators, social scientists, and the inquiring public to find, in one set of volumes, summaries of the state of all major aspects of education, gathered from worldwide sources. The present Encyclopedia has been designed to perform such a service.[4]

It is evident that the time now has come to bring together the dispersed set of knowledge constituting the field of international and comparative education, and to demonstrate its usefulness. Who could be better suited to do this than 'the grand old man of education,' Torsten Husén? The first edition of IEE was a 10-volume thick encyclopaedia consisting of a multi-level subject index with 45,000 entries and 160 overarching entry topics divided into 25 sections. Nearly 1448 larger articles were written by experts from over 100 countries. The two editors-in-chief worked closely

---

[3] American Educational Research Association, *Encyclopedia of Educational Research: A Project of the American Educational Research Association* 4th ed. (London: Macmillan, 1969).

[4] Torsten Husén and T. Neville Postlethwaite, 'Preface,' in *The International Encyclopedia of Education* vol. 1, ed. Torsten Husén and T. Neville Postlethwaite (Oxford: Pergamon, 1985), xii.

6 EDITING THE *INTERNATIONAL ENCYCLOPEDIA OF EDUCATION...* 111

with a larger editorial board of 15 people[5] and an international honorary board of 11 people were appointed to guarantee articles from 'the Third World.'[6] The second edition from 1994 was 90 percent rewritten, according to the editors, and contained more than 1200 larger articles from experts in 95 countries.[7]

Encyclopaedic facts are often perceived as truthful and fair representations of reality. However, this chapter investigates the impact of discursive trends and practical realities on the writing and editing of one of the most influential education encyclopaedias.[8] Special attention is given to the issue of how research can strengthen public education globally, and therefore some 90 country system reports from Asia, the Americas and the Caribbean and Europe are compared and analysed.[9] Since the IEE was intended as a resource for development, especially in the Third World, and as a unifier as the Cold War was approaching its end, the ways in which 'the international scene' was constructed are highly interesting from a historical perspective. The IEE can in many ways be seen as a representation of the field of comparative education during the 1980s and 1990s. At the same time, it is equally important to understand the conditions and limitations of describing a foreign country's educational system in a fair way. Also, modern encyclopaedias face the challenges of representation and translation.[10] Combining modern text analysis with archive studies of editorial documents, the difficulties and challenges of keeping a project like this to agreed standards will be revealed. It is also possible to show a learning curve between the first and second editions, even though the project

---

[5] Most of these 15 experts worked in the United States, some in the UK while only two were employed in non-Anglo-Saxon countries.

[6] Husén and Postlethwaite, 'Preface.'

[7] Torsten Husén and T. Neville Postlethwaite, 'Preface,' in *The International Encyclopedia of Education* vol. 2, ed. Torsten Husén and T. Neville Postlethwaite (Oxford: Pergamon, 1994).

[8] Jürgen Schriewer and Carlos Martínez Valle, 'Constructions of Internationality in Education,' in *The Global Politics of Educational Borrowing and Lending*, ed. Gita Steiner-Khamsi (New York: Teachers College Press, 2004) pp. 29–53.

[9] See also Christian Lundahl, 'The Scholarship of the International Encyclopaedia of Education 1980—1994: Learning how to Produce Knowledge in a Public Genre' (paper presentation, American Educational Research Association, Washington, D.C., USA, April 8–12, 2016).

[10] E.g. Sverre Tveit and Christian Lundahl, 'New Modes of Policy Legitimation in Education: (Mis) using Comparative Data to Effectuate Assessment Reform,' *European Educational Research Journal* 17, no. 5 (2018).

112   S. GREK ET AL.

met great challenges in rewriting the world of education during the closing years of the Cold War.

The work on the International Encyclopaedia of Education is a very clear example of the disembedded laboratory, and illustrates processes of knowledge production over multiple sites, spaces, and networks. It is also a good illustration of the messiness and circumstantiality in knowledge construction, but also of its sophistication. In the work on the Encyclopaedia, Husén and Postlethwaite made use of the huge network of international scholars and organisations they collaborated with for over four decades as described in the previous chapters. After introducing 'encyclopaedic thinking,' this chapter describes the initial editorial process for determining the scope and structure of the Encyclopaedia, including the assignment of section editors. The following section discusses the efforts to make the Encyclopaedia international by finding authors with a global perspective, making it the first truly international encyclopaedia. In an analysis of 90 country system reports in IEE, we will show how the selection of authors and the use of standardising guidelines provided stability in the proceedings of this laboratory. Finally, we argue that the disembedded nature of the work presented challenges but also helped to legitimise it.

WHAT CONSTITUTES AN ENCYCLOPAEDIA?

The term 'encyclopaedia' comes from the Greek notion of *enkyklios paideia*, 'learning within the circle' or 'all-round education.' Historically, its roots have been traced to antique texts some 100 years BC.[11] Despite its commonality and high rank among 'knowledge books,' it is surprisingly difficult to find research about the actual work of editing such books. There exist of course several guidelines on how to edit encyclopaedias,[12] but systematic research on them is rare. Much of what can be found takes

---

[11] Simon Garfield, *All the Knowledge in the World. The Extraordinary History of the Encyclopaedia* (New York: Weidenfeld & Nicolson, 2022).

[12] E.g. Harry S. Ashmore, 'Editing the Universal Encyclopedia,' *American Behavioural Scientist* 6, no. 15 (1962); David L. Sills, 'Editing a Scientific Encyclopedia,' *Science*, 163, no. 3872 (1969); Benjamin R. Beede,' Editing a Specialized Encyclopedia,' *Journal of Scholarly Publishing* 33, no. (2001); Louise Edwards, 'Editing Academic Books in the Humanities and Social Sciences: Maximizing Impact for Effort,' *Journal of Scholarly Publishing* 44, no. 1 (2012).

6 EDITING THE *INTERNATIONAL ENCYCLOPEDIA OF EDUCATION...* 113

the form of biographical notes.[13] Katharine Schopflin argues that the field of book history neglected the construction process of an encyclopaedia, partly because it's not really a book, in the sense of a single authored text around a few topics.[14] At the same time encyclopaedias have been treated within the history of knowledge and science, as being part, more or less, as an instrument of the enlightenment.[15] Modern time encyclopaedias are rarely dealt with.[16] Today encyclopaedias can be said to have belonged to 'the print paradigm,' more and more succeeded by digital 'wikis.'[17] The main audiences for today's encyclopaedias are schools, universities and libraries.[18]

When considering research encyclopaedias, one may ask why take on such a time-consuming and demanding project as editing an encyclopaedia. A common response in biographical notes is that it provides the opportunity to bring attention to a subject that has been worked on extensively. Editors of scholarly encyclopaedias tend to be prominent within their field of knowledge.[19]

The Torsten Husén archive comprises around three feet (eight volumes) of IEE material. An additional volume has been discovered in the Husén Library at Växjo University in southern Sweden. This chapter is based on approximately 4000 documents of IEE material and mainly focuses on the editorial correspondence, as well as 90 country system reports in the completed IEE. These reports have been scanned into digital copies for the 1985 edition, but were already digitised for the 1994

---

[13] Christian Lundahl, 'The Book of Books: Encyclopaedic Writing in the Science of Education in the 1980s,' in *Transnational Policy Flows in European Education*, ed. Andreas Nordin and Daniel Sundberg (London: Symposium Books, 2014).

[14] Katharine Schopflin, 'The Encyclopaedia as a Form of the Book,' PhD diss., (University College London, 2014); Katherine Schopflin, 'What do we Think an Encyclopaedia is?,' *Culture Unbound* 6, no. 3 (2014).

[15] Peter Burke, *A Social History of Knowledge. Volume II. From the Encyclopédie to Wikipedia* (Cambridge: Polity Press, 2011).

[16] For exceptions see Maria Simonsen, *Den skandinaviske encyklopædi: Udgivelse og udformning af Nordisk familjebok & Salmonsens Konversationsleksikon* (Göteborg, Makadam: 2016).

[17] Olof Sundin and Jutta Haider, 'The Networked Life of Professional Encyclopaedias: Quantification, Tradition and Trustworthiness,' First Monday 18, no. 6 (2013); Linn Holmberg and Maria Simonsen, *Stranded Encyclopedias, 1700–2000* (Cham: Palgrave Macmillan, 2021).

[18] Sundin and Haider, 'Networked Life.'

[19] Cf. Carol A. Chapelle, 'Why Would Anyone Want to Edit an Encyclopedia?,' *The Modern Language Journal* 95, no. 4 (2011); Edwards, 'Editing Academic Books.'

114   S. GREK ET AL.

CD-ROM edition. The objective of comparing the country reports is to demonstrate the differences in the reports based on their construction circumstances. Is it correct to assume that all IEE countries are equally represented and has IEE effectively addressed the ethnocentrism that the AERA encyclopaedias were criticised for?

The International Encyclopaedia of Education Takes Form

The International Encyclopaedia of Education: Research and Studies was first published in April 1985 at the AERA conference. Pergamon Press, a publisher of scientific journals and encyclopaedias since the 1960s, published the encyclopaedia.

In 1986, the IEE was awarded the Dartmouth Award by the American Library Association for being the best reference work of the year. The IEE received mixed reviews from scholarly reviewers, despite their recognition of the effort put into it. In the Oxford Review of Education, five researchers evaluated major articles in four sections. After identifying strengths and weaknesses, the reviewer of the country entries and articles related to comparative education concluded that 'the entries on comparative education are so uneven and so unbalanced.'[20]

The criticism may have been unsettling for Husén and Postlethwaite, as this area could be considered their own prime expertise.[21] The editors made significant changes in the editorial process for the second edition released in 1994, which had evident effects on the comparative education sections of the encyclopaedia. This illustrates the 'laboratory' nature of knowledge production; it is modelled, worked on, evaluated, and reworked.

Producing and Indexing the Content

The editorial work of an encyclopaedia begins with a classificatory system and ends with the production of a functional index. A well-organised index is crucial for ease of use. This raises the question of the origin and development of the organisational principles behind the content and index

---

[20] David Phillips et al., 'Review of International Encyclopedia of Education,' *Oxford Review* 12, no. 1 (1986): 82.

[21] The reviewers of the section of teaching and teacher training (Kenneth Wilson), and of research policy and methodology (John K. Backhouse) were also more critical than praising, while the reviewer of the headings under Curriculum, Karl-Heinz Gruber, was much more impressed. Philips et al., 'Review.'

6 EDITING THE *INTERNATIONAL ENCYCLOPEDIA OF EDUCATION...* 115

of the IEE. In practical editorial work, this process is referred to as 'deciding on the entry topics' or 'general headings.'[22] How did the editors of IEE decide on the organisation of their encyclopaedia and what options did they consider? Who should be selected as section editors? When it comes to the IEE, we can clearly see how many options here were elaborated upon.

In the summer of 1979, Robert Maxwell (1923–1991),[23] who was a publisher at Pergamon Press, proposed to Torsten Husén that he, with the assistance of Dr. James Botkin at Harvard, should edit a multivolume work that would draw together all available internationally significant recent work in education. It would mainly be acquired by libraries, and some 25–40 authors would prepare it.[24] As described by Husén in his book *Möten* [Meetings], he met Maxwell coincidently at a hotel bar in Salzburg.[25]

However circumstantial the first meeting between Maxwell and Husén was, several experts were subsequently invited to Maxwell's Mansion, Headington Hill Hall, to participate in an initial meeting. The purpose, structure, organisation, and time frames of the IEE were discussed at this meeting. Those invited except for Husén and Postletwaite were Dr. J. Botkin, Harvard, Massachusetts; Professor M. Debeauvais, International Institute for Educational Planning, Paris; Professor N. L. Gage, Stanford University, California; Dr. H. Judge, University of Oxford; Dr. F. N. Kerlinger, University of Amsterdam, and Dr. Gilbert de Landsheere, University of Liege.[26]

The invitation to the Oxford meeting included a seven-page note from Botkin.[27] In May 1980, Botkin and Professor Gage met with Torsten

[22] Jeffrey I. Ross and Frank Shanty, 'Editing Encyclopedias for Fun and Aggravation,' *Publishing Research Quarterly* 25, no. 3 (2009).

[23] Maxwell was a Czechoslovakian-born British media proprietor who rose from poverty to build a publishing empire. After his death, it was revealed that he had had stolen hundreds of millions of pounds from his own companies' pension funds. See further John Preston, *Fall: The Mystery of Robert Maxwell* (London. Penguin Books, 2021).

[24] The international encyclopaedia for educational research. Invitation letter to Oxford June 11–14, 1980 (The Husén archive, 2.194).

[25] Torsten Husén, *Möten men psykologer, pedagoger och andra* (Lund: Wiken, 1992): 313.

[26] Husén, *Möten*, 313.

[27] Botkin was first assigned as a co-editor in chief together with Husén, but for some reason that is not revealed in the archive material he was exchanged with Postlethwaite during the fall of 1980. A letter from Pergamon, shows that Botkin had been offered a section editor position instead, but did not find this financially rewarding enough, so he was released from the project (C. R. Ellis to Postlethwaite, September 30, 1980 (The Husén archive, 1.279)). In Husén's autobiography, Botkin is not even referred to by name, but as 'some young man from Harvard' (Torsten Husén, *Möten*, 313).

116   S. GREK ET AL.

Husén to discuss the content for the June meeting. They established that the audience for the IEE should be broader than the research community. It should be 'a state of the art report on all aspects of worldwide educational research and its relevance to educators, lifelong consumers of education, administrators, politicians, civil servants, and industrialists.'[28]

Botkin suggested establishing some 'ground rules' before the meeting.[29] Therefore, he, Husén, and Gage discussed the meaning of the four main title words: international, encyclopaedia, educational, and research. For instance, by 'international' they meant that the articles should come from many countries, that the IEE should be distributed to many countries, and maybe even translated. Further they discussed if 'the geographic scope [should] include not only developing countries ... but also socialistic countries?'[30] Since a majority of the research on education was from the U.S., Botkin and his fellow researchers also wanted to discuss how valid it was for the rest of the world.[31]

At the Oxford meeting, eight subject editors (also called section editors) were decided upon, of whom six were attending the meeting.[32] To clarify the scope of the encyclopaedia, Maxwell proposed distributing a questionnaire worldwide with the assistance of Pergamon's field offices. He also suggested that he himself would interview a past British Minister of Education, Shirley Williams, who he thought would have good opinions. It was also suggested that they should make contact with the editors of the Encyclopaedia of Educational Research that was simultaneously being prepared by AERA.[33]

The personal reflections of the participants in their notes to Maxwell from the Oxford meeting contain various suggestions on how to organise the content of the IEE. These suggestions differ from those of Botkin, Gage, and Husén. Postlethwaite listed a number of people and institutions from different parts of the world that he himself recognised had a generally good overview, but when it came to content he just noted that the

---

[28] James Botkin, 'Notes for participants, May 15, 1980. Oxford Meeting, June 11–14' (The Husén archive, 2.194), 1.

[29] Botkin, 'Notes for participants.'

[30] Botkin, 'Notes for participants,' 3.

[31] Botkin, 'Notes for participants,' 3.

[32] Meeting at Oxford, June 11–14, 1980. Working session I, morning June 12, part 1 (The Husén archive, 2.194).

[33] Meeting at Oxford, June 11–14, 1980. Working session I, morning June 12, part 2 (The Husén archive, 2.194).

6 EDITING THE *INTERNATIONAL ENCYCLOPEDIA OF EDUCATION...* 117

AERA encyclopaedia and a dictionary that de Landsheere edited could be good starting points.[34] De Landsheere himself suggested three methods of selecting entries: 'Judgments choice, 'Logical' semantic tree, and Computerised approach,' upon which he did not elaborate further.[35] Harry Judge suggested that the principal targets for an encyclopaedia are professional teachers and educationalists. Judge believed that the encyclopaedia would be used to answer basic questions, and he listed 37 tentative *Who*, *What*, *How* and *When* questions teachers might have, for example, What are the uses and limitations of the questionnaire? What is human capital theory? What is regression analysis? What is Behaviourism? Do schools make a difference? Who is Thorndike? What is formative evaluation?[36]

De Landsheere stressed, 'There must be no place for educational bla-bla-bla' and suggested a structure similar to that of medical handbooks where 'one finds an up to date presentation of say heart physiology and pathology. Why not a similar approach for reading, music learning, ...?' He also wanted to make room for contemporary issues like: 'Hard vs. soft evaluation, Optimum class size, The failure of new math, Impact of new technology (specially videodisc + computer + larger beam reading)' etc.[37] Professor Gage found a way of expressing these kinds of needs. The purpose of the encyclopaedia should be to serve as a 'resource of the first resort' where users could find information concerning 'facts, concepts, principles, controversies, theories, methods, trends, historical backgrounds and specific educational findings from educational studies and research.'[38] This expression was used in several other documents,[39] and one gets the impression that it demonstrates the project members' intentions regarding the content well. We can clearly see that the initial editorial board had different suggestions as to what would be the best underlying organisational

---

[34] Note from T. Neville Postlethwaite to Robert Maxwell, June 12, 1980 (The Husén archive, 2.194).

[35] Note from Gilbert de Landsheere to Robert Maxwell, Notes on the Encyclopaedia Project, June 12, 1980 (The Husén archive, 2.194).

[36] Note from Harry Judge to Robert Maxwell, Notes on the Encyclopaedia Project by Harry Judge, June 12, 1980 (The Husén archive, 2.194).

[37] De Landsheere, 'Note to Robert Maxwell.'

[38] Note from Nathanael L. Gage to Robert Maxwell, The Proposed International Encyclopaedia of Education, June 12, 1980 (The Husén archive, 2.194).

[39] For example, in what appears to be a press release on the project sent out from the Nassau meeting, March 20, 1981 (The Husén archive, 2.194, stamped May 5, 1981).

118 S. GREK ET AL.

principle here; from earlier classifications as Postlethwaite suggested, or departing from purposes of use as put forward by Judge. An inventory of issues, as was suggested early on by Botkin and his fellow researchers, finally became the guiding principle to organise for a 'resource of the first resort.' Regardless, this process reflects the circumstantial and somewhat messy aspects of this kind of knowledge production. It did not follow on strict epistemological principles.

Deciding upon Section Editors

During the Oxford meeting, it was decided to create a manual to assist authors and subject/section editors. Robert Maxwell expressed his preference for subject editors or advisors to be selected from among the meeting attendees.[40] A comparison between the Oxford attendees and the subject editors in Nassau, Bahamas, in March 1981 reveals several changes in this regard.

Of the first participants from the Oxford meeting only Husén, Postlethwaite, and de Landsheere remained in the editorial main group of sector editors[41]:

Bruce H. Choppin	Evaluation and assessment
University of California, Los Angeles, USA	
Luvern Cunningham	Educational administration
Ohio State University, Columbus, Ohio, USA	
Gilbert L. de Landsheere	
University of Liège, Liège, Belgium	
Michael J. Dunkin	Teaching and teacher education
University of Sydney, Sydney, New South Wales, Australia	
Michael Eraut	Educational technology
University of Sussex, Brighton, Sussex, UK	
Torsten Husén	Editor in chief
University of Stockholm, Stockholm, Sweden	

(continued)

[40] Meeting at Oxford—June 11–14, 1980. Working session IV, afternoon June 13, part 2 (The Husén archive, 2.194).

[41] Record of the main points of achievement and agreement reached at a meeting of section editors and the editors-in-chief in, see Anonymous, 'Press Release.'; Torsten Husén and Neville Postlethwaite, eds., *The International Encyclopedia of Education* vol. 10 (Oxford: Pergamon, 1985), ix.

6 EDITING THE *INTERNATIONAL ENCYCLOPEDIA OF EDUCATION...* 119

(continued)

John P. Keeves Australian Council for Educational Research, Hawthorn, Victoria, Australia	Research methodology
J. Roby Kidd Ontario Institute for Studies in Education, Toronto, Ontario, Canada	Adult, recurrent, and lifelong education
Arieh Lewey University of Tel Aviv, Tel Aviv, Israel	Curriculum
Raphael O. Nystrand University of Louisville, Louisville, Kentucky, USA	
A. Harry Passow Teachers College, Columbia University, New York, USA	Special education
T. Neville Postlethwaite University of Hamburg, Hamburg	Editor in chief
George Psacharopoulos World Bank, St Paul, Minnesota, USA	Economics of education
Gordon I. Swanson University of Minnesota, St Paul, Minnesota, USA	Vocational and industrial education
R. Murray Thomas University of California, Santa Barbara, California, USA	Human development
Colin J. Titmus Goldsmith's College, University of London, London, UK	
Hans N. Weiler Stanford University, Stanford, California, USA	Educational policy and planning

From Pergamon Press Barbara Barrett and A. J. Steel had joined the editorial board as administrative staff.[42] With these section editors at place, the international field of education was divided into 14 different sections. But until the final version of the IEE these sections were split and re-organised several times. In the IEE volume 10, there are 25 sections.[43]

---

[42] Barbara Barrett was a publishing manager at Pergamon and came to be the administrative co-ordinator.

[43] Namely: Administration of education; Adult, recurrent, and lifelong learning; Comparative and international education; Counselling and guidance; Curriculum; Developing countries and education; Disciplinary approaches to education; Early childhood education; Economics of education; Educational institutes, organisations, and societies; Educational policy and planning; Educational technology; Evaluation and assessment; Higher education; Human development; Motivation and attitudes to education; National systems of education; Occupationally oriented education; Research policy and methodology; Sex roles and gender in education; Social stratification and education; Special education; Teaching and teachers' education; Vocational and institutional education; and Women and education.

120   S. GREK ET AL.

The further division of the sections probably evolved from the articles that were finally produced.[44] In the first edition of 1985, there were no women in the editorial board, and in the 1994 edition 3 out of 22 section editors were women: Gabriele Lakomski, Lorin W. Andersson, and Margret C. Wang.[45]

At the Oxford meeting, the autonomy of subject editors was a significant topic of discussion. Ultimately, authors were granted considerable freedom in designing their articles. Tentative suggestions were made that topics should generally include theories, issues, and results of empirical studies from around the world, along with descriptions of research methods where appropriate, as well as educational applications and implications.[46]

Looking at the section editors selected especially for the first edition, five of them had worked together with Husén and Postlethwaite at IEA.[47] They were mainly Europeans, and some Americans. These men met to construct the 'world of education.' They were elaborative at the start, and during the process. The 'world of education' grew as they worked, for example, also to include female perspectives. Nevertheless, 'the source of the first resort' when it came to international education were clearly constructed by someone, an old network of male scholars, under very specific conditions.

A World of Educational Knowledge and Knowledge of the Educational World

Encyclopaedias are often criticised due to their inevitable obsolescence. They claim to contain vast amounts of knowledge, but the sheer amount of information available means that they can quickly become outdated. Additionally, many encyclopaedia projects never make it to publication, as evidenced by the work of Holmberg and Simonsen.[48] When beginning work on an encyclopaedia, editors must determine its coverage. In the case

[44] See Chapelle, 'Why Would Anyone.'

[45] Franziska Primus and Christian Lundahl, 'The Peripherals at the Core of Androcentric Knowledge Production: An Analysis of the Managing Editor's Knowledge Work in The International Encyclopedia of Education (1985),' *Paedagogica Historica* 57, no 6 (2021).

[46] IEEP editors-in-chief to Section editors, November 11, 1980. (The Husén archive, 2.194).

[47] Namely, de Landsheere, Choppin, Keeves, Lewy, Passow; see chapter 3.

[48] Holmberg and Simonsen, 'Stranded Encyclopedias.'

6 EDITING THE *INTERNATIONAL ENCYCLOPEDIA OF EDUCATION...* 121

of IEE, this involved selecting globally relevant topics and deciding how to write about the global world of education. The previous section focused on determining the scope and general structure of the IEE, as well as assigning section editors. This section focuses on producing the actual content and ensuring global coverage.

In a general guideline to authors of the 1985 edition, the editors wrote that the encyclopaedia 'will consist of a strictly alphabetical review and repository of our current knowledge about all aspects of schooling and learning from birth to death.'[49] This included formal and non-formal education from pre-school through university level. The editors stated that the encyclopaedia will be, with the familiar phrase, 'a resource of the first resort' on qualitative as well at quantitative results of studies and research throughout the 'world in the field of education.'[50]

To what extent they lived up to these claims might be reflected in the general guidelines of the 1994 edition. The editors wrote that 'the review of the Encyclopedia were laudatory in terms of coverage, quality of content, and cross-referencing.'[51] The reviews, however, also indicated that some topics were not sufficiently covered, such as sociology of education, vocational and technical education, women's studies, nonformal education, special education, and the history of education. Finally, it was felt that more effort should be made to achieve a fuller international coverage of many themes.[52] In the 1994 ed. guidelines, the editors stress that their attempt is to provide 'a storehouse' of knowledge for faculty members, students, and researchers at the universities, and in teacher training programs as well as for policymakers.

> In summary, the aim of the encyclopedia is to provide a comprehensive up-to-date international overview of the state-of-the-art of education at a time when the developed knowledge of the twentieth century becomes, in the 1990s, the basis of ideas and policies for the twenty-first.[53]

---

[49] Torsten Husén and Neville Postlethwaite, *Guideline Report: The International Encyclopedia of Education: Studies and Research. Aims, Scope, Organization and Recommendations to Authors* (Linnéuniversitets bibliotek, Husénsamlingen, T. Husén International Encyclopedia of Education, 2nd ed.), 6.

[50] Husén and Postlethwaite, *Guideline Report*.

[51] Husén and Postlethwaite, *Guideline Report*, 1.

[52] Husén and Postlethwaite, *Guideline Report*, 1.

[53] Husén and Postlethwaite, *Guideline Report*, 1.

122   S. GREK ET AL.

These claims for the twenty-first century relevance clearly meant covering more of the world, being truly international at a time when global movements in education grew in strength.[54]

In a letter of 21 January 1991, to the managing editor of IEE Mrs. Barbara Barrett, before a meeting with section editors, Husén and Postlethwaite suggest to her to include a rather long paragraph on international coverage:

> It is of utmost importance that authors are chosen because of their knowledge of their field of speciality of what goes on in different countries. Scientific principles, methods and technical procedures in educational research are cross-nationally valid and less culture-bound than educational practices and procedures. Critical reviewers have indicated that authors of entries (particularly those from North America), even though they are outstanding scholars in their respective fields have limited knowledge about what goes on in the rest of the world. It is not sufficient to produce an article which deals with what goes on in the US plus one peripheral study from Israel.
>
> A working 'rule of thumb' when dealing with educational practices and procedures is to include material from at least 3–4 countries of which one should be a non-English speaking country. When it comes to structural arrangements in education (school-structure, pre-service teaching training, administration, etc.) authors should consider to cover as many structures as possible.
>
> Authors should also realize that there is a strong Anglo-Saxon (particularly US) dominance in education research, as can be seen from the existing data-bases, such as ERIC. But one should also consider that several data-bases are biased because of limitation of coverage to material in English.
>
> If two authors possess the same competence to write up an entry but belong to two different languages areas (e.g., German and English) one should prefer the one with non-English mother tongue in spite of the fact that he or she may cause more trouble when editing the article.[55]

What we see in this paragraph is an example of how constructing 'the international' in the encyclopaedia wasn't easy. Lessons learned from the

---

[54] Martin Lawn and Sotiria Grek, *Europeanising Education* (London: Symposium Books, 2012).

[55] Torsten Husén and T. Neville Postlethwaite to Barbara Barrett, 21 January, 1991. (Linnéuniversitets bibliotek, Husénsamlingen, T. Husén International Encyclopedia of Education (second edition).

6 EDITING THE *INTERNATIONAL ENCYCLOPEDIA OF EDUCATION...* 123

first edition, the editors-of-chief took on some precautions when demanding three to four different examples on each topic from different countries. They also point at biases in research data bases and finally, if everything else equal, they also suggested invoicing non-English mother-tongue authors.

Finding all authors needed was a difficult task and here the personal networks, active networking and NGOs' networks came into use. This made it difficult to find a broader international representation. In a letter to Barrett dated 29 April 1989, Husén reveals some of his strategies in finding authors:

Dear Barbara,
In my letter to you on April 24 I forgot to mention the charge I undertook in connection with the meeting in Princeton, May 3-5, of the US National Academy of Education.[56]

Since so many 'Encylopedia relevant' people are turning up at the Princeton meeting, I should seize the opportunity to talk to those, whose participation we want to enlist for the future. It is much easier to persuade people when you have them face to face, than by mail (not to speak of the time you save).

Thus, I will try to approach the following (without firm obligations):

1. Urie Bronfenbrenner, Cornell University (for Human Development)
2. Burton Clark, as Section Editor for Sociology of Education
3. Larry Cremin, as Section Editor for the History of Education. If he refuses I will try to persuade Carl Kaestle, Wisconsin.

/.../
I will be back in Stockholm on Monday, May 8, and be ready to report on my efforts to recruit people. If you want to contact me in Princeton, I will be staying at the Henry Chauncy Center.

Best wishes, Torsten[57]

The letter tells about the strategic work in finding authors, but at the same time also some of the highly social and circumstantial aspects of this so crucial part of the knowledge production contributing to some

---

[56] Husén became a fellow the US National Academy of Education in 1967 which obviously granted him an important American network (Husén, *Incurable Academic*).

[57] Torsten Husén to Barbara Barrett April 29, 1989 (Linnéuniversitets bibliotek, Husénsamlingen, T. Husén International Encyclopedia of Education (second edition).

124 S. GREK ET AL.

ethnocentrism. An example of other circumstances was that authors and section editors got sick or in some cases also actually died during the process.[58]

Of special importance for the international coverage of the encyclopaedia were the national systems reports. For both editions, Professor Postlethwaite was appointed as the section editor of 'National systems of education' and he provided the authors, who often were not researchers, with a section manual, *Description of Country Systems of Education*, inspired to some extent by the UNESCO Statistical Yearbook.[59] Following a system of 11 sub-headings, the country education system articles were built up from rather basic data and information.[60] In the preface to the first edition, the editors also acknowledge the importance of large international organisations for their help and support in reaching out to people and countries: 'Contacts made through the networks of UNESCO, the International Association for the Evaluation and Educational Achievement (IEA), and the International Institute for Educational Planning (IIEP) were especially valuable' (IEE 1985, p. xiii). We can assume though that the way of describing a country from this perspective did not suit every country equally well, and in the draft preface of the supplementary volumes it is clear that Husén and Postlethwaite realised that they had been *too* ethnocentric, despite their efforts not to be (this self-reflection is edited out in the final version).[61] However, in the second edition of IEE they used an even more standardised procedure, which will be described in the following.

Seen in a laboratory perspective these challenges with the first edition represents a messiness, or instability, in the inscription process of the 'world of education,' that the editors had to manage and eventually overcome.[62] Their main tools for stabilising these processes where the selection of authors, and to provide them standardising guidelines.

---

[58] Lundahl, 'Book of Books;' Primus and Lundahl, 'Peripherals at the Core.'

[59] Description of Country Systems of Education (The Husén archive, 2.279).

[60] The basic structure of the countries system in IEE is: (1) Present-day data about the country, (2) Goals of the education system, (3) General structure and size of the education effort, (4) Administrative and supervisory structure and operation, (5) Education finance, (6) Supplying personnel for the education system (including teacher education), (7) Curriculum Development and Teaching Methodology, (8) The systems of examinations, promotions and certification, (9) Educational Research, (10) Major problems for the next two decades, (11) Bibliography and further reading.

[61] Preface, 1987, 1st draft. In a letter from Torsten Husén to Barbara Barrett dated July 14, 1987. (The Husén archive, 2.279)

[62] See Appendix A.

WORLD 'FACTS': THE COUNTRY SYSTEM REPORTS

Looking back, it was challenging to achieve equal quality in the country system reports, particularly in the 1985 edition. The statements about the world of education were highly unstable in laboratory terms.[63] This was due, in part, to its disembedded nature, which required many different scholars to understand their objects in similar ways. This analysis highlights variations between the country system reports of Asia, the Americas and the Caribbean, and Europe. Explanations for these variations will also be provided.

As shown in Appendix B, some country reports are significantly longer than others, potentially due to external writers being asked to limit their word count in reports from smaller countries. Taking this into consideration, a clear pattern emerges where Asian countries are described using the fewest words on average, while descriptions of countries in the Americas and the Caribbean are slightly longer, and European descriptions are by far the longest. Surprisingly, smaller countries such as Austria, Finland, and Sweden are at the top, alongside larger countries such as France and West Germany. The top-ranking countries in Europe are expected to be included, but why are China, the Soviet Union, or the USA not represented among the longer country system reports? One possibility is that the IEE project was focused on the European educational research community, making it easier for the editors to locate the most suitable writers for the articles.

However, there are also other intriguing disparities in the country system reports, which are linked to the author's affiliation. There are four types of affiliations for the authors of the country reports: national university, national agency or ministry, NGO (often UNESCO or the World Bank), or external university in another country. In this analysis, national and external university authors are treated as one population (N 87). Officials account for 58 texts and NGOs for 7.

Figure 6.1 shows a greater difference between university authors and official authors in Europe compared to the other two continents. This may be due to the fact that many authors who wrote about smaller countries in Asia, the Americas, and the Caribbean were employed at foreign

---

[63] Latour and Woolgar, *Laboratory Life*; Karin Knorr-Cetina, 'Laboratory Studies: The Cultural Approach to the Study of Science,' in *Handbook of science and technology studies*, ed. Sheila Jasanoff (Los Angeles: Sage, 1995); see Appendix A.

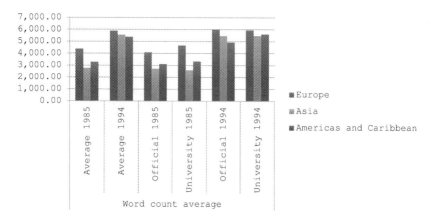

Fig. 6.1 Word count average in Europe, Asia, and the Americas and the Caribbean, depending on official or university author

universities. In 1994, external writers were used 40 percent less, enabling smaller countries to provide more detailed descriptions of their own country, which were now written by own government officials.

Figure 6.1 also shows that the differences between the three continents were smaller in 1994 than in 1985. Clearly, there had been an overall learning curve between the first and second edition. As pointed out by Knorr-Cetina, laboratories tend to 'reconfigure' scientists to become 'workable' (feasible) in relation to the object of the laboratory.[64] In a proposal for a second edition Husén, Postlethwaite, and Barrett wrote as one of their USPs for a new edition:

> Much hard work went into The International Encyclopedia of Education and routines for the writing-up and production of such a source work were thereby established. The field was also mapped out. One can expect that the momentum gained and the routines established would make it possible to produce a second edition more efficiently.[65]

In 1994, Postlethwaite, the editor of the country system reports, worked more strategically with these routines to stabilise the work in the

[64] Knorr-Cetina, 'Laboratory Studies;' see also Appendix A.
[65] Torsten Husén, T. Neville Postlethwaite, Barbara Barrett, *Proposal* (The International Encyclopedia of Education. Second edition. Linnéuniversitets bibliotek, Husénsamlingen, T. Husén International Encyclopedia of Education (second edition).

6 EDITING THE *INTERNATIONAL ENCYCLOPEDIA OF EDUCATION...* 127

disembedded laboratory, compared to his approach in 1985. Almost all of the 144 entries were approved by the ministers of education of each country. The authors, whether officials or university employees, followed a specific text structure decided upon by the editors (preface 1994 XVIII). Postlethwaite also ensured that the authors were followed-up on. For example, in a letter to Dr. Hajdaraga in Tirana, Albania, on 24 October 1991, Postlethwaite wrote:

> Dear Dr. Hajdaraga
> Thank you for your letter of 12 October. 1991.
> Having read your article I am not sure if you received the Guidelines that I wrote for each entry. I therefore enclose:
>
> a) The Guidelines for the article;
> b) A 'model' article (i.e. the structure required) about Australia.
>
> It is very important that you follow the guidelines and use the same major heads and sub-heads. /.../[66]

Even though this extra work resulted in an increased standardisation of headings and increased length of the articles (word count), other differences between official and university authors remained. We can, for example, see that they differ according to the number of references to 'research,' 'charts' and 'tables,' and the number of posts in their bibliography. They also differ, if only slightly, in how much they refer to NGOs such as OECD, or the World Bank.

Content-wise there is an interesting difference between the country reports in the 1985 and 1994 editions, where it is possible to see a more prevalent discourse in 1994. This discourse, or standard of stabilisation, 'prescribes' the countries' educational system in terms of: the influence of economic and political structure, the importance of a developed school administration, curriculum development procedures, teacher training, the enrolment in preschool ['percent'], primary school, secondary school, vocational—and adult education, and finally—future challenges.

One example that illustrates the growing importance of economy, efficiency and quality in international education policy discourse during the 1980s and 1990s is the frequency with which the term 'evaluation' appears (Fig. 6.2).

---

[66] T. Neville Postlethwaite to Dr. Hajdaraga. International Encyclopedia of Education. Korrespondens N. Postlethwaite. 1980–tidigt 90-tal (The Husén archive, 2.279).

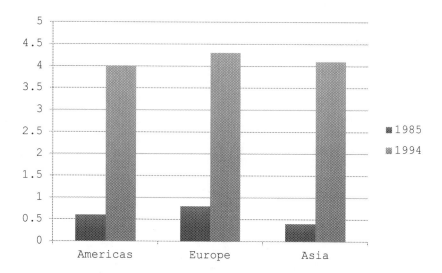

Fig. 6.2 Average mentions of the term 'evaluation' in 1985 and 1994

The increased frequency of 'evaluation' and 'quality control' in 1994 is evident for all three regions and indicates the presence of a new global discourse on management by objectives and results-oriented school systems. A legitimate question is whether this actually describes the reality or if it is a consequence of the increased influence on these country system reports by, on one side, NGOs like OECD, UNESCO and the World Bank, and on the other, of national ministers of education.

Thus, turning to authors representing the national agencies for education, and providing them with detailed guidelines caused some stabilisation to occur in the disembedded laboratory creating facts about the world of education. This is also related to a discourse connecting education with policies that value economy, efficiency, and quality in the public sector.

Unwrapping International Encyclopaedic Knowledge

With the production of IEE, the world of educational knowledge became comprehensive, at least enough to fit in ten volumes. A large number of authors were contracted to write an enormous amount of articles and entries, both on topics they had expert knowledge about, and on things they knew less about (Torsten Husén by the way wrote seven articles

6 EDITING THE *INTERNATIONAL ENCYCLOPEDIA OF EDUCATION...* 129

himself).[67] Yet, what makes an encyclopaedia an encyclopaedia is for one thing its authority of knowledge, being 'a resource of the first resort.'[68] Today we see a 'de-authorisation of the cult of experts' in particular through *Wikipedia*, which since 2001 has offered encyclopaedia-style articles, written by voluntary contributors and editable by almost anyone, but also social media and platforms like EURYDICE makes knowledge construction a more open endeavour.[69] On the positive side, knowledge becomes less fixed to time and individuals, on the negative side all knowledge production risks becoming valued as equally solid. As this chapter illustrates, there are good grounds to scrutinise authoritative knowledge, since also that is circumstantial, but at the same time, the chapter illustrates the amount of time and work that goes into the production of an international encyclopaedia of education. Unwrapping *international* and *encyclopaedic* knowledge thus is both about a sound and reflexive de-authorisation of experts visualising the social and circumstantial aspects of facts, and a re-authorisation made possible through highlighting that this knowledge production is comparatively global, systematic and reliable.

A major motivation to undertake the work of editing the IEE was to show the potential of comparative and international education. The editors-in-chief, Torsten Husén and Neville Postlethwaite, believed that by showing this, they could really help the Third World to develop, not, as many earlier encyclopaedias had, from a particular ethnocentric perspective but from the global perspective of a united educational research community. The first edition of IEE also had the purpose at the end of the Cold War of creating a sense of objectivity and coherence in an increasingly diversified discipline, in a less divided world.[70] The second one aimed at laying a foundation of knowledge on education as a preparation for the twenty-first century. The IEE thus appears clearly as an example of the globalisation of scientific knowledge, but the project as a whole is not an 'epistemic object' in a strict sense—it was not based on theory or on a well-defined methodology.[71] If we understand the IEE as the product of

---

[67] Husén, *Printed Publications.*

[68] Schopflin, 'What Do We Think.'

[69] Mike Featherstone and Couze Venn, 'Problematizing Global Knowledge and the New En-cyclopaedia Project: An Introduction,' *Theory Culture Society* 23, no. 2/3 (2006).

[70] Lundahl, 'Book of Books;' Zaki Laïdi, *A World Without Meaning: The Crisis of Meaning in International Politics* (London: Routledge, 1998).

[71] Karin Knorr-Cetina, Karin, 'Objectual practice, 'in *The Practice Turn in Contemporary Theory*, ed. Theodore R. Schatzki, Karin Knorr-Cetina and Eike von Savigny (New York: Routledge. 2001).

an epistemic culture,[72] then looking at early decision points and the structure of this knowledge, the final content of the encyclopaedia to some extent seems contingent and personal and is definitely not only a product of thorough scientific research. The division of educational knowledge into different sub-categories sometimes seemingly just happened, but we can also see how the encyclopaedia developed from collegial deliberations and experienced judgements. The selection of section editors and of authors was clearly vital, yet not all text were written by the foremost experts in the field.[73] An encyclopaedia helps to bring structure to a discipline—illustrating that different paradigms in educational thinking coexist—but without telling much about the processes of constructing its structure and categories. In the English version of Husén's autobiography the work with the encyclopaedia is mentioned as an example of his own lifelong learning, in which he had realised what an amorphous field educational enquiry actually was.[74]

One condition the editors had to work under, especially in the first edition, was the lack of autonomously produced country descriptions. Many of the countries on Postlethwaite's list probably would have had quite poor data on their school systems if it had not been for the help of OECD, UNESCO, the World Bank, IEA and IIEP. The way to systematise basic facts and knowledge in these country reports departed from an interest within international organisations in comparing countries' development and progress.[75] On the positive side, this offered the country reports some kind of standardisation, or stability, without which the encyclopaedia might have felt very disjointed. In this regard, we clearly see a higher degree of standardisation in the second edition compared to the first. Anyway, this poses the question of what is being displayed for comparison here—education ministry officers' skills in adapting to standards set by international organisations and/or good mirrors of each, and respective countries' real education systems? Laboratories rarely work with objects as they occur in reality, but with images of them,[76] and in case of IEE country reports these images were related to who could bring what into the labo-

---

[72] Knorr-Cetina, *Epistemic Cultures*.

[73] Primus and Lundahl, 'Peripherals at the Core.'

[74] Husén, *Incurable Academic*, 205.

[75] See Sotiria Grek et al., 'Travel, Translation, and Governing in Education: The Role of Swedish Actors in the Shaping of the European Education Space,' *Paedagogica Historica* 58, no. 1 (2020).

[76] Knorr-Cetina, 'Laboratory Studies.'

6 EDITING THE *INTERNATIONAL ENCYCLOPEDIA OF EDUCATION...* 131

ratory, and Postlethwaite's ability to oversee the complexity of disembeddedness.

The production of IEE was a social process that involved a large and dispersed network of people, objects, and locations. The language used is clear, objective, and value-neutral, with a formal register and precise word choice. The text adheres to conventional structure and format, with a logical flow of information and causal connections between statements. The text is free from grammatical errors, spelling mistakes, and punctuation errors. This network included hundreds of individuals, as well as devices like pencils, computers, and writing paper. It also involved places such as international conferences where new contacts were established and arrangements were made. The network is viewed as a social science laboratory where facts are negotiated and constructed. In contrast to the hard science laboratory, which aims to eliminate social context and stabilise the environment, the IEE's social science laboratory was disembedded; an unstable environment. This means that it was not tied to a specific, centralised location for fact production. The encyclopaedia's objective was to present factual information without a particular ethnographical viewpoint. It aimed to have an international outlook and production process. The laboratory's legitimacy was derived from its production in an internationalised world, which included conferences, airports, hotels, and correspondence via postal mail and telefax.

CHAPTER 7

Words for the World: Writing and Publishing Strategies for an International Book Market

The previous chapters have looked at the various contexts in which Husén engaged with his fellow scholars, be it in the form of workshops, conferences, international organisations or the editing of encyclopaedias. As we have seen, this was largely collective work, requiring the ability to collaborate across national, cultural, and linguistic boundaries, as well as between scientific disciplines. This chapter zooms in on another crucial aspect of Husén's work: his academic writings. Husén published a large number of texts in the form of reports, books and journal articles throughout his career (see further Appendix A). Many of these publications—especially the journal articles—were single-authored. But even texts produced in solitude must be seen in relation to a larger social context that created a need for them and influenced the specific issues that they addressed. This chapter, based mainly on Husén's correspondence, aims to shed light on how we can understand Husén as a writer of academic books and journal articles, focusing in particular on how international experiences, networks and collaborations made him a prolific and relatively versatile writer throughout six decades.[1]

In other words, the chapter discusses the relationship between international networks and academic productivity. Husén travelled extensively, and it is sometimes difficult to see how academic writing was made possible amidst all the travel and related meetings, seminars and

---

[1] For a statistical overview of Husén's publications, see Appendix A.

© The Author(s), under exclusive license to Springer Nature Switzerland AG 2024
S. Grek et al., *The World as a Laboratory*, Global Histories of Education, https://doi.org/10.1007/978-3-031-68090-8_7

133

134   S. GREK ET AL.

conferences. Nevertheless, the chapter demonstrates that international travel and academic publishing were closely linked. The chapter is divided into three parts. The first discusses the various ways in which Husén used his international experience, either to strengthen his position at home or on the international stage. The second part focuses on Husén's writing practices and the third part on dissemination strategies.

Making Use of International and International Experiences: Three Major Phases

Husén's academic career spanned a major part of the twentieth century, with his first academic publication in 1940 and his first international academic contacts in the 1930s. Thus, his intellectual life reflects some of the remarkable social changes that the twentieth century brought.

From Germany to Sweden

Husén's first international experiences that had an importance for his academic career were from Germany. This phase is significant since he actively came to use his experiences in Germany and by implication built his career on it. Since it was during the Nazi years, it is a part of his life that is sensitive and that he has somewhat downplayed, without entirely erasing it, from his own narrative of his life.

In the summers of 1938 and 1939, Husén studied in Marburg, Germany. Husén has commented on this experience in an autobiographical article. He argues that the choice of Marburg was partly a coincidence. Originally, he planned to go to Leipzig but for various reasons opted for Marburg instead, where Ernst Kretschmer was professor of psychiatry. At Marburg, Husén he also found out that one of the professors was a Nazi:

> Erich Jaensch held the chair of psychology. I did not know until I came to Marburg that he was a Nazi who had been made president of the German Psychological Association. Thus, in one respect Marburg was a bad choice.[2]

This is a somewhat polished picture of his actual experiences, omitting the fact that he actually returned to Marburg the following year, and the

[2] Torsten Husén, 'A Marriage to Higher Education,' *The Journal of Higher Education* 51, no. 6 (1980): 621.

7 WORDS FOR THE WORLD: WRITING AND PUBLISHING STRATEGIES... 135

fact that there was a close connection between Jaensch's research and Husén's licentiate thesis. Jaensch was an expert in eidetic imagery, the subject of Husén's licentiate thesis and Husén had at least three of Jaensch's books in his personal library. That there was a connection between the two is furthermore indicated by the fact that Husén received at least one letter from Jaensch, in which he asked Husén for a favour in disseminating a political message regarding alleged peace proposals by Adolf Hitler.[3]

The German connection soon proved to be important in establishing Husén as a major player in Swedish military knowledge. At that time Husén had not yet established himself as a writer and academic, but the summers spent in Germany provided him with some expertise to build on. In 1941 he submitted his first article on military psychology to the journal *Ny militär tidskrift* [New Military Journal]. In his letter to the editor, he referred to his studies in experimental psychology in Germany during the summers of 1938 and 1939. He wrote that he during his visit had noticed that German military psychology had reached a very high level, especially when it came to finding the right man in the right place, and that this had convinced him that Sweden could also make use of military psychology.[4] Husén's article was accepted, followed by 12 more articles in 1941 and 1942 for the magazine, and he also published books on the topic. His publication in *New Military Journal* was the start of his career as a military psychologist and he was later hired by the army to conduct military tests. As the letter in which he initially contacted the journal indicates, the summers in Germany were important in establishing Husén as an authority in military psychology in Sweden.

During the war, in November 1940, Husén also attended an academic conference in Rostock, a meeting between Swedish and German academics. During the meeting several lectures were held by Swedish and German

---

[3] In the letter, signed in October 1939, Jaensch claimed that Hitler had made peace proposals in a Reichtag speech but that the speech had been misrepresented abroad. Therefore, the German government had translated the speech to various European languages, and Jaensch asked Husén to forward it to appropriate organizations in Sweden. Erich Jaensch to Torsten Husén, October 13, 1939. The letter is not available in the Husén archive but is kept in Husén's personal copy of a book by Jaensch, *Der Gegentypus*, available at the Husén library (Husénsamlingen) at Linneuniversitetet, Växjö. A similar letter was the same day sent from Jaensch to Husén's supervisor John Landquist, who also knew Jaensch. Erich Jaensch to John Landquist, October 13, 1939 (Kungliga biblioteket).

[4] Torsten Husén to Arvid Eriksson, February 12, 1941 (The Husén archive, 1.115).

scholars. Many were professors, but the relatively inexperienced Husén, 24 years old at the time, gave a speech as well, entitled 'Über die Erforschung der eidetischen Anlage.'[5] He soon wrote an account of the meeting in a Swedish pro-German journal, in which he described the conference enthusiastically. The report contains no criticism of German policy during the Nazi era. Nor does it contain any direct endorsements, but it does have positive things to say about the German national character.[6] This article was probably not something Husén was proud of in the long run, and it is not mentioned in his later bibliographies or in his self-biographical writings. These experiences might raise questions on how to characterise Husén's political sympathies in his early 1920s but lack of sources make it complicated to establish his position.[7] The archive does not shed any further light on the issue, partly because it doesn't cover sources from the 1930s and few from the 1940s, but also because political aspects in general are absent. What on the other hand is clear in this case is that Husén demonstrated an ability and willingness to use knowledge developed in an international context in his home country. This would strengthen his role in the development of military testing and military psychology in Sweden, an expertise that he could later, in the post-war period, transform into an expertise in educational testing and large-scale testing, in a social and political context that was very different from the previous years. This ability, to take experiences made somewhere and then apply them elsewhere, was something that he would later demonstrate, albeit in a radically different context, when his knowledge about Sweden became of international interest.

---

[5] *Jahrbuch des Auslandsamtes der deutschen Dozentenschaft, Deutsch-Schwedische Akademikertagung in Rostock 24 bis 30 November 1940*, Heft 2 (Leipzig: Verlag Bibliographisches Institut, 1943), 8.

[6] Torsten Husén, 'Svensk-tyska akademikermötet i Rostock,' *Sverige-Tyskland* 2 (1941): 16–18.

[7] Peter Bennesved and Marie Cronqvist have briefly commented on this issue and argue that there are no signs of Husén having the same warm feelings for Nazi Germany as his supervisor and mentor John Landquist, and that there are indications that he politically and scientifically developed in other directions during his time in Lund, for example through contacts with radical historians and Marxist scholarship. 'En humanistiskt skolad kunskapsstrateg på ett samhällsvetenskapligt fält: Torsten Husén och framväxten av. ett svenskt psykologiskt försvar,' in *Humaniora i välfärdssamhället: Kunskapshistorier om efterkrigstiden*, eds. Johan Östlin, Anton Jansson and Ragni Svensson Stringberg (Göteborg: Makadam, 2023), 255–256.

World-wide Expert on Sweden

After the Second World War, Husén gradually moved away from military psychology and into education, becoming in 1953 professor of education and educational psychology at Stockholm University College. He got involved in the development of the comprehensive school reform and was in that sense an example of an academic involved in educational policy. It was partly in this capacity that he made a name for himself abroad.

In the 1960s, Husén established himself as a world expert on Swedish education. During this period there was a marked increase in the number of English-language texts describing the Swedish school system, written by Husén and other mainly Swedish scholars. In some ways this was a new situation. If we go back to the situation in 1956, we get a clear example of how the lack of English texts limited the possibilities for international networking. In that year Husén was contacted by W. D. Wall, the newly appointed director of the National Foundation for Educational Research in England and Wales (NFER). The internationally minded Wall wrote to Husén suggesting that his institute and Husén's could work together. In terms of international exchange, Wall asked for two things. First, he mentioned research reports and asked if his foundation could be put on a regular mailing list for research reports produced at Husén's department. Secondly, he wanted to exchange tests. He sent Husén two catalogues of tests published by the NFER and said that he wanted to build up a collection of tests from other countries.[8] Husén's enthusiastic reply indicates a willingness to cooperate, while acknowledging that Sweden unfortunately had little to offer.

> I was delighted to hear that we could establish an exchange between our institutes. I am afraid, however, that our contributions cannot come up to the same qualitative and quantitative standard as yours. A good deal of our stuff is printed or mimeographed in Swedish, which limits its availability.[9]

However, this linguistic limitation was soon to change, at least when it comes to research publications, and especially regarding Husén. Gradually, he became more engaged in international publishing, particularly in describing the Swedish comprehensive school reform. Sweden was increasingly seen as an interesting case of how educational policy and educational

---

[8] W. D. Wall to Torsten Husén, November 23, 1956 (The Husén archive, 1.17).
[9] Torsten Husén to W. D. Wall, December 5, 1956 (The Husén archive, 1.17).

138 S. GREK ET AL.

research developed in tandem. Husén's position in the field of comparative education was thus not based on a broad knowledge of different educational systems, but on a specialised knowledge of what was going on in his own country. In 1966, a bibliography was published in *Comparative Education Review*, with the title 'The Swedish Comprehensive School Reform: A Selected Annotated Bibliography.' It contained 61 items published between 1948 and 1965, most of them being in English. Husén had written or co-written 15 of those publications, published in reports, edited books and the following journals: *International Review of Education, Comparative Education, Comparative Education Review, Phi Delta Kappan, Educational Research, Review of Educational research.*[10] Most of the journals were fairly new, established in the 1950s or 1960s,[11] and illustrates that scholarly journals were expanding and that international dimensions and the field of comparative education was becoming institutionalised (Fig. 7.1).

Husén entering the international scene as an expert on Sweden was a transformation that began in the late 1950s, and American contacts in particular were crucial. Husén's first visit to the US was in 1954, and in 1959 he was a visiting professor in Chicago, working closely with C. Arnold Anderson at the newly established Comparative Education Center. The field of comparative education was growing as a scientific field at the time, as evidenced by the establishment of organisations such as CESE and CES (later CIES). The Chicago Centre, which opened in July 1958, proved to be influential in the field.[12] As early as December 1957, Husén received an invitation to become a visiting professor at the Centre.[13] During his time as a visiting professor in the autumn term of 1959, Husén gave a series of lectures on the Swedish educational system, which he later collected in a small book entitled *Problems of Differentiation in Swedish Compulsory Schooling*. This was the first, but not the last, example of a visit abroad resulting in a book. In the same year that he was in Chicago, he was also

[10] Rolland G. Paulston, 'The Swedish Comprehensive School Reform: A Selected Annotated Bibliography,' *Comparative Education Review* 10, no. 1 (1966).

[11] *Phi Delta Kappan* was established in 1916; *Review of Educational Research* in 1931; *International Review of Education* in 1955; *Comparative Education Review* in 1957; *Educational Research* in 1958; and *Comparative Education* in 1964.

[12] Erwin H. Epstein, 'C. Arnold Anderson,' in *North American Scholars in Comparative Education: Examining the Work and Influence of Notable 20th Century Comparativists*, ed. Erwin H. Epstein (London: Routledge, 2019), 73–81.

[13] Francis S. Chase to Husén, December 23, 1957 (The Husén archive, 1.14).

Fig. 7.1 Comparativist and expert on Sweden. The quest for Husén's writings in the field of comparative education was initially related to his expertise on Swedish educational policy. This 1961 report was published by the US Office of Education

140 S. GREK ET AL.

contacted by the *Comparative Education Review*, a journal founded in 1957. In a letter signed by George Bereday, a professor of comparative education, Husén was asked to write an article on the Swedish school reforms of 1950.[14] These are just two examples of how Husén's role changed in the late 1950s and 1960s, making him an international expert on Sweden.

Another example from the European scene is when the journal *Comparative Education*, founded in 1964, contacted Husén to write an article. In 1965, the journal asked Husén to write an article on the Swedish comprehensive school, and wanted it done quickly to be ready for the Comparative Education Conference in Berlin that year. Husén was given about a month to write the article, which the editor admitted was very short notice, but added that Husén hopefully 'had something available.'[15] He was right. Husén submitted his article just a week after the journal's letter was sent from England. The fact that he managed to finish it in such a short time suggests that it was not an original piece of work. In fact, Husén mentioned that it had been prepared as a lecture for teachers from abroad.[16] The article was subsequently published in the June issue of *Comparative Education* in the same year.[17] By today's standards it is hardly a scholarly article—the bibliography includes two titles, one by Husén himself. Instead, it is a fairly descriptive piece on the political developments leading up to the comprehensive school reform. Nevertheless, it was published in an academic journal devoted to comparative education. Thus, in the mid-1960s, Husén was in a position where he was asked to write about his homeland, a task he accomplished without much difficulty.

Overview of the World

After a while, the interest in Sweden as a model country lost its appeal, probably partly because some countries had already introduced comprehensive school reforms and the Swedish development was no longer a significant novelty to showcase for the world. Gradually, Husén also

[14] George Bereday to Torsten Husén, April 3, 1959 (The Husén archive, 1.14).

[15] Alec Peterson to Torsten Husén, February 25, 1965 (The Husén archive, 1.27).

[16] Torsten Husén to A.D.C. Peterson, March 2, 1965 (The Husén archive, 1.4).

[17] Torsten Husén, 'Educational Change in Sweden,' *Comparative Education* 1, no. 3 (1965).

7 WORDS FOR THE WORLD: WRITING AND PUBLISHING STRATEGIES... 141

developed a greater expertise in comparative studies of different education systems.

His position as chairman of the IEA was crucial in this respect. Leading an international organisation that focused on school performance clearly placed him in a position of having an overview of education more broadly, including the developing world. In terms of academic publications, it should be stressed that the IEA reports were collective products and Husén's role should not be overstated. Nevertheless, as the chairman of the association he got a certain public visibility. He was also active in terms of publications: he was the main editor of the mathematics reports published in 1967, he wrote the foreword to the reports of the Six Subject Survey, and he also published individually written journal articles based on the IEA surveys.

His interest in international and comparative studies was also evident in books like *The School in Question: A Comparative Study of the School and its Future in Western Society* from 1979, and *The Learning Society* from 1974. In those books he zoomed out to reflect on the school as an institution on a more general plane, while also discussing its future.[18]

Husén's position as a person attracted to the bird's eye view of the educational world was also demonstrated when he retired in 1982 and his collaborators discussed to make a festschrift. Instead of producing a festschrift, it was decided to organise an international symposium on a topic close to the heart of Husén—on the relationship between educational research and educational policy. The results were reported in a volume, edited by Husén himself and Maurice Kogan, which featured contributions by James S. Coleman, Hellmut Becker, James A. Perkins and others.[19] Effectively editing his own festschrift, the book was a testament to a long career devoted to work and international networks. It was a process that would continue, and perhaps reach its apogee, after retirement, with the editing of the *International Encyclopedia of Education* (see Chap. 6) that he conducted in the 1980s and 1990s together with his long-time colleague and friend, Neville Postlethwaite.

---

[18] Torsten Husén, *The Learning Society* (London: Methuen, 1974).
[19] Torsten Husén and Maurice Kogan, *Educational Research and Policy. How Do They Relate?* (Oxford: Pergamon, 1984).

Writing Practices

Having briefly characterised the different ways in which Husén used his international experiences in scholarly publications, it is now time to focus on a slightly different question: his actual writing practices. Understood in its broad sense, writing practices can encompass attitudes to writing, tools for writing, and making time and space for writing. Looking at such things can enhance our understanding of the scientific productivity of scholars who make it on the international arena.

Breaking the Language Barrier

There was a linguistic component to Husén's ability to transform himself and enter the international arena. In the beginning of his career, he was more at home in German, while he considered English to be his third language. However, as the twentieth century progressed, the ability to communicate in English became increasingly important for international networking and collaboration. While other languages, such as German and French, were also used to communicate, English was becoming more or less the standard language.[20] It is clear that the ability to master the English language was unevenly distributed, which could affect the extent to which international collaborations could be successfully initiated. As he reoriented himself towards the Anglo-Saxon world, he had to confront his linguistic limitations, which he himself considered to be considerable. As late as 1955 (two years after becoming a professor, one year after his first trip to the United States), he publicly expressed strong doubts about his ability to communicate clearly with his audience. It was the summer of 1955, and he was invited to speak at a summer school at Worcester Training College. He began his talk with a long apology for his poor English. Quoting a professor who had remarked that when one lectures to a competent audience, one runs the risk of exposing one's intellectual deficiencies, he added that when one lectures in a foreign language one

---

[20] 'In the 1950s and 1960s nearly half of the publications registered in the International Bibliography of the Social Sciences were in English, by 2005 their share had gone up to over 75 per cent.' Johan Heilbron, Thibaud Boncourt and Gustavo Sorá, 'Introduction: The Social and Human Sciences in Global Power Relations', in *The Social and Human Sciences in Global Power Relations*, eds. Johan Heilbron, Gustavo Sorá and Thibaud Boncourt (Cham: Springer, 2018), 6.

runs the risk of exposing one's linguistic deficiencies. Lingering on the theme of language, he went on to say:

> I feel a good deal of hesitation giving a lecture to this audience not only because of my linguistic shortcomings but also because the topic I have been hazardous enough to speak about is a very extensive one. As far as I know you have no or very few speech improvement clinics at your universities which does not give me an opportunity to get a quick course, say at Birmingham University before being sent here. In the U.S. my situation would have been more favourable in that respect. I hope indeed that you will compensate my poor verbalization by asking me questions after the lecture. I shall be extremely pleased to give a little series of supplementary lectures which might add to the information I am trying to give you in this lecture.[21]

There is a great deal of ambivalence in this quote. Husén was clearly aware of his linguistic limitations (which he probably exaggerated), but he also seems to have been proud of what he was about to say, with the subject being described as bold, as 'hazardous.' He was apparently not paralysed by his shortcomings, he really wanted to communicate, which is why he urged his audience to ask questions and why he looked forward to giving 'a little series of supplementary lectures after the lecture.'

He held a similar view on language regarding the publication of his speeches as articles. When *Educational Review* asked him to condense his speeches, he described the challenges of adapting an oral presentation into a written format. However, instead of being altogether discouraged, he sought help from the journal with writing the articles.

> I am not quite sure that I will be able to make an adequate script of my two lectures. It is easy to write a lecture in a more conversational style than to formulate a more condensed and strict article. Therefore, I think I better send you my first scripts and ask you to abbreviate as you like.[22]

Asking the editor to abbreviate the article was arguably a radical strategy, but one that made the publication possible. A letter to Philip

---

[21] Torsten Husén, 'A Swedish point of view. Paper given on July 27th at the Birmingham University Summer School at Worcester Training College' (The Husén archive, 2.253).

[22] Torsten Husén to Mr. Tubbs, October 14, 1955. (The Husén archive, 1.1).

144 S. GREK ET AL.

E. Vernon a few months earlier demonstrates that Husén had previously asked for linguistic assistance.[23]

Gradually, Husén became more proficient and experienced in English, and despite some self-doubt, he was never hampered in his writing and apparently never suffered from writer's block. Nevertheless, correspondence shows that he was sometimes criticised for his writing style. On one occasion, for example, Neville Postlethwaite was asked to comment on Husén's writing. An unusually frank reader, Postlethwaite wrote in a letter that he had tried his best to correct the bad English and gross errors of style, but admitted that it was a challenge to maintain his high standards: 'One problem with this sort of work is that by the time you have read half the book, you are so used to Swenglish ways of writing, that you no longer recognize the fact that it is Swenglish!' He also added that one of the chapters was 'extremely badly written' and would have to be rewritten.[24] Such comments were probably a reminder to Husén of his non-English origins, and also adds to our understanding of scientific reports not just as representation of objects, but also of the author as subject.

An Atlantic Crossing: Bringing the Typewriter to the US

The twentieth century has been described as the century of the typewriter. Using a specific machine to write was a means of accelerating writing.[25] For Husén, it was a tool that would accompany him for much of his life. In fact, he learned to type on his father's old Remington before he learned

---

[23] 'Thank you also for reading my paper. I am quite aware of the fact that its present style is not adequate for a publication. I was in a hurry to prepare it before I left Sweden, and perhaps it must be thoroughly revised before being sent to the printer. If you think that I had better wait to publish it I shall do so. On the other hand, if there is anybody at your institute who can spend time to give it a better style I should be very grateful. There is a possibility of sending a certain fee to the person who is willing to do this job.[…] Anyhow, I think it should be up to you to decide whether it is worthwhile to 'wash' the English of my paper or if you think it better to publish it in a more comprehensive monograph.' Torsten Husén to Philip E. Vernon, September 20, 1955 (The Husén archive, 1.1).

[24] Neville Postlethwaite to Torsten Husén, January 20, 1969 (IEA projektet, Institutionen för internationell pedagogik, Stockholms universitet, F2A), 14.

[25] Martyn Lyons, *The Typewriter Century: A Cultural History of Writing Practices* (Toronto: University of Toronto Press, 2021).

7 WORDS FOR THE WORLD: WRITING AND PUBLISHING STRATEGIES... 145

Fig. 7.2 Husén's portable typewriter Erika. (Photo: Mats Husén. According to his children, he typed all his work using only two fingers)

to write by hand. When he started school, he told his teacher that he had no need for handwriting as he was already good at typing (Fig. 7.2).[26]

He bought his own personal typewriter in the 1930s, shortly after graduating from Lund University. The machine—an Erika portable typewriter—accompanied him through the decades and across continents. The fact that it was portable meant that he could take it with him on his travels. His host at the University of Chicago, C. Arnold Anderson, may not have been aware of this. When Husén was about to become a visiting professor in Chicago in 1959, Anderson wrote a letter where he promised to rent a Swedish typewriter for Husén in Chicago:

---

[26] Arild Tjeldvoll and Hans G. Lingens, eds., *Torsten Husén: Conversations in Comparative Education* (Bloomington, Indiana: Phi Delta Kappa, 2000), 4.

146 S. GREK ET AL.

We will rent a typewriter for your use. Please send me a copy of the keyboard of a Swedish typewriter (I assume you prefer that keyboard) and we can get a machine so equipped. There are many Swedes in the city and the typewriter people will have had previous requests. However, you may prefer an English keyboard.[27]

Anderson's offer indicates a willingness to remove some of the obstacles that can arise when a scholar moves from one country to another. Husén, however, replied that it was not necessary as he would bring his own typewriter. He added that he couldn't take it on the plane, so he arranged to have it sent by ship instead.

Since I am allowed to bring with me only 20 kilos in the plane, I have sent most of the stuff ahead. Mr. Norman, who is superintendent of the public schools in Stockholm, is leaving Gothenburg by boat on Monday the 21 and is expected to arrive on October the 5. He is bringing my typewriter and a lot of books.[28]

In his autobiography Husén commented on his writing habits and his relationship with his typewriter. The one he bought in the 1930s had proved to be very durable. When the autobiography was published, in the early 1980s, he was still writing on the same typewriter he had bought in his twenties and he had developed a strong emotional attachment to it. It was a machine that he had used for most of his publications, as well as for all of his letters, which were numerous. 'It has been an extraordinarily durable machine, and my emotional ties to it has in some ways taken on a symbolic significance. As long as it carries on, so will its owner.'[29] Such affective engagements are not uncommon among writers. As Lyons notes in his history of the typewriter, writers have expressed a wide range of emotions, from the positive to the extremely negative—Hunter S. Thompson, for example, first shot his typewriter and later himself.[30] For Husén the feelings seem mainly to have been positive. Initially, Husén used to start his writing directly by writing on his typewriter. Later, as he

[27] C. Arnold Anderson to Torsten Husén, July 27, 1959 (The Husén archive, 1.14).
[28] Torsten Husén to C. Arnold Anderson, September 19, 1959 (The Husén archive, 1.14).
[29] Torsten Husén, *An Incurable Academic: Memoirs of a Professor* (Oxford: Pergamon Press, 1981), 179.
[30] Lyons, *Typewriter Century*, 3.

7 WORDS FOR THE WORLD: WRITING AND PUBLISHING STRATEGIES... 147

started to publish in English, he found it more convenient to first make an outline by hand. His shift of language involved a shift in writing practices.[31]

Time and Space for Writing

One of the reasons why travel and productivity were compatible was that Husén made a number of journeys that were essentially about reading and writing. Visiting professorships in Chicago (1959), Hawaii (1968), Stanford (1965/66; 1973/74) and Ontario (1973) gave him the opportunity to focus his energies on writing new monographs and rewriting older ones.

Getting away from home for an extended period of time allowed him to delve deeper into a subject and get away from distractions. While there were some responsibilities at home that he still had to attend to, others could be neglected. For example, in a letter to one of his doctoral students, Husén admitted that supervising doctoral students had been a low priority during his time in the US. Husén explained that this was due to his urgent need to finish a book that he would never be able to complete in Sweden.[32]

So, writing books abroad had the advantage of allowing time off to concentrate. In the case of Stanford and the Center for Advanced Study in the Behavioral Sciences, they provided various kinds of support for its visiting scholars: secretaries, research assistants, a library, and various kinds of office equipment, including typewriters, dictaphones, and tape recorders. One potential drawback was that certain library resources could be limited. The Stanford Centre, therefore, informed its visiting scholars that they should bring books that they intended to use on a more or less regular basis.[33] While a visiting professor in Ontario, Husén wrote the book *Social Background and Educational Career*, published by the OECD in 1972. Two years later, as a visiting scholar at Stanford University, he was busy revising the book, which by then was practically out of print. One reason for the revision was that during his time in Ontario he had had very little access to relevant literature on countries such as Germany and the Netherlands.[34] The book was heavily revised and, therefore, published

---

[31] Husén, *Incurable Academic*, 180.
[32] Torsten Husén to Ian Dunlop, April 17, 1974 (The Husén archive, 1.56).
[33] 'Financial information form' (The Husén archive, 1.48).
[34] Torsten Husén to Denis Kallen, February 15, 1974 (The Husén archive, 1.140).

148 S. GREK ET AL.

under a new title: *Social Dimensions of Scholastic Attainment*. He also completed a book as part of the Europe 2000 project entitled *Talent, Equality and Meritocracy*. After his stay, he remarked: 'The year at the Center made it possible for me to write up, in its entirety, my report.'[35]

As mentioned above, Husén managed to visit the Stanford centre twice. This was unusual because the centre gave priority to admitting new people every year. When Husén approached the Stanford Centre for a second time in 1972 with a request for a research fellowship, he was first told that it would be difficult to justify the return of a former fellow.[36] Husén did not conceal his deep disappointment, and stressed his need for a place and time to focus on his writing, in this case an IEA report. 'I am sorry to insist but a stay at the Center would in so many respects be ideal for me. It would enable me to write up a monograph for which I have tried to gain momentum during ten years of research in evaluation.'[37]

DISSEMINATION

Being a prolific writer is not in itself a sufficient condition for gaining a position on a global arena of scholarship. To understand how a scholar such as Husén could reach a global audience, we also need to look at patterns of dissemination. Making translations, finding publishers, and circulating published texts to a network of interested scholars were important aspects of dissemination.

Finding Publishers and Making Translations

Several of Husén's books were translated. While the majority of his works were in Swedish, his works also appear in several languages, including English, German, Spanish, Italian, Hungarian, Polish, Norwegian, Hindi, and Russian. In the beginning of his career, he mainly wrote in Swedish, but subsequently he shifted to English as his default language. This shift occurred during a year in the middle of the 1960s when he was a visiting professor at Stanford.[38] Among the books that he wrote in English was

---

[35] Torsten Husén to Preston S. Cutler, August 9, 1974 (The Husén archive, 1.56).
[36] Preston S. Cutler to Torsten Husén, March 20, 1972 (The Husén archive, 1.48).
[37] Torsten Husén to Preston S. Cutler, March 29, 1972 (The Husén archive, 1.48).
[38] Husén, *Incurable Academic*, 199.

The School in Question, which was translated into six languages.[39] His first English book, entitled *Psychological Twin Research*, was published in 1959 and was based on a study of 500 twins with the primary aim of discussing the relation between heredity and environment. The book had originally been published in Swedish in 1953 but sold only about a dozen copies.[40] In order to reach a broader audience, Husén decided to translate the book himself. The English translation is said to have sold 2000 copies.[41]

One of the books that was translated was *Skolans sociologi* [The sociology of the school], coauthored with the Swedish sociologist Gunnar Boalt in 1964, and translated into at least four languages.[42] When the book was translated, the title was changed in all cases but one (Norwegian). In English, the book was given the title *Educational Research and Educational Change: The Case of Sweden*, which was similar to the Italian title *Ricerca educativa e riforme scolastiche: L'esempio svedese*, while the German title was somewhat simpler: *Bildungsforschung und Schulreform in Schweden*. Thus, these three translated versions did not stress the role of sociology, but instead highlighted the relation between educational research and educational reforms. This shift in meaning is consistent with Husén's emerging role as an expert on Sweden and its comprehensive school reforms.

The international launch of this book was facilitated by international networks. In the USA, Torsten Husén's Chicago-based friend and colleague C. Arnold Anderson supported a translation, and in Germany the close colleague Hellmut Becker was involved in the issue of translation, among others.[43] Still, the publishers had to be persuaded. In the US, it was first envisaged that Chicago University Press would publish *Skolans sociologi*. However, the publisher's assessment was that the work had little relevance in an American context because the education system was so different. 'We do not, as do Boalt and Husén, need to prove the merits of comprehensive schooling.' The publisher's reviewer felt that the book aimed to convince teachers, especially at the higher age levels, of the value of comprehensive schooling reform, which in an American context was

---

[39] Husén, *Incurable Academic*, 178.

[40] Husén, *Incurable Academic*, 92.

[41] Torsten Husén, *Möten med psykologer, pedagoger och andra: anteckningar* (Lund: Wiken, 1992), 190.

[42] Gunnar Boalt and Torsten Husén, *Skolans sociologi* (Stockholm: Almqvist & Wiksell, 1964).

[43] Rolf Neuhaus to Torsten Husén, November 3, 1967 (The Husén archive, 1.33).

150 S. GREK ET AL.

superfluous.[44] However, the book was translated into English anyway, via the Swedish publisher, and was later published by both a Swedish publisher, Almqvist & Wiksell, and an American publisher, John Wiley.[45]

Reprints and Other Ways of Spreading Publications

The existence of international scientific journals was an important means of communicating research. Some of the journals in which Husén published himself in were new, other had longer historical roots. One of the reasons that journals was an effective means of disseminating research was the fact that journals made reprints of articles. A common figure seems to have been about 50 reprints per article. However, it was also possible to order an extra number of reprints, and correspondence reveals that Husén frequently used this opportunity. Sometimes he paid extra to get more reprints than what was given for free from the journal. For example, when he wrote an article for *Phi Delta Kappan* in 1961, he wanted to have 150–200 reprints. In his letter to the journal, he explained that this number of reprints had to do with international dissemination: 'They will be valuable when we have visitors from abroad.'[46] He could also send reprints to colleagues by mail. For instance, he sent a reprint of his 1951 article 'The Influence of Schooling upon IQ' to Lewis Terman at Stanford University. Terman replied that he had read the piece carefully and congratulated Husén for having done 'such an objective and careful piece of work,' and returned the favour by sending a couple of reprints of his own recent articles.[47]

Sometimes Husén also distributed books in his international network. In the 1970s, he wrote a book for OECD. A letter to James Ronald Gass, the director of CERI at the OECD, shows that Husén was somewhat frustrated over OECD's inability to send him copies of the book that Husén could distribute when he participated in international events. In

---

[44] Anders Richter to Karl-Åke Kärnell, February 12, 1965 (The Husén archive, 1.28).

[45] For a fuller discussion on the Swedish and international launch of *Skolans sociologi*, see Joakim Landahl and Anna Larsson, 'Discipliner, politik och vetenskap i tidig svensk utbildningssociologi,' in *Pedagogikens politik: Historiska perspektiv på relationen mellan utbildningsforskning och utbildningspolitik*, eds. Anders Burman, Joakim Landahl and Anna Larsson (Huddinge: Södertörns högskola, 2024).

[46] Torsten Husén to Gerald H. Read. December 5, 1961 (The Husén archive, 1.2).

[47] Lewis Terman to Torsten Husén, September 19, 1951. The letter is saved in Husén's personal copy of Terman's book *The Intelligence of School Children*, and is available at the Husén library at Växjö University, Sweden.

7 WORDS FOR THE WORLD: WRITING AND PUBLISHING STRATEGIES... 151

the letter to Gass, he claimed that their publications department 'seems to have run mad.' He referred to international meetings with key people in the field of education in the United States where he had brought some 15 books with him. After those meetings he had tried to get some more copies from the OECD without success. 'I have repeatedly tried to get at least 40 copies, which I want to send to colleagues around the world who might want to use it as a textbook.'[48]

A final way in which Husén's publications became known across the world was through his printed bibliography. In 1966, when he turned 50, his graduate students congratulated him by compiling his publications in a bibliography. That bibliography was subsequently updated, with new, expanded editions and supplements, printed in 1972, 1976, 1981, 1986, and 1996. For Husén the bibliography became a tool for dissemination of research; he used to send it to people he knew or had met. For example, when he came home from a round-the-world trip in 1967, he thanked his host in Japan, Michi Kagawa at the National Institute for Educational Research, with the following words:

> Thanks to your and your colleagues' kindness our stay in Japan was no doubt the high light of our round-the-world-trip. As a small token of our deep appreciation I am sending a bibliography which my coworkers and former graduate students prepared as a surprice (*sic*) birthday present.[49]

The bibliography, meant as a gift to Husén from his students, was thus passed forward as a gift to people Husén encountered. His vast network, ever expanding as he travelled across the world, became useful in spreading knowledge about his writings (Fig. 7.3).

Another example of international dissemination, one that might have been proved important in the long run, is when Husén in 1972 noticed that a seminar at the International Council for Educational Development (ICED) was set to deal with futurological issues, namely the prospects for education by the year 2000. At the time Husén was just about to finish a report on education in the year 2000 for the Swedish Board of Education, and he sent over three copies of the report to the organisers.[50] The ICED was chaired by Jim Perkins, who also chaired yearly seminars on

---

[48] Torsten Husén to James Ronald Gass, December 8, 1975 (The Husén archive, 1.57).
[49] Torsten Husén to Michi Kagawa, July 18, 1967 (The Husén archive, 1.32).
[50] Torsten Husén to Ebba K. Concoran, March 10, 1972 (The Husén archive, 1.48).

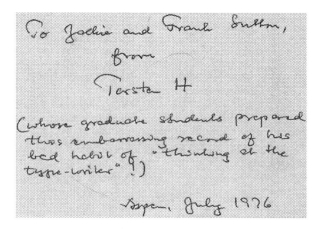

Fig. 7.3 Dedication to Jackie and Frank Sutton in Husén's bibliography *Tryckta skrifter: 1940–1975*, in which he refers to his 'bad habit of thinking at the typewriter.' Frank Sutton was deputy vice president of the Ford Foundation, a major funder of the IEA (private photo)

education at the Aspen Institute for Humanistic Studies. Some years later, as Chap. 5 details, Husén would be responsible for discussing futurological issues of education at a series of Aspen seminars, leading up to the publication of *The School in Question* in 1979.

Knowledge Strategies and Publications in Times of Change

Torsten Husén has been described as a 'knowledge strategist,' someone who was skilled at using his knowledge and networks to further his career.[51] Academic publishing was one way in which Husén managed to do this. He was not the kind of scholar who suffered from writer's block or who dedicated his time to administrative issues: he was a prolific writer. He was also a person with an extensive network, an avid traveller, and with major engagements in international organisations. In order to understand how Husén managed to 'make it' in the international arena, it is obvious that his publishing patterns were related to the way in which he established social connections with other scholars in the field. These connections were

[51] Cronqvist and Bennesved, 'En humanistiskt skolad kunskapsstrateg,' 255–256.

facilitated by the fact that a key phase of his career coincided with the institutionalisation of comparative education in universities in different countries, as well as the rise of the Swedish educational system as an international model. These conditions, however, were not a permanent feature of his career, which spanned several decades, beginning in the 1930s and continuing well beyond his formal retirement in 1982. Spanning the period from the inter-war years through the Second World War, the Cold War and beyond, his professional life coincided with dramatic changes in society and in academic life. Because of these changes, the role and importance of international experience changed for every scholar, and in order to maintain his role in the academic field, Husén had to adapt. Reinventing himself as society renewed itself, whether it was for strategic reasons or not, was a way of constantly recreating scientific relevance.

Seen from a wider perspective, the case of Husén's publications is an illustration of how the role of printed materials in the forms of books, articles, and reports grew increasingly important as a means of transnational exchange and collaboration during the twentieth century. The circulation of ideas in the field of education had the circulation of academic texts as a prerequisite. As books, articles, and reports were written, disseminated, read, and reviewed, networks across borders were strengthened.

Correction to: The Rise of a Global Expert Network: The International Institute for Educational Planning, 1963–1973

Correction to:

Chapter 4 in: S. Grek et al., *The World as a Laboratory*,
Global Histories of Education,
https://doi.org/10.1007/978-3-031-68090-8_4

The year [1963] was misspelled in the initially published version of this chapter and has been corrected.

The corrections have been carried out in the chapter and the updated chapter has been approved by the author.

The updated version of this chapter can be found at
https://doi.org/10.1007/978-3-031-68090-8_4

© The Author(s), under exclusive license to Springer Nature
Switzerland AG 2024
S. Grek et al., *The World as a Laboratory*, Global Histories of
Education, https://doi.org/10.1007/978-3-031-68090-8_8

C1

EPILOGUE: THE DISEMBEDDED LABORATORY

This book has focused on the production, circulation, and use of comparative educational research for policy, using Torsten Husén's archive as a lens. The metaphor of a 'disembedded laboratory' is employed to describe archive studies as a textual ethnography of a social science laboratory, providing insight into the working life of scientists and the culture of research. The Husén archive texts are not only considered as filtered representations of a practice but also as the practice itself.[1] The vast amount of correspondence in the archive between Husén and his peers is a testimony to how ideas are exchanged and circulated in an ever-growing network. Letterheads from hotels all over the world bear witness to travels and visits. Letterheads from various universities, national agencies, international organisations, and research institutes indicate the development of a global network, not only on an individual level but also on an organisational level. Conference proceedings, meeting protocols, manuals, and guidelines provide insight into the daily work of scholarly life. There are also notes on technical, financial, and material needs and challenges. Plentiful examples of social relationships are provided on a friendly and personal level, including spouses and family. Even if we have centred our chapters around the work of Torsten Husén, we don't see comparative education as a field of

---

[1] See also Richie Nimmo, 'Actor-Network Theory and Methodology: Social Research in a More-Than-Human World,' *Methodological Innovations Online* 6, no. 3 (2011).

© The Author(s), under exclusive license to Springer Nature   155
Switzerland AG 2024
S. Grek et al., *The World as a Laboratory*, Global Histories of
Education, https://doi.org/10.1007/978-3-031-68090-8

156   EPILOGUE: THE DISEMBEDDED LABORATORY

distinguished individuals, but rather as a shared scientific endeavour entangled in cross-border networks and materiality.

We have argued that the growth of international and comparative education during the post–Second World War period and throughout the twentieth century can be understood as a disembedded laboratory. Traditional laboratory studies of science view the laboratory as a place where statements and ideas are stabilised through various material actions, as described by Latour and Woolgar.[2] The researcher becomes a tool for 'bringing home' objects in nature and manipulating them in the laboratory, and for producing inscriptions of the results, as described by Knorr Cetina.[3] The concept of a disembedded laboratory allows for scientific constructions to be temporarily and spatially detached from a single physical location. These constructions can take place in both disembedded and embedded locales.[4] See further Appendix A.

The disembedded laboratory here is presented as a multilayered network with a structural level network of ideas about educational opportunities, goals, evaluations, etc. On another level, there is a network of nations, states, and international organisations. In relation to this network, there are individual actors who have their own network and are also part of others. These individuals are often part of a network of national institutions, universities, agencies, research centres, and similar organisations. Flows in this multilevel network are created by actions, funds, technologies, and other non-human actors, as well as by places, travel, communication, and translations. In this case, the multilevel network functions as a laboratory for the production and circulation of knowledge to be used in educational policy.

As we move through the chapters in this book we show how a comparative movement, and network, develops. New journals and societies of comparative education were formed, and a new generation of scholars like Husén entered the field. As demonstrated in Chaps. 2 and 3, the

---

[2] Bruno Latour and Steve Woolgar, *Laboratory Life: The Construction of Scientific Facts* (Princeton: Princeton University Press, 1979/1986).

[3] Karin Knorr-Cetina, 'Laboratory Studies: The Cultural Approach to the Study of Science,' in *Handbook of Science and Technology Studies*, ed. Sheila Jasanoff (Los Angeles: Sage, 1995).

[4] Martina Merz, "Nobody Can Force You When You Are across the Ocean': Face to Face and E-mail Exchanges between Theoretical Physicists,' in *Making Space for Science: Territorial Themes in the Shaping of Knowledge*, eds. Crosbie Smith and Jon Agar (London: Palgrave Macmillan, 1998).

opportunity to travel abroad, attend international conferences, and establish relationships with peers from around the world provides valuable perspectives on education. During their meetings, scholars with diverse educational backgrounds were able to share their expertise and gain new insights into education. This exchange of knowledge allowed them to enhance their own learning and thinking. It is important to note that personal experiences as both students and teachers played a role in shaping their perspectives. As shown, English (and American) concepts and statistical methods were used to translate and exchange ideas and develop new insights. These methods included probability, reliability, diagnostic tests, standardisation, sampling, test construction, and questionnaire items. The researchers could then apply these insights to their own work. During the expansion of secondary education and the rise of comprehensive schooling, international expertise proved valuable for national educational policy and international policy recommendations. This was recognised by organisations such as UNESCO, the World Bank, IIEP, IEA, and later the OECD.

The comparative network of education was influenced by several factors, including the growing interconnectedness of the world due to air travel and decolonisation, as well as the increasing competition resulting from the tensions of the Cold War. In the 1960s, educational research underwent a significant increase, leading to the establishment of national research institutes and international networks such as IEA and later IIEP. There was a notable rise in secondary schooling, which sparked an interest in exploring various methods of organisation. The Swedish model of comprehensive schooling here become very influential. Additionally, technological advancements, such as the creation of more powerful computers, have made it easier to conduct large-scale surveys, as outlined in Chap. 3. They have also allowed for the organisation of knowledge, such as in the International Encyclopaedia of Education (Chap. 6). Comparative education has become relevant not only for researchers but also for policymakers due to various factors. It provides answers to present policy-relevant questions and is believed to be helpful in anticipating the future. Chapter 5 demonstrates that the early organisation of education and number-making became a way of imagining a political future, not only the probable but also the desired one. The use of data to create a utopian society has become a popular political concept, often linked to economic growth and success. The IIEP is an early example of this idea, which has since become a common theme in the work of many international

158 EPILOGUE: THE DISEMBEDDED LABORATORY

education organisations. It translates education research into specific policy recommendations and uses teaching courses, internships, and other processes of socialisation to promote particular ways of thinking about education (Chap. 4).

Husén entered a strand of comparative education that emphasised collaboration among a large number of scholars. His work on the IEA, IIEP, and the IEE shared this feature, as they were all large-scale projects that involved numerous individuals. As a result, there was a significant amount of communication through meetings, correspondence, and other means. The collaborative nature of these projects tended to attract scholars who appreciated the demands of working with others. Husén's contributions as a research leader are more noteworthy than his individual written works in education (see Chap. 7, Appendix A).

The knowledge produced in the comparative network utilised the comparative perspective as leverage. Comparison is a crucial tool in isolating variables and factors that make a difference in all data production. Given that the 1950s–1960s was a period of Western reconstruction, where material resources and finance were scarce, academics could offer a fair and equitable way of distributing facts and knowledge about the state of affairs. Education could provide the necessary means to build both economic and social capital. Furthermore, there was an increasing demand to comprehend the interconnected world and its potential.

The building of research networks like those described in this book seems to rest on circumstances not commonly considered as scientific routines. An encyclopaedia, for example, helps to bring structure to a discipline—illustrating that different paradigms in educational thinking coexist—but without talking much about the processes of constructing its structure and categories, how the relation between societal internationalisation and the internationalisation of social sciences is developed, and finally how educational research functioned as an engine in the modernisation of education systems. A high-level seminar like the ones held in Aspen helps to draw together knowledge and produce a forward-looking report. The more international in its data work and networking, the more likely it will change disciplinary practices. However, although Husén and his colleagues in the IEA thought they had created the first steps in a new science-based comparative education, they did this in a period when the comparison of single country case studies was the dominant methodology in that discipline. The nation-state had been the dominant unit of analysis since the emergence of the field as a distinct domain of inquiry. Husén claimed for

EPILOGUE: THE DISEMBEDDED LABORATORY   159

the IEA a major leap forward in comparative education, as did others, for example, Edmund King:

> the chief value of the I.E.A. survey for a specialist in comparative education is that it produces more (and more reliable) evidence than had previously been possessed, evidence of newer and sharper kinds; that it demands a better contextual explanation than had previously been provided by comparative education specialists; that it invites them too to participate—first in suggesting hypotheses for further empirical enquiry, and secondly in continuous evaluation whatever these admirable empirical methods can offer to serious researchers.[5]

But if there is one interesting omission here it is that there is a contradiction between comparativists welcoming the fine data of the IEA studies and admiring the analysis, and the inability to affect that discipline, instead becoming an ever more technical and specialised list of required actions.

Torsten Husén has been described as a 'state intellectual.'[6] From a current perspective, Pettersson and Popkewitz compare Husén's expertise with that of Andreas Schleicher, the head of OECD's PISA studies (the Programme for International Student Assessment). Husén, and his peers, got their position as 'state intellectuals,' based on a strong position as scholars. This changes when looking at Schleicher as an 'expert' on education. Rather than deriving legitimacy from scholarly achievements, Pettersson and Popkewitz argue that the individual's authority stems from affiliation with a well-established organisation equipped with ample resources for disseminating findings and exerting influence over national educational frameworks through indirect means.[7] In this context, the traditional notion of an 'expert' engaged in academic research gives way to a model characterised by large-scale research conglomerates. Within these conglomerates, expertise in education no longer hinges on scholarly pursuits but rather on the capacity to effectively communicate educational insights. Consequently, the validation of one's expertise no longer relies

---

[5] Edmund King, 'International Study of Achievement in Mathematics. Phase I. A Comparison of Twelve Countries by Torsten Husén,' *International Review of Education* 13, no. 3 (1967): 361.

[6] Daniel Pettersson and Thomas S. Popkewitz, 'A Chimera of Quantifications and Comparisons: The Changing of Educational 'Expertise',' in *New Practices of Comparison, Quantification and Expertise in Education: Conducting Empirically Based Research*, eds. Christina Elde Mølstad and Daniel Pettersson (London: Routledge, 2019).

[7] Pettersson and Popkewitz, 'Chimera.'

160   EPILOGUE: THE DISEMBEDDED LABORATORY

on academic credentials but rather on the adoption of methodologies aligned with information and communication technologies (ICT) and the dynamics of a media-driven landscape.

Another difference would be to focus on their role as knowledge producers and knowledge brokers, where Husén and his peers may be seen as 'issue advocates,' trying to *reduce* the scope of choices in policy,[8] while today's educational knowledge in policy tends to be less fixed. It is, as Pettersson and Popkewitz argue, medialised and visualised in a scope and pace we have not seen before and more open for interpretations and policy choices.[9]

In contemporary knowledge production and circulation, traditional institutions and authorities are being challenged or complemented by what we might call a 'disembodied knowledge.' This refers to a more free-floating knowledge production process where educational scholars based on their personal knowledge, established reputations and peer opinion are less involved in the construction, dissemination, or interpretation phases. The relationship between traditional educational research and educational policy has been decoupled.

Afterword

During our research in the Husén archive, we were contacted by Husén's daughter, a retired scholar of education whom we had informed about our project. She told us that she possessed some of Husén's tapes from a micro-recorder and offered them to us. We obtained an old micro-recorder from eBay and began listening to the tapes, which only had some names and dates on the cover. Most of the content on the tapes were related to a project Husén began working on during his 'retirement' in the 1980s (he retired formally in January 1982 at the age of 65 and 10 months). The project aimed to provide a comparative perspective on the relationship between educational researchers and policymakers in Sweden, the UK, Germany, France, and the US. There is no evidence that he ever wrote about this project, and the collection only contains a few tapes of interviews on the topic.

---

[8] Rodger A. Pielke junior, *The Honest Broker: Making Sense of Science in Policy and Politics* (Cambridge: Cambridge University Press, 2007).

[9] Pettersson and Popkewitz, 'Chimera.'; Christian Lundahl & Margareta Serder, "Is PISA more important to school reforms than educational research? The selective use of authoritative references in media and in parliamentary debates,' *Nordic Journal of Studies in Educational Policy*, 6:3, 193-206 (2020).

EPILOGUE: THE DISEMBEDDED LABORATORY   161

The relationship between research and policy is a recurring theme in Husén's work, as described in previous chapters. He spent most of his career informing policy with educational research knowledge and information. However, this position is not universally accepted in the social sciences. Additionally, Husén faced criticism for his perceived alignment with the Swedish social democrat party.[10] It is unclear whether Husén intended to justify the work as a 'state intellectual' with this final project. Regardless, it is interesting in several ways that Husén at this age decided to conduct an interview study with his old friends and colleagues. Not least does it illustrate that he could not stop working.

One of the interviews conducted was with Ralph W. Tyler (1902–1994), a renowned educational scholar, who was 87 years old at the time of the interview. Tyler is famous for his work on curriculum and evaluation, and is credited with developing Tyler's rationale, which outlines four basic principles of curriculum and instruction that can be used to organise a curriculum.[11]

The conversation with Tyler covers Tyler's experience working in Lyndon B. Johnson's so-called task force on education,[12] as well as his work on national assessments during the 1960s. The interview concludes after just over 25 minutes, and Husén regrets that his wife, Ingrid, could not have joined them and that she had asked him to document the

---

[10] In a review of a textbook Husén published on educational sociology, Wilhelm Sjöstrand wrote: 'To the extent that they aimed for a textbook, which should be useful for people other than students, who under their auspices should acquire what they consider to be 'the right view', their book must therefore be regarded as worthless. It will then no longer be an account of research results of a certain type—one that everyone is free to present, but rather a propaganda account of the kind that one would not expect to find in a Western democracy. Possibly can the petition be a kind of incense and myrrh for the so-called state-bearing party. But even in this direction, one would not yet dare to defend, for example, a textbook in social studies, especially the development and position of the political parties, where it was based exclusively on scientific literature about the socialist ideology but neglected the research concerning the meaning and argumentation of liberal and conservative views, etc.' Wilhelm Sjöstrand, 'Från den pedagogisk-sociologiska författarfabriken,' *Svenska Dagbladet*, June 14, 1964 (transl. here); see also Joakim Landahl, 'Polemik och pedagogik under strecket: Wilhelm Sjöstrand som skoldebattör och vetenskapskritiker,' in *Humaniora i välfärdssamhället. Kunskapshistorier om efterkrigstiden*, ed. Johan Östling, Anton Jansson and Ragni Svensson Stringberg (Göteborg: Makadam, 2023).

[11] Ralph W. Tyler, *Basic Principles of Curriculum and Instruction* (Chicago: University of Chicago Press, 1949).

[12] See also William D. Leuchtenburg, ed., *Task Force Reports of the Johnson White House, 1963–1969: Research Collections in American Politics* (New York: LexisNexis, 2004).

162 EPILOGUE: THE DISEMBEDDED LABORATORY

meeting with a photograph. Husén takes out his camera and shoot two pictures and says, 'This is typical of the Japanese. They're always taking pictures!'[13]

The interview with Tyler represents in brief a history where some few mainly male scholars had great influence on educational policy nationally and internationally. The network they developed over many years of collaboration was their immediate strength when learning from each other and bringing international perspectives back home. This network also grew in strength due to the fact of friendship evolving on personal levels, often also involving the wives.

While there are limitations to a history that relies mainly on one archive, we have attempted to overcome this by connecting our work to other scholarly research on the development of comparative education. Husén has been our lens by purpose giving this history of clear focus. No doubt Torsten Husén made a significant impact on the field of comparative education and educational reforms both in Sweden and internationally. This achievement was made possible by his collaboration with a team of competent individuals who helped to ease his workload. One such individual is Neville Postlethwaite, who worked with Husén at IEA, IIEP, IIE in Stockholm, and with IEE. Regarding IEE, it appears that the technical manager Barbara Barret played a significant role.[14] Additionally, Husén received significant support from his wife Ingrid. In his memoir *An Incurable Academic*, Husén describes how she not only took care of the children but also helped him with intellectual work such as translations to and from English.[15] This also becomes evident by a book he wrote to her memory two years after her passing.

> Another question I often asked myself is: How could I be so intensely absorbed by my own actions that the family was so horribly neglected? The neglect may not have been total, as evidenced by the letters from me to Ingrid in the fall of 1959 [when Husén was in Chicago], but the career was a high priority. A little forgiving compensation was that I always found it important that we both could be together during the more lavish journeys.

[13] Recorded conversation between Torsten Husén and Ralph Tyler, 1989.

[14] See Franziska Primus and Christian Lundahl, 'The Peripherals at the Core of Androcentric Knowledge Production: An Analysis of the Managing Editor's Knowledge Work in The International Encyclopedia of Education (1985),' *Paedagogica Historica* 57, no 6 (2021).

[15] Torsten Husén, *An Incurable Academic: Memoirs of a Professor* (Oxford: Pergamon Press, 1983).

EPILOGUE: THE DISEMBEDDED LABORATORY   163

But even during these, she was responsible for the ground service. This said as a 'foreword' to what should, and probably also partly is, an attempt at confession of sins.[16]

Husén was not just married to Ingrid. He was also, as he confessed in an article, 'married to higher education'[17]—as it was proven, this was a very productive arrangement for him and for the internationalisation of education research.

[16] Torsten Husén, *Av och om Ingrid: En Kvinna: Stycken för en trängre krets* (Stockholm: Lindströms tryckeri, 1993), 3–4. (transl. here)

[17] Torsten Husén, 'A Marriage to Higher Education,' *The Journal of Higher Education* 51, no. 5 (1980).

Appendix A: Torsten Husén and His Archive as a Disembedded Laboratory

A Brief Biography

Torsten Husén (1916–2009) was prominent in Swedish educational research, as well as an internationally acknowledged researcher and a key figure in international and comparative educational research. While this book mainly highlights Husén's standing in comparative and international education, it is important to remember that the position he got on an international scene also evolved in relation to his work on a national level. He has, with certain righteousness, been called a 'state intellectual,' that is, a by governments often 'appointed' expert.[1] He was much involved in the Swedish comprehensive school reform during the 1950s and onwards, he was engaged in *Folkuniversitet* ('The people's university') and lifelong learning, he worked on improving conditions for higher education in Sweden and so forth. He had more than 40 PhD candidates over the years and equally many licentiate candidates (Fig. A.1).[2]

---

[1] Daniel Pettersson and Thomas S. Popkewitz, 'A Chimera of Quantifications and Comparisons: The Changing of Educational 'Expertise',' in *New Practices of Comparison, Quantification and Expertise in Education: Conducting Empirically Based Research*, ed. Christina Elde Mølstad and Daniel Pettersson (London: Routledge, 2019).

[2] Torsten Husén, *An Incurable Academic: Memoirs of a Professor* (Oxford: Pergamon Press, 1983).

© The Author(s), under exclusive license to Springer Nature Switzerland AG 2024
S. Grek et al., *The World as a Laboratory*, Global Histories of Education, https://doi.org/10.1007/978-3-031-68090-8

165

Fig. A.1 Torsten Husén in his office. (Photo Yukiko Sawano 2001. With courtesy of the Husén family)

In brief, Husén became a master of arts in 1938, was an assistant at the Department of Psychology at Lund University from 1938 to 1943, received his PhD at Lund in 1944, and was appointed associate professor of education at Stockholm University in 1947. He was professor of education and educational psychology at Stockholm University from 1953 to 1956, professor of practical education at Stockholm Institute of Education from 1956 to 1971, and professor of international education at Stockholm University from 1971 to 1981. The Institute of International Education (IIE) at Stockholm University was founded by a government decision in 1971 with Torsten Husén as the first chair holder. Husén was also a visiting professor at the Universities of Chicago (1959), Hawaii (1968), Ontario (1971), Stanford University (1981), and California (1984). He worked as a consultant to the OECD and the World Bank (1968–1985), and was a member of the Governing Board at the Max Planck Institute in Berlin, 1964–1982. Torsten Husén was elected as a member of the Royal Swedish Academy of War Sciences in 1956, of the Royal Swedish Academy of Sciences in 1972, of the Finnish Academy of Sciences in 1973, of the

Polish Academy of Sciences in 1977, and of the Russian Academy of Educational Sciences in 1991. He also received several honours, medals, and awards.[3]

Husén got involved with comparative education in the late 1950s, when he became one of the key people in the International Association for the Evaluation and Educational Achievement (IEA), where he served as its second chairman from 1962 to 1978. Between 1970 and 1980, he was also the chairman of the governing board for International Institute for Educational Planning (IIEP). His work in IEA and IIEP is thoroughly described in Chaps. 3 and 4.

He has authored more than 1200 publications between 1940 and 2008 in various genres, for example, 148 books, 160 newspaper articles, 200 scientific articles, and a several encyclopaedia articles (Fig. A.2). His texts were also stretching over many different themes. During his most productive years he covered over 50 various topics related to education and psychology (Fig. A.3), and was written in/translated to more than 20

Fig. A.2 Number of publications by Husén 1940–2008, based on Husén 1981, 1996, and a library search (Torsten Husén, ed., *Torsten Husén: Tryckta skrifter 1940–1980* (Uppsala: Almqvist & Wiksell, 1981); Torsten Husén, ed., *Torsten Husén: Printed Publications 1981–1995* (Stockholm: Institute of International Education, 1996))

---

[3] For a full list of his credentials, see Europa Publications, ed., *The International Who's Who 2001*, 64th ed. (London: Europa Publications, 2000), 724.

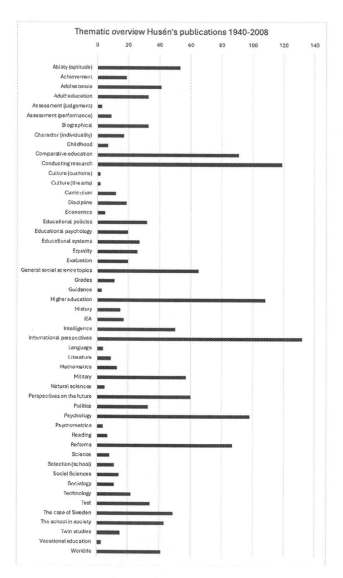

Fig. A.3 This thematic overview of Husén's writings between 1940 and 2008 is based on Husén 1981, 1996, and a library search. (Husén, *Tryckta skrifter*; Husén, *Printed Publications*.) Some publications are classified under more than one theme. The total number of classifications are 1619

APPENDIX A: TORSTEN HUSÉN AND HIS ARCHIVE AS A DISEMBEDDED... **169**

Table A.1 Husén's publications between 1940 and 2008 in different languages, based on Husén 1981, 1996, and a library search

Language	Number of publications
Arabic	1
Bosnian	1
Chinese	3
Croatian	1
Czech	2
Danish	23
Dutch	3
English	336
Finnish	5
French	24
German	49
Hindi	1
Hungarian	6
Italian	38
Japanese	8
Korean	1
Norwegian	12
Polish	7
Portuguese	1
Romanian	1
Russian	5
Slovenian	1
Spanish	27
Swedish	623
Yugoslavian (cited as)	1

Husén, *Tryckta skrifter*, Husén, *Printed Publications*

languages (Table A.1). During the last decades of his career, he used his generalist knowledge on education as the editor-of-chief of the two editions of the International Encyclopaedia of Education, 1985 and 1994 (see Chap. 6).

Husén's publications peaked during two periods of his career: between 1959 and 1975, and between 1985 and 1995, after he had retired (Fig. A.2). There are no significant content differences between these two peaks; he covers a broad range of topics throughout his career. However, towards the end of his career, he becomes slightly more interested in higher education. After his retirement, his publications in scientific journals also decrease.

Although some themes in Fig. A.3 overlap, it is safe to say that Husén covered a broad range of educational topics, including most aspects of education except for maybe kindergarten and early childhood. The most common themes were general education, international and comparative education reforms, educational research, higher education, and psychology. Husén published most of his work in Swedish, followed by English and German, which were languages he was proficient in. Additionally, many of his publications were translated (see Table A.1).

The width of Husén's work exemplifies not only that Husén was a well-established and productive *international* scholar, with a long career, but also the collective nature of his work (see further Chap. 7). In fact, what distinguishes Husén is not his individual contributions to educational research, but rather as we have seen throughout the chapters, his role as an organiser and a research leader. It was his ability to organise large-scale international projects that came to be his foremost and lasting footprint in the field of comparative education. He is described in memoranda not only as a high-capacity scholar but also a good administrator and research leader.

Alan Purves, who worked with Husén at IEA, wrote the following about Husén's sense of leadership:

> Torsten operates in such a fashion that a group of disparate people can come together to work hard for a period of time and finish the working session with a feeling of true collegiality. Everyone becomes equally important when he chairs a meeting, and people from different disciplines are scrupulously heeded. His closing 'Dear friends ...' is always heartfelt and welcome. It is thanks in great measure to Torsten Husén that IEA has survived into the second and third generation of researchers.[4]

Here we might find a key to understanding Husén as a comparativist—he managed to bring very different people from different countries and disciplines together and work towards a common goal, which we have seen many examples of in this book.

---

[4] Alan Purves quoted in T. Neville Postlethwaite and Torsten Husén, *International Educational Research: Papers in Honor of Torsten Husén* (Oxford: Pergamon, 1986), xi.

APPENDIX A: TORSTEN HUSÉN AND HIS ARCHIVE AS A DISEMBEDDED... 171

1.1 The Husén Archive

Torsten Husén retired formally in 1982. In the fall of 1983, he contacted the National Archives to deposit his personal archive. The first delivery was planned for the beginning of June of the same year. However, the archive was not established until 1993, with the last change made in 2012. Initially, this archive was organised by Torsten Husén's son, Sven-Torsten Husén, historian and archivist at the National Archives. After his own retirement in 2006, he worked on the archive for another two years when a colleague took over. The deposited documents include a few documents from the 1940s, for example, working materials for his doctoral thesis, defended in 1944, but mostly from the 1950s and to 2000 and comprise two series: 159 volumes of correspondence and 285 volumes of thematic documents, totalling over 200,000 pages. As with many personal archives of researchers, this archive primarily pertains to Husén's professional career as an academic, researcher, and civil servant spanning 50 years. The archive appears to be structured according to various professional roles, which is in line with the self-image presented in the introduction to Husén's autobiography, *The Incurable Academic*.[5] In this work, Husén explains that the idea of writing an autobiography arose while he was working on the article 'A Marriage to Higher Education.'[6]

The division of the archive into two series may appear somewhat loosely defined when compared to other personal archives with more series. However, the archive's limited scope makes it challenging to navigate without a more detailed understanding of Husén's career. However, the series division reflects large parts of Husén's professional life with material from different areas and offices over 50 years. The correspondence supplements the subject-organised documents by means of correspondence commenting on or directly linking to various projects. In correspondence, private information may occasionally emerge. For instance, Husén often included his wife Ingrid in his greetings to scholars and their families. However, the majority of the material in Husén's archive is not private. Based on the archive list, it is difficult to conclude that the archive reflects a specific activity. Instead, it appears to be a collection of projects and

---

[5] Torsten Husén, *An Incurable Academic: Memoirs of a Professor* (Oxford: Pergamon Press, 1983).

[6] Torsten Husén, 'A Marriage to Higher Education,' *The Journal of Higher Education* 51, no. 5 (1980).

172 APPENDIX A: TORSTEN HUSÉN AND HIS ARCHIVE AS A DISEMBEDDED...

Table A.2 Thematic overview of the Torsten Husén archive, *Riksarkivet* Stockholm

Category	Volumes (1 volume appr. 500–1000 pages)
Correspondence	159
International originations/collaborations	113
National agencies/state institutions	40
Higher education admin	28
National/Government investigations	22
Seminars and courses	17
Miscellaneous	16
Travel and conferences	13
Book manuscripts/editorial	11
Military	9
Subject specific	7
PhD students	4

activities that are connected by Husén's professional life. However, a significant aspect of Husén's professional career was his involvement in international projects, as evidenced by the archive. The subject-arranged documents, totalling at least 120 volumes, are clearly linked to various international projects, travels, and conferences. Table A.2 provides a general overview of the archive's contents.

This archive is, to our knowledge, in its structure and rich content very unusual when it comes to educational scholarship, and possibly also when seen in a wider contemporary social science perspective.

1.2 Archive Studies as the Textual Ethnography of a Social Science Laboratory

Upon initial examination of the Torsten Husén archive, it becomes apparent that it contains a plethora of materials, including conversations, meeting protocols, memos, drafts, manuscripts under revision, conference documents, travel documents, tickets, and carefully labelled and dated recipes, all stored in brown boxes. Upon closer inspection, it becomes clear that these documents represent a variety of research processes, actors, actions, and mediated knowledge, both as a whole and in detail. The archive can be seen as a documentation of a disembedded laboratory.

Despite the concept of a 'disembedded laboratory' may seem contradictory, given that locality is a fundamental aspect of laboratory research,

APPENDIX A: TORSTEN HUSÉN AND HIS ARCHIVE AS A DISEMBEDDED...   173

it is used in this book. As defined by Bruno Latour and Steve Woolgar in their seminal work 'Laboratory Life—The Construction of Scientific Facts,' a laboratory is a local, a place, where statements and ideas stabilises through various material actions, being it applied methods and operationalisation or inscriptions, such as data production and publications.[7] We see though, that this kind of stabilisations doesn't require a fixed place such as a physical laboratory.

Laboratory studies in the wake of Latour and Woolgar have often been ethnographical studies of the actual work life of the scientists; the processes and culture of research, rather than on ideas and experiment that has so often been in focus in the history of science and ideas, and in earlier sociology of science (Ludwik Fleck, Thomas Kuhn, Robert Merton, David Bloor, and others).

In the wider sense of knowledge production, the laboratory, according to Karin Knorr-Cetina, also needs to be understood in its socio-political and historical context. This broad view of the laboratory has some theoretical implications when it comes to how it reconfigures objects, subjects, time, and space. A good way to describe this is as a reconfiguration of the system of self-other-things in which the researcher becomes a method for 'bringing home' objects in nature and manipulate them in ways that also change the world of the researcher. Laboratories rarely work with objects as they occur in reality, but with images of them. They do this in three ways. First, they transform the object as such. Laboratorians extract a visual, audial, graphical version of the object, in a purified form so to speak, to work with. Second, the object is moved from its natural environment, to be manipulated in the laboratory. Third, the object is moved from its natural cycles of occurrence, and might be put into new processes, and time cycles.[8]

It is important here to see the self-other-things reconfiguration as a mutual process where the laboratory work "'align' the natural order with the social order by creating reconfigured, 'workable' objects in relation to agents of a given time and place."[9] In this reconfiguration, also the scientist becomes 'workable'; they learn and adapt in relation to the objects the work within the laboratory.

---

[7] Bruno Latour and Steve Woolgar, *Laboratory Life: The Construction of Scientific Facts* (Princeton: Princeton University Press, 1979/1986), 243.

[8] Knorr-Cetina, 'Laboratory Studies,' 145–45.

[9] Knorr-Cetina, 'Laboratory Studies,' 146–47.

With this understanding of a laboratory, how can we then understand transnational social science work, as laboratory? Social scientists also bring home objects, being it recorded interviews, surveys, test, notes/pictures of archive material or written texts. The laboratory might not so much be a physical one as a network of actions and interactions using various kinds of 'mediators' and 'intermediators' such as international colleagues and correspondences, conferences, workshops, seminars, and the like. The objects are removed from their natural time cycle, data can be extracted and read over and over again or put into 'frozen' boxes and charts. They can even be used to forecast future developments or imageries of the future (see Chap. 5). In this process, also the social scientists are reconfigured. They learn and develop new skills; make smarter calculations, write and rewrite, review and edit. They produce 'inscriptions' in forms of articles, reports, and books.

One question that puzzled Latour is how objective knowledge comes into being. The fact that he (or anyone) can't exactly explain that process raises questions about the relationship between the scholar and her or his object. In laboratory studies, 'measurability' of objects is expressed rather in terms of how something is made measurable. Latour's point is that objects, 'things,' are made relevant to the language. This process is not simple, the objects 'protest' all the time against how they are spoken about—they strike back: 'Objectivity does not refer to a special quality of the mind, an inner state of justice and fairness, but to the presence of objects which have been rendered 'able' ... to object to what is told about them.'[10]

The point is that there is a messiness in knowledge production where knowledge production struggles with reality in two major ways, that of the scientists and their material conditions, and that of the objects, how they behave and can be described in language.

Here the social science laboratory isn't that different from the natural science ones. Of course, it often has a less clinical character, uses fewer high-tech instruments and less experimental design. Maybe, the biggest difference, just looking at the laboratory and not the work, is its disembeddedness; the social science laboratory is rarely a fixed local but can rather be described as a network of actors (human and non-human) in interaction across time and space. This social science laboratory derives its

---

[10] Bruno Latour, 'When Things Strike Back: A Possible Contribution of 'Science Studies' to the Social Sciences,' *The British Journal of Sociology* 51, no. 1 (2000): 115.

APPENDIX A: TORSTEN HUSÉN AND HIS ARCHIVE AS A DISEMBEDDED... 175

legitimacy not from a central lab and fixed structures, but from the claim that it produces knowledge in a highly internationalised world; constituted by communication and other social activities, for example, at international conferences and proceedings.

One difficulty when it comes to observe social science laboratories is their lack of specific locality and materiality. While a traditional laboratory is easily observable, even sometimes behind glass walls, social science is often much messier. Interviews, surveys, and observations are usually carried out at the place of the research object, in classrooms, workspaces, or at home. Textual analyses, or archive work, can be carried out at libraries, archives, or at university offices (or home offices). All this makes social science less visible, less easily observable. It is here, however, that we have found a source that enables us to in retrospect observe the work of social science in the archives of Torsten Husén. Thus, we use the archive as an ethnographical lens in understanding the social science laboratory. The archive, it shows, provides us with many examples of the messiness in knowledge production; Husén and his peers correspond on circumstantial challenges like funding, locality, travelling, and so on, and we see how texts are revised and re-written in efforts of clarity. Things strike back in the laboratory.

An ethnographic perspective on historical texts has its limitations though. In contrast to the messiness of physical laboratory practices and their multidimensionality, historical texts appear rather one-dimensional and organised, offering an already filtered version of reality. However, in the light of STS, texts are not considered as filtered representations of a practice, but rather also as practice itself. Especially in research contexts, texts are mobile and become 'active agents which assemble, shape and connect practices, and in doing so enact objects, constitute subjects, and inscribe relations, ontological boundaries and domains.'[11]

Hence, in our studies of the archive, we understand the sources as being both a network and inscriptions. It consists of several hundred individuals in different positions and practices in relation to each other interacting with material, economical, practical conditions performing a network that is inscribed in an article, a book or report, that, through references, becomes part of new networks.

---

[11] Richie Nimmo, 'Actor-Network Theory and Methodology: Social Research in a More-Than-Human World,' *Methodological Innovations Online* 6, no. 3 (2011): 114.

176   APPENDIX A: TORSTEN HUSÉN AND HIS ARCHIVE AS A DISEMBEDDED...

Of course, there are a lot of limitations to an archive like this. Jacques Derrida, for example, claims that if Freud and his contemporaries had had access to telephones, tape recorders, fax machines, computers, printers, and e-mail, it would have completely transformed the history and development of psychoanalysis.[12] Many scholars have come to understand the historical record, whether it consists of books in libraries or records in archives, not as an objective representation of the past, but rather as a selection of objects that have been preserved for a variety of reasons (which include sheer luck). Daniel Tröhler have argued that the archive rather should be seen as a place for reconstructing rather than gathering data.[13] Because there is never sufficient archival material Carolyn Steedman contends that 'historians [also must] read for what is not there: the silences and the absences of the documents always speak to us.'[14] With that in mind, some examples of what we have not found in this archive are private notes, private correspondence; anything prior to 1940 (e.g. student years, his German visits); Husén's library; most of Husén's manuscripts; photographs; voice memos; external administration like budgets; machines; datasets; phone calls; personal meetings, supervision; *smells*, and *sounds*.

The lack of these kinds of sources affects with which complexity we can understand the work of Husén and his peers as a social science laboratory. Social interactions of flesh and blood cannot be observed in an archive. However, social relations, ideas, thoughts, and feelings can be part of the text, the inscriptions, we find at the archive. And the archive itself tells a story—of a very text-intensive social practice where textual correspondence of various kind is at heart, and that Husén, as well as archivists in Sweden and elsewhere thought that these texts were worth preserving.

It could be argued that the inclusion of interviews, as an element of oral history, would have provided this book with nuances, personal perspectives, and a greater emotional depth. Oral history interviews allow individuals to share their memories, experiences, and emotions in a way that written documents cannot capture, and there are people still alive who

---

[12] Jaques Derrida, *Archive Fever: A Freudian Impression*, trans. Eric Prenowitz (Chicago: University of Chicago Press, 1995).

[13] Daniel Tröhler, *Languages of Education: Protestant Legacies, National Identities, and Global Aspirations* (New York: Routledge, 2011).

[14] Carolyn Steedman, 'Something She Called a Fever: Michelet, Derrida, and Dust,' *American Historical Review* 106, 5 (2001): 1165.

were involved in the events described. It is important to recognise that archives may only contain information that has been recorded or preserved, leaving gaps in the historical record. Oral history interviews can serve to fill in these gaps by capturing the experiences and perspectives of individuals who may not have left a written record. At the same time, archives can provide a wealth of detailed information on a particular topic or event, allowing researchers to delve deeply into a subject and explore it from various angles. Here oral history may be limited to the recollections of a few individuals, which may also be subject to memory lapses or biases.[15] As is the case with all laboratory studies, the level of interaction with the subjects of study can vary. Given the vast material in the Husén archive, the textual analyses were given full priority with both its strengths and limitations in mind.

---

[15] See Alessandro Portelli, 'The Peculiarities of Oral History,' *History Workshop Journal*, 12, no. 1 (1981); Alessandro Portelli, 'What Makes Oral History Different,' in *The Oral History Reader*, ed. Robert Perks and Alistair Thomson, 3rd ed.(London: Routledge, 2016).

Appendix B

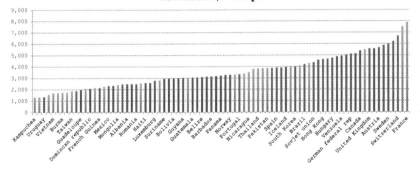

SOURCE MATERIAL

ARCHIVES

Husén library [Husénsamlingen], Linné University, Växjö.

IEA-projektet, Institutionen för internationell pedagogik, Stockholms universitet, F2A.

International Association for the Evaluation of Educational Achievement records, Hoover Institution Library & Archives.

Kungliga biblioteket [The Royal Library], Stockholm.

Professor Torsten Husén's archive, Riksarkivet [The national archive], Stockholm.

UNPRINTED

MEETING NOTES AND MEMORANDA

Anonymous. 1966. Criteria for National Centres Participating in the IEA Study (Extract from Minutes of Standing Committee Meeting. November 21). IEA archive/Hoover institution/357.

———. 1967. *Arrangements for data processing* (undated, ca.). IEA Archive/ Hoover Institution/ 243.

Botkin, James. 1980. *Notes for participants.* May 15. Oxford Meeting. June 11–14. SE/RA/720869/2.194.

Director of the UNESCO Institute. 1962. *Memorandum concerning the position of the Institute in the I.E.A.* Project 5/6, SE/RA/720869/2.237.

© The Author(s), under exclusive license to Springer Nature Switzerland AG 2024
S. Grek et al., *The World as a Laboratory*, Global Histories of Education, https://doi.org/10.1007/978-3-031-68090-8

182   SOURCE MATERIAL

Husén, Torsten. Telegram quoted at IEA Council meeting in Stockholm 1967a. (IEA archive/Hoover institution/ 357).

———. *Notes taken at a meeting in Chicago on May 20, 1968a, with Professor Benjamin S. Bloom on IEA business.* IEA archive/Hoover institution/ 357.

International Institute for Educational Planning. 9th Session of the Governing Board. December 1–2, 1970, Paris. SE/RA/720869/2.53.

———. 10th Session of the Governing Board. November 22–24, 1971, Santiago de Chile. SE/RA/720869/2.53.

———. 11th Session of the Governing Board. November 28–30, 1972a, Paris. SE/RA/720869/2.56.

Meeting at Oxford. June 11–14, 1980a. Working session I, morning June 12, part 1. SE/RA/720869/2.194.

———. June 11–14, 1980b. Working session I, morning June 12, part 2. SE/RA/720869/2.194.

———, 1980c. Working session IV, afternoon June 13, part 2. SE/RA/720869/2.194.

LETTERS

A.D.C. Peterson to Torsten Husén. February 25, 1965. SE/RA/720869/1:27.

Anderson, C. Arnold. 1959. *Letter to Torsten Husén.* July 27. SE/RA/720869/1:14.

Anderson, C. Arnold to Saul B. Robinsohn. January 16, 1963. SE/RA/720869/1.21.

Bereday, George. 1959. *Letter to Torsten Husén.* April 3. SE/RA/720869/1:14.

Bloom, Benjamin. 1961. *Letter to William C. Wall.* August 25. SE/RA/720869/1:20.

Chase, Fracis S. 1957. *Letter to Torsten Husén.* December 23. SE/RA/720869/1:14.

Choppin, Bruce. 1968a. *Letter to Douglas Pidgeon.* February 29. IEA archive/Hoover institution/vol 299.

———. 1968b. *Letter to T. Neville Postlethwaite.* March 18. IEA archive/Hoover institution/vol 399.

Cutler, Preston S. 1972. *Letter to Torsten Husén.* March 29. SE/RA/720869/1:48.

De Landsheere, Gilbert. 1980. *Note to Robert Maxwell.* Notes on the Encyclopaedia Project. June 12. SE/RA/720869/194.

Ellis, C.R. 1980. *Letter to Postlethwaite.* September 30. SE/RA/720869/279.

Gage, Nathanael L. 1980. *Note to Robert Maxwell.* The Proposed International Encyclopaedia of Education. June 12. SE/RA/720869/194.

Husén, Torsten. 1941b. *Letter to Arvid Eriksson.* February 12. SE/RA/720869/1:115.

———. 1955a. *Letter to Mr Tubbs.* October 14. SE/RA/720869/1:1.

———. 1955b. *Letter to Philip E. Vernon.* September 20. SE/RA/720869/1:1.

SOURCE MATERIAL   183

———. 1956. *Letter to William D. Wall.* December 5. SE/RA/720869/1:17.
———. 1959. *Letter to C. Arnold Anderson.* September 19 SE/RA/720869/1:14.
———. 1961a. *Letter to Gerald H. Read.* December 5. SE/RA/720869/1:2.
———. 1961b. *Letter to William D. Wall.* October 9. SE/RA/720869/1:20.
———. 1962. *Letter to William D. Wall.* August 27. SE/RA/720869/1:24.
———. 1963. *Letter to C. Arnold Andersson.* April 4. SE/RA/720869/1.21.
———. 1965b. *Letter to A.D.C. Peterson.* March 2. SE/RA/720869/1:4.
———. 1968b. *Letter to T. Neville Postlethwaite.* May 21. IEA archive/Hoover institution/vol 357.
———. 1972a. *Letter to Ebba K. Concoran.* March 10. SE/RA/720869/1:48.
———. 1972b. *Letter to Preston S. Culter.* March 29. SE/RA/720869/1:48.
———. 1974a. *Letter to Ian Dunlop.* April 17. SE/RA/720869/1:56.
———. 1974b. *Letter to Denis Kallen.* February 15. SE/RA/720869/1:140.
———. 1974c. *Letter to Preston S. Culter.* August, 9. SE/RA/720869/1:56.
———. 1975. *Letter to J.R. Gass.* December 8. SE/RA/720869/1:57.
———. 1987. *Letter to Barbara Barrett.* July 14. SE/RA/720869/279.
———. 1989. *Letter to Barbara Barrett.* April 29. SE/RA/720869/279.
Husén, Torsten, and T. Neville Postlethwaite. 1991. *Letter to Barbara Barret.* January 21. Linnéuniversitets bibliotek/Husénsamlingen/T. Husén International Encyclopedia of Education (second edition).
IIEP Editors-in-Chief. 1980. *Letter to the Section Editors.* November 11. SE/RA/720869/194.
Jaensch, Erich. 1939. *Letter to John Landquist.* October 13. Kungliga biblioteket.
Judge, Harry. 1980. *Note to Robert Maxwell.* Notes on the Encyclopaedia Project. June 12. SE/RA/720869/194.
Neuhaus, Rolf. 1967. *Letter to Torsten Husén.* November 3. SE/RA/720869/1:33.
Pidgeon, Douglas. 1968. *Letter to Torsten Husén.* May 27. IEA archive/Hoover institution/vol 357).
Postlethwaite, T. Neville. 1966a. *Letter to Torsten Husén.* January 1. IEA archive/Hoover institution/vol 299.
———. 1966b. *Letter to Torsten Husén.* April 22. IEA archive/Hoover institution/vol 299.
———. 1966c. *Letter to Torsten Husén.* March 22. IEA archive/Hoover institution/vol 357.
———. 1969b. *Letter to Torsten Husén.* January 20. IEA archive/Stockholm [*Reference to be completed*].
———. 1980a. *Letter to Dr Hajdaraga.* International Encyclopedia of Education. Korrespondens N. Postlethwaite. tidigt 90-tal. SE/RA/720869/2:279).
———. 1980b. *Note to Robert Maxwell.* June 12. SE/RA/720869/194.
Richter, Anders. 1965. *Letter to Karl-Åke Kärnell.* February 12. SE/RA/720869/1:28.

184 SOURCE MATERIAL

Robinsohn, Saul B. 1961a. *Letter to Aleksei Leontiev.* May 19. IEA archive/ Hoover institution/vol 299.

———. 1961b. *Letter to Aleksei Leontiev.* June 20. IEA archive/Hoover institution/vol 299.

———. 1963. *Letter to Torsten Husén.* January 4. SE/RA/720869/1:23.

Terman, Lewis. 1951. *Letter to Torsten Husén.* September 19. Husén library/ Växjö University.

The International Encyclopaedia for Educational Research. 1980. Invitation letter to Oxford June 11–14. SE/RA/720869/194.

Wall, William D. 1956b. *Letter to Torsten Husén.* November 23. SE/ RA/720869/1:17.

———. 1961. *Letter to Torsten Husén.* June 29. SE/RA/720869/1:24.

Wolf, Richard M. undated. *Letter to T. Neville Postlethwaite.* IEA archive/Hoover institution/vol 399.

REPORTS, PRESENTATIONS, AND DRAFTS

Husén, Torsten. A Swedish point of view. Paper given on July 27th at the Birmingham University Summer School at Worcester Training College. SE/ RA/720869/2.253.

Husén, Torsten, and Neville Postlethwaite. *Guideline Report: The International Encyclopedia of Education: Studies and Research. Aims, Scope, Organization and Recommendations to Authors.* 2 edn. Linnéuniversitets bibliotek, Husén samlingen, T. Husén, International Encyclopedia of Education.

Husén, Torsten, T. Neville Postlethwaite and Barbara Barrett. *Proposal.* The International Encyclopedia of Education. 2 ed. Linnéuniversitets bibliotek/ Husénsamlingen/T. Husén International Encyclopedia of Education.

International Association for the Evaluation of Educational Achievement. 1968. *Information on the International Association for the Evaluation of Educational Achievement (IEA) 1968.* Hamburg: UNESCO Institute for Education.

Noonan, Richard, and T. Neville Postlethwaite. 1970. Confidential: Personnel problems and location of IEA office (First draft). IEA archive/Hoover institution/403.

Office of the U.S. High Commission for Germany, Office or Public Affairs, Division of Cultural Affairs. 1952. *A cooperative report of the workshop 'Modern psychologies and German education' held at Die Hochschule für International Pädagogische Forschung, Frankfurt am Main.* August 4–29. SE/ RA/720869/2.198.

Postlethwaite, T. Neville. 1969a. *IEA Major Decisions Reached at the New York Meeting.* June 17. IEA archive/Hoover institution/14.

SOURCE MATERIAL 185

OTHER

Anonymous. 1981. *Press Release on the IEE Project*. March 20. Nassau, Bahamas. SE/RA/720869/2.194.

'Financial information form.' SE/RA/720869/1.48.

Morella, Arthur. 2011. This is Futurama! *American History*. January 5. https://americanhistory.si.edu/explore/stories/futurama.

Office of Military Government for Germany, United States (OMGUS). 1947. Education and Cultural Division, Information Bulletin. September. 'Education for Democracy'.

PRINTED

American Education Research Association. *Report of the First International Conference on Educational Research Atlantic City, New Jersey, U.S.A.*, 1956. Paris: UNESCO.

American Educational Research Association. 1969. *Encyclopedia of Educational Research: A Project of the American Educational Research Association*. 4th ed. London: Macmillan.

Axelrod, Joseph. 1956. International Meeting on School Reform, Hamburg. *International Review of Education* 2 (2): 245–249.

Beeby, Clarence E., ed. 1969. *Qualitative Aspects of Educational Planning*. Paris: UNESCO.

Boalt, Gunnar, and Torsten Husén. 1964. *Skolans sociologi*. Stockholm: Almqvist & Wiksell.

Broadfoot, Patricia. 1978. Review of The IEA Studies in Evaluation: Some Views on the Six Subject Surveys. *Prospects* 8 (1): 121–126.

Bullock, Alan. 1979. Foreword. In *The School in Question: A Comparative Study of the School and Its Future in Western Societies by Torsten Husén*, ix–xxii. London: Oxford University Press.

Coombs, Philip H. 1965. *Educational Planning: An Inventory of Major Research Needs*. Paris: UNESCO.

———. 1968. *The World Educational Crisis: A Systems Analysis*. London: Oxford University Press.

Council of Europe. 1968. *Educational Research, European Survey*. Vol. 1. Strasbourg: Documentation Centre for Education of Europe.

De Landsheere, Gilbert. 1997. IEA and UNESCO: A History of Working Coorperation. In *UNESCO: Fifty Years of Education [CD-ROM]*. Paris: UNESCO.

De Solla Price, Derek J. 1963. *Little Science, Big Science*. New York: Columbia University Press.

186 SOURCE MATERIAL

De Solla Price, Derek J., and Donald Beaver. 1966. Collaboration in an Invisible College. *American Psychologist* 21 (11): 1011–1018.

Epstein, Erwin H. 2019. C. Arnold Anderson. In *North American Scholars in Comparative Education: Examining the Work and Influence of Notable 20th Century Comparativists*, ed. Erwin H. Epstein, 73–81. London: Routledge.

Fischer, Hardi. 1958. Réunion d'experts sur l'évaluation en éducation, Hambourg, Mars 1958. *International Review of Education* 4 (4): 492–493.

Gal, Roger. 1962. L'Institut de l'Unesco pour l'Education à Hambourg. Dix ans d'activité. *International Review of Education* 8 (1): 1–12.

Gallusser, U.M. 1957. Réunions d'experts sur les causes des échecs scolaires, Hambourg, mai/juin 1956. *International Review of Education* 3 (1): 114–116.

Halls, W.D. 1968. Review of International Study of Achievement in Mathematics. *Comparative Education Review* 12 (1): 87–89.

Hans, Nicholas. 1958. *Comparative Education*. 3rd ed. London: Routledge.

Hotyat, Fernand. 1958. *Evaluation in Education: Report on an International Meeting of Experts, held at the UNESCO Institute for Education, Hamburg 17–22 March 1958*. Hamburg: UNESCO Institute for Education.

Husén, Torsten. 1941a. Svensk-tyska akademikermötet i Rostock. *Sverige-Tyskland* 2.

———. 1965a. Educational Change in Sweden. *Comparative Education* 1 (3): 181–191.

———, ed. 1967b. *International Study of Achievement in Mathematics: A Comparison of Twelve Countries*. Vol. 1. Stockholm and New York: Almqvist & Wiksell and John Wiley & Sons.

———. 1968c. *Skola för 80-talet: Framtidsperspektiv på utbildningssamhället*. Stockholm: Almqvist & Wiksell.

———. 1968d. Talent, Opportunity, and Career: A Twenty-Six-Year Follow-Up. *The School Review* 76 (2): 190–209.

———. 1970. Two Decades of Educational Research. *Interchange* 1: 86–98.

———. 1971. *Utbildning är 2000: En framtidsstudie*. Bonnier: Stockholm.

———. 1974. *The Learning Society*. London: Methuen.

———. 1979a. An International Research Venture in Retrospect: The IEA Surveys. *Comparative Education Review* 23 (3): 371–385.

———. 1979b. *The School in Question: A Comparative Study of the School and its Future in Western Society*. London: Oxford University Press.

———. 1980. A Marriage to Higher Education. *Journal of Higher Education* 51 (5): 616–649.

———, ed. 1981. *Torsten Husén: Tryckta skrifter 1940–1980*. Uppsala: Almqvist & Wiksell.

———. 1983a. *An Incurable Academic: Memoirs of a Professor*. Oxford: Pergamon Press.

SOURCE MATERIAL 187

———. 1983b. Educational Research and the Making of Policy in Education: An International Perspective. *Minerva* 21 (1): 81–100.

———. 1983c. The International Context of Educational Research. *Oxford Review of Education* 9 (1): 21–29.

———. 1986. *The Learning Society Revisited*. Oxford: Pergamon.

———. 1992. *Möten men psykologer, pedagoger och andra*. Lund: Wiken.

———. 1993. *Av och om Ingrid: En Kvinna: Stycken för en tängre krets*. Stockholm: Lindströms tryckeri.

———. 1995. Thomas Neville Postlethwaite: A Doctorfather's Subjective Portrait. In *Reflections on Educational Achievement: Papers in Honour of T. Neville Postlethwaite to Mark the Occasion of his Retirement from His Chair in Comparative Education at the University of Hamburg*, ed. Wilfried Bos and Rainer H. Lehmann, 1–7. New York: Waxmann Münster.

———, ed. 1996. *Torsten Husén: Printed Publications 1981–1995*. Institute of International Education: Stockholm.

Husén, Torsten, and Maurice Kogan. 1984. *Educational Research and Policy. How Do They Relate?* Oxford: Pergamon.

Husén, Torsten, and T. Neville Postlethwaite. 1985. Preface. In *The International Encyclopedia of Education*, ed. Torsten Husén and T. Neville Postlethwaite, vol. 1, xi–xxii. Oxford: Pergamon.

———. 1994. Preface. In *The International Encyclopedia of Education*, ed. Torsten Husén and T. Neville Postlethwaite, vol. 2, xi–xx. Oxford: Pergamon.

Husén, Torsten, and Neville Postlethwaite, eds. 1985. *The International Encylopedia of Education*. Vol. 10. Oxford: Pergamon.

International Institute for Educational Planning. 1972b. *IIEP 1972*. Paris: UNESCO.

———. 1980. *IIEP Medium-Term Plan 1979–1983*. Paris: UNESCO.

———. 2003. *40th Anniversary of the IIEP*. Paris: UNESCO.

Jahrbuch des Auslandsamtes der deutschen Dozentenschaft. 1943. *Deutsch-Schwedische Akademikertagung in Rostock 24 bis 30 November 1940, Heft 2*. Leipzig: Verlag Bibliographisches Institut.

King, Edmund. 1967. Review of International Study of Achievement in Mathematics. Phase I. A Comparison of Twelve Countries by Torsten Husén. *International Review of Education* 13 (3): 359–636.

Lauwerys, Joseph A. 1958. General Education, a Conference of the Unesco Institute for Education, Hamburg. November 1957. *International Review of Education* 4 (3): 372–373.

Malmqvist, Eva, and Hans U. Grundin. 1976. International Co-Operation in Educational Research. *International Review of Education* 22 (3): 339–356.

Noll, Victor H. 1957. Introduction: Educational Research in Countries Other than the U.S.A. *Review of Educational Research* 27 (1): 5–6.

188 SOURCE MATERIAL

———. 1958. International Cooperation in Educational Research. *International Review of Education* 4 (1): 77–87.

Paulston, Rolland G. 1966. The Swedish Comprehensive School Reform: A Selected Annotated Bibliography. *Comparative Education Review* 10 (1): 87–94.

Phillips, David, Vernon Mallison, Kenneth Wilson, Karl-Heinz Gruber, and John K. Backhouse. 1986. Review of International Encyclopedia of Education. *Oxford Review* 12 (1): 77–93.

Postlethwaite, T. Neville. 1966. International Project for the Evaluation of Educational Achievement (I.E.A.). *International Review of Education* 12 (3): 356–369.

———. 2004. *Monitoring Educational Achievement*. Paris: UNESCO.

———. 2012. A Man of Principle. In *Benjamin S. Bloom: Portraits of an Educator*, ed. Thomas R. Guskey, 70–72. Lanham: Rowman & Littlefield Education.

Postlethwaite, T. Neville, and Torsten Husén. 1986. *International Educational Research: Papers in Honor of Torsten Husén*. Oxford: Pergamon.

Purves, Alan C. 1987. The Evolution of the IEA: A Memoir. *Comparative Education Review* 31 (1): 10–28.

———. 1991. The World as an Educational Laboratory. *IEA Guidebook*: 35–40.

Sjöstrand, Wilhelm. 1964. Från den pedagogisk-sociologiska författarfabriken. *Svenska Dagbladet*. June 14.

Tjeldvoll, Arlid, and Hans G. Lingens, eds. 2000. *Torsten Husén: Conversations in Comparative Education*. Bloomington: Phi Delta Kappa Educational Foundation.

Tyler, Ralph W. 1949. *Basic Principles of Curriculum and Instruction*. Chicago: University of Chicago Press.

Wall, William D. 1956a. *Psychological Services for Schools*. Hamburg: UNESCO Institute for Education Publications.

———. 1970. Research and Educational Action. *International Review of Education* 16 (4): 484–501.

———. 1979. Psychology of Education. *International Review of Education* 25 (2/3): 367–391.

BIBLIOGRAPHY

Aradau, Claudia, and Tobias Blanke. 2017. Politics of Prediction: Security and the Time/Space of Governmentality in the Age of Big Data. *European Journal of Social Theory* 20 (3): 373–391.

Aradau, Claudia, and Rens van Munster. 2011. *Politics of Catastrophe: Genealogies of the Unknown*. London: Routledge.

Ashmore, Harry S. 1962. Editing the Universal Encyclopedia. *American Behavioural Scientist* 6 (15): 15–18.

Aspen Institute. 2024. *A Brief History of the Aspen Institute*. Aspen Institute. February 22. https://www.aspeninstitute.org/about/heritage/.

Aspen Institute Germany. 2024. *Aspen History*. Aspen Institute. February 22. https://www.aspeninstitute.de/aspen-history/.

Beede, Benjamin R. 2001. Editing a Specialized Encyclopedia. *Journal of Scholarly Publishing* 33: 1–10.

Bennesved, Peter, and Marie Cronqvist. 2023. En humanistiskt skolad kunskapsstrateg på ett samhällsvetenskapligt fält: Torsten Husén och framväxten av ett svenskt psykologiskt försvar. In *Humaniora i välfärdssamhället: Kunskapshistorier om efterkrigstiden*, ed. Johan Östlin, Anton Jansson, and Ragni Svensson Stringberg, 241–265. Göteborg: Makadam.

Bijker, Wiebe, Thomas P. Hughes, and Trevor Pinch, eds. 1987. *The Social Construction of Technological Systems: New Directions in the Sociology and History of Technology*. Cambridge: MIT Press.

© The Author(s), under exclusive license to Springer Nature 189
Switzerland AG 2024
S. Grek et al., *The World as a Laboratory*, Global Histories of
Education, https://doi.org/10.1007/978-3-031-68090-8

190 BIBLIOGRAPHY

Bourdieu, Pierre. 1993. *The Field of Cultural Production: Essays on Art and Literature*. New York: Columbia University Press.

———. 1999. The Social Conditions of the International Circulation of Ideas. In *Bourdieu: A Critical Reader*, ed. Richard Shusterman, 220–228. Oxford: Blackwell.

Bray, Mark. 2008. The WCCES and Intercultural Dialogue: Historical Perspectives and Continuing Challenges. *International Review of Education* 54 (3/4): 299–317.

Broome, André, Alexandra Homolar, and Matthias Kranke. 2017. Bad Science: International Organizations and the Indirect Power of Global Benchmarking. *European Journal of International Relations* 24 (3): 514–539. https://doi.org/10.1177/1354066117719320.

Burke, Peter. 2011. *A Social History of Knowledge. Volume II. From the Encyclopédie to Wikipedia*. Cambridge: Polity Press.

———. 2015. *What Is the History of Knowledge?* Hoboken, NJ: Wiley.

Camic, Charles, Neil Gross, and Michèle Lamont, eds. 2011. *Social Knowledge in the Making*. Chicago: University of Chicago Press.

Carnoy, Martin. 2019. *Transforming Comparative Education: Fifty Years of Theory Building at Stanford*. Stanford: Stanford University Press.

Chapelle, Carol A. 2011. Why Would Anyone Want to Edit an Encyclopedia? *The Modern Language Journal* 95 (4): 632–633.

Condliffe Lagemann, Ellen. 2000. *An Elusive Science: The Troubling History of Educational Research*. Chicago: University of Chicago Press.

Cortada, James W. 2019. *IBM. The Rise and Fall and Reinvention of a Global Icon*. Cambridge, MA: MIT Press.

Danzinger, Kurt. 1990. *Constructing the Subject: Historical Origins of Psychological Research*. Cambridge: Cambridge University Press.

Daston, Lorraine. 2015. The History of Science and the History of Knowledge. *KNOW: A Journal on the Formation of Knowledge* 1 (1): 131–154.

Derrida, Jaques. 1995. *Archive Fever: A Freudian Impression*. Trans. Eric Prenowitz. Chicago: University of Chicago Press.

Edwards, Louise. 2012. Editing Academic Books in the Humanities and Social Sciences: Maximizing Impact for Effort. *Journal of Scholarly Publishing* 44 (1): 61–74.

Elfert, Maren. 2013. Six Decades of Educational Multilateralism in a Globalising World: The History of UNESCO Institute in Hamburg. *International Review of Education* 59: 263–287.

Elfert, Maren, and Christian Ydesen. 2023. *Global Governance of Education: The Historical and Contemporary Entanglements of UNESCO, the OECD and the World Bank*. London: Springer.

Espeland, Wendy Nelson, and Mitchell Stevens. 1998. Commensuration as a Social Process. *Annual Review of Sociology* 24: 312–343.

BIBLIOGRAPHY 191

Europa Publications, ed. 2000. *The International Who's Who 2001.* 64th ed. London: Europa Publications.

Ewald, Francois. 2002. The Return of Descartes' Malicious Demon: An Outline of a Philosophy of Precaution. In *Embracing Risk: The Changing Culture of Insurance and Responsibility*, ed. Tom Baker and Jonathan Simon, 273–302. Chicago: University of Chicago Press.

Featherstone, Mike, and Couze Venn. 2006. Problematizing Global Knowledge and the New En-cyclopaedia Project: An Introduction. *Theory Culture Society* 23 (2/3): 1–20.

Fenwick, Tara, and Richard Edwards. 2010. *Actor-Network Theory and Education.* London: Routledge.

———, eds. 2012. *Researching Education through Actor-Network Theory.* Oxford: Wiley-Blackwell.

Fleck, Christian. 2011. *A Transatlantic History of the Social Sciences: Robber Barons, the Third Reich and the Invention of Empirical Social Research.* London: Bloomsbury Academic.

Fuchs, Eckhardt. 2004. Educational Sciences, Morality and Politics: International Educational Congresses in the Early Twentieth Century. *Paedagogica Historica* 40 (5/6): 757–784.

Fuchs, Eckhart, and Eugenia Roldán Vera, eds. 2019. *The Transnational in the History of Education: Concepts and Perspectives.* Cham: Palgrave McMillan.

Garfield, Simon. 2022. *All the Knowledge in the World. The Extraordinary History of the Encyclopaedia.* New York: Weidenfeld & Nicolson.

Ghosh, Arunabh. 2020. *Making it Count: Statistics and Statecraft in the Early People's Republic of China.* Princeton/Oxford: Princeton University Press.

Gieryn, Thomas F. 1999. *Cultural Boundaries of Science: Credibility on the Line.* Chicago: University of Chicago Press.

———. 2000. A Space for Place in Sociology. *Annual Review of Sociology* 26: 463–496.

———. 2018. *Truth-Spots: How Places Make People Believe.* Chicago and London: University of Chicago Press.

Gorur, Radhika. 2011. Policy as Assemblage. *European Educational Research Journal* 10 (4): 611–622.

———. 2015. Situated, Relational and Practice-Oriented: The Actor-Network Theory Approach. In *Educational Policy and Contemporary Theory: Implications for Research*, ed. Kalervo N. Gulson, Matthew Clarke, and Eva Bendix Petersen, 87–98. London: Routledge.

Gorur, Radhika, Mary Hamilton, Christian Lundahl, and Elin Sundström Sjödin. 2019. Politics by Other Means? STS and Research in Education. *Discourse: Studies in the Cultural Politics of Education* 40 (1): 1–15.

Graham, S.E. 2006. The (Real)politiks of Culture: U.S. Cultural Diplomacy in Unesco, 1946–1954. *Diplomatic History* 30 (2): 231–251.

192 BIBLIOGRAPHY

Grek, Sotiria. 2024. *The New Production of Expert Knowledge: Education, Quantification and Utopia.* London: Springer.

Grek, Sotiria, Joakim Landahl, Martin Lawn, and Christian Lundahl. 2020. Travel, Translation, and Governing in Education: The Role of Swedish Actors in the Shaping of the European Education Space. *Paedagogica Historica* 58 (1): 32–53.

Grosse Stein, Janice, and Richard Stren. 2001. Knowledge Networks in Global Society: Pathways to Development. In *Networks of Knowledge: Collaborative Innovation in International Learning,* ed. Janice Grosse Stein, Richard Stren, Joy Fitzgibbon, and Melissa Maclean, 3–28. Toronto: University of Toronto Press.

Gümüsay, Ali Aslan, and Juliane Reinecke. 2022. Researching for Desirable Futures: From Real Utopias to Imagining Alternatives. *Journal of Management Studies* 59 (1): 236–242.

Hacking, Ian. 1990. *The Taming of Chance.* Cambridge: Cambridge University Press.

Heilbron, Joha, Gustavo Sorá, and Thibaud Bancourt, eds. 2018a. *The Social and Human Sciences in Global Power Relations.* Cham: Palgrave Macmillan.

Heilbron, Johan, Thibaud Boncourt, and Gustavo Sorá. 2018b. Introduction: The Social and Human Sciences in Global Power Relations. In *The Social and Human Sciences in Global Power Relations,* ed. Johan Heilbron, Gustavo Sorá, and Thibaud Boncourt, 1–25. Cham: Springer.

Hewson, Martin. 1999. Did Global Governance Create Informational Globalism? In *Approaches to Global Governance Theory,* ed. Martin Hewson and Timothy J. Sinclair, 97–116. Albany, NY: State University of New York Press.

Hofstetter, Rita, and Bernhard Schneuwly. 2002. Institutionalisation of Educational Sciences and the Dynamics of Their Development. *European Educational Research Journal* 1 (1): 3–26.

———. 2004. Introduction: Educational Sciences in Dynamic and Hybrid Institutionalization. *Paedagogica Historica* 40 (5/6): 569–589.

Holmberg, Linn, and Maria Simonsen. 2021. *Stranded Encyclopedias, 1700–2000.* Cham: Palgrave Macmillan.

Johnson, Terry. 1993. Expertise and the State. In *Foucault's New Domains,* ed. Mike Gane and Terry Johnsson, 139–152. London: Routledge.

Kaika, Maria. 2017. 'Don't Call Me Resilient Again!': The new Urban Agenda as Immunology … Or … What Happens When Communities Refuse to be Vaccinated With 'Smart Cities' and Indicators. *Environment and Urbanization* 29 (1): 89–102.

Kaloyannaki, Pella, and Andreas M. Kazamias. 2009. The Modernist Beginning of Comparative Education: The Proto-Scientific and the Reformist-Meliorist Administrative Motif. In *International Handbook of Comparative Education,* ed. Robert Cowen and Andreas M. Kazamias, 11–36. Dordrecht: Springer.

BIBLIOGRAPHY 193

Keim, Wiebke, Ercüment Çelik, Christian Ersche, and Veronika Wöhrer, eds. 2014. *Global Knowledge Production in the Social Sciences: Made in Circulation*. Farnham: Ashgate.

Kingsbury, Benedict, Sally Engle Merry, and Kevin E. Davis. 2012. Indicators as a Technology of Global Governance. *Law & Society Review* 46 (1): 71–104.

Knorr Cetina, Karin. 1999. *Epistemic Cultures. How the Sciences Make Knowledge*. Cambridge: Harvard University Press.

Knorr-Cetina, Karin. 1995. Laboratory Studies: The Cultural Approach to the Study of Science. In *Handbook of Science and Technology Studies*, ed. Sheila Jasanoff, 140–166. Los Angeles: Sage.

———. 2001. Objectual Practice. In *The Practice Turn in Contemporary Theory*, ed. Theodore R. Schatzki, Karin Knorr-Cetina, and Eike von Savigny, 175–188. New York: Routledge.

Krajewski, Markus. 2014. *World Projects: Global Information Before World War I*. Minneapolis: University of Minnesota Press.

Krige, John. 2008. *American Hegemony and the Postwar Reconstruction of Science in Europe*. Cambridge: MIT Press.

———, ed. 2019. *How Knowledge Moves: Writing the Transnational History of Science and Technology*. Chicago: University of Chicago Press.

———, ed. 2022. *Knowledge Flows in a Global Age: A Transnational Approach*. Chicago: University of Chicago Press.

Lahn, Bård, and Göran Sundqvist. 2017. Science as a 'Fixed point'? Quantification and Boundary Objects in International Climate Politics. *Environmental Science & Policy* 67: 8–15.

Laïdi, Zaki. 1998. *A World Without Meaning: The Crisis of Meaning in International Politics*. London: Routledge.

Landahl, Joakim. 2018. De-scandalisation and International Assessments: The Reception of IEA Surveys in Sweden during the 1970s. *Globalisation, Societies and Education* 16 (5): 566–576.

———. 2020. The Pisa Calendar: Temporal Governance and International Large-scale Assessments. *Educational Philosophy and Theory* 52 (6): 625–639.

———. 2023a. Data Friction and Precarious Knowledge: IEA and the Movement of Data in the 1960s and 1970s. *On Education: Journal for Research and Debate* 6, no. 18. https://doi.org/10.17899/on_ed.2023.18.1.

———. 2023b. Polemik och pedagogik under strecket: Wilhelm Sjöstrand som skoldebattör och vetenskapskritiker. In *Humaniora i välfärdssamhället. Kunskapshistorier om efterkrigstiden*, ed. Johan Östling, Anton Jansson, and Ragni Svensson Stringberg, 165–185. Göteborg: Makadam.

———. 2023c. 'The Punched Cards Were Sent Yesterday, We Hope They Arrive Undamaged': Computers and International Large-Scale Assessments During the 1960s and 1970s. *Learning, Media and Technology* 49 (1): 93–108. https://doi.org/10.1080/17439884.2023.2218644.

194 BIBLIOGRAPHY

Landahl, Joakim, and Anna Larsson. 2022. Pedagogy and the Humanities: Changing Boundaries in the Academic Map of Knowledge 1860s–1960s. In *The Humanities and the Modern Politics of Knowledge: The Impact and Organization of the Humanities in Sweden 1800–2020*, ed. Anders Ekström and Hampus Östh Gustafsson, 81–103. Amsterdam: Amsterdam University Press.

———. 2024. Discipliner, politik och vetenskap i tidig svensk utbildningssociologi. In *Pedagogikens politik: Historiska perspektiv på relationen mellan utbildningsforskning och utbildningspolitik*, ed. Anders Burman, Joakim Landahl, and Anna Larsson, 95–114. Södertörn Studies in Intellectual and Cultural History. Huddinge: Södertörns högskola.

Landahl, Joakim, and Christian Lundahl, eds. 2017. *Bortom PISA: Internationell och jämförande pedagogik*. Natur och Kultur: Stockholm.

Latour, Bruno. 1987. *Science in Action: How to Follow Scientists and Engineers Through Society*. Cambridge: Harvard University Press.

———. 2000. When Things Strike Back: A Possible Contribution of 'Science Studies' to the Social Sciences. *The British Journal of Sociology* 51 (1): 107–123.

———. 2005. *Reassembling the Social: An Introduction to the Actor-Network Theory*. Oxford: Oxford University Press.

Latour, Bruno, and Steve Woolgar. 1979/1986. *Laboratory Life: The Construction of Scientific Facts*. Princeton: Princeton University Press

Lawn, Martin. 2004. The Institute as Network: The Scottish Council for Research in Education as a Local and International Phenomena in the 1930s. *Paedagogica Historica* 40 (5/6): 720–732.

———, ed. 2008. *An Atlantic Crossing? The Work of the International Examinations Inquiry: Its Researchers, Methods and Influence*. Oxford: Symposium Books.

———. 2017. Europeanizing Through Expertise: From Scientific Laboratory to the Governing of Education. In *Uneven Space-Times of Education: Historical Sociologies of Concepts, Methods and Practices (World Yearbook of Education 2018)*, ed. Julie McLeod, Noah W. Sobe, and Terri Seddon, 53–69. London: Routledge.

———. 2018. Governing Through Assessment Data in the UK During the late 20th Century: An Extreme Outlier? In *Assessment Cultures: Historical Perspectives*, ed. Cristiana Alarcón López and Martin Lawn, 397–413. New York: Peter Lang.

Lawn, Martin, and John Furlong. 2009. The Disciplines of Education in the UK: Between the Ghost and the Shadow. *Oxford Review of Education* 35 (5): 541–552.

Lawn, Martin, and Sotiria Grek. 2012. *Europeanising Education*. London: Symposium Books.

Lehmann, Rainer. 2011. The Scientific Contributions of Torsten Husén and Neville Postlethwaite to the Development of International Comparative Research on Educational Achievement. In *IEA 1958–2008: 50 Years of*

BIBLIOGRAPHY 195

Experiences and Memories, ed. Constantinos Papanastasiou, Tjeerd Plomp, and Elena C. Papanastasiou, vol. 1, 515–529. Amsterdam: International Association for the Evaluation of Educational Achievement.

Leuchtenburg, William D. ed. 2004. *Task Force Reports of the Johnson White House, 1963–1969: Research Collections in American Politics*. New York: LexisNexis. https://www.lexisnexis.com/documents/academic/upa_cis/LBJ%20 Task%20Force%20Reports%201963-69.pdf.

Levitas, Ruth. 2013. *Utopia as Method: The Imaginary Reconstitution of Society*. London: Palgrave Macmillan.

Livingstone, David N. 2003. *Putting Science in Its Place: Geographies of Scientific Knowledge*. Chicago: University of Chicago Press.

Louis, Marieke, and Lucile Maertens. 2021. *Why International Organisations Hate Politics: Depoliticising the World*. London: Routlegde.

Lundahl, Christian. 2006. *Viljan att veta vad andra vet: Kunskapsbedömning i tidigmodern, modern och senmodern skola*. Stockholm: Arbetslivsinstitutet.

———. 2014. The Book of Books: Encyclopaedic Writing in the Science of Education in the 1980s. In *Transnational Policy Flows in European Education*, ed. Andreas Nordin and Daniel Sundberg, 79–103. London: Symposion Books.

———. 2016. *The Scholarship of the International Encyclopaedia of Education 1980–1994: Learning how to Produce Knowledge in a Public Genre*. Paper presented at the American Educational Research Association, Washington, DC. April 8–12.

Lyons, Martyn. 2021. *The Typewriter Century: A Cultural History of Writing Practices*. Toronto: University of Toronto Press.

MacKenzie, Donald. 2008. *An Engine, Not a Camera: How Financial Models Shape Markets*. Cambridge: MIT Press.

McCulloch, Gary. 2014. Fred Clarke and the Internationalization of Studies and Research in Education. *Paedagogica Historica* 50 (1/2): 123–127.

Mehrpouya, Afshin, and Rita Samiolo. 2016. Performance Measurement in Global Governance: Ranking and the Politics of Variability. *Accounting, Organisations and Society* 55: 12–36. https://doi.org/10.1016/j.aos.2016.09.001.

Mennicken, Andrea, and Robert Salais, eds. 2022. *The New Politics of Numbers: Utopia, Evidence and Democracy*. Cham: Springer.

Merz, Martina. 1998. 'Nobody Can Force You When You Are across the Ocean': Face to Face and E-mail Exchanges between Theoretical Physicists. In *Making Space for Science: Territorial Themes in the Shaping of Knowledge*, ed. Crosbie Smith and Jon Agar, 313–329. London: Palgrave Macmillan.

Meyer, Christoph O. 2005. Convergence Towards a European Strategic Culture? A Constructivist Framework for Explaining Changing Norms. *European Journal of International Relations* 11 (4): 523–549.

Michalopoulou, Catherine. 2016. Statistical Internationalism: From Quetelet's Census Uniformity to Kish's Cross-National Sample Survey Comparability. *Statistical Journal of the IAOS* 32 (4): 545–554.

196 BIBLIOGRAPHY

Miller, Riel. 2018. *Transforming the Future: Anticipation in the 21st Century.* London: Routledge.

Nespor, Jan. 1994. *Knowledge in Motion: Space, Time and Curriculum in Undergraduate Physics and Management.* London: Routledge.

Newman, Janet. 2013. Beyond the Deliberative Subject? Problems of Theory, Method and Critique in the Turn to Emotion and Affect. *Critical Policy Studies* 6 (4): 465–479.

Nimmo, Richie. 2011. Actor-Network Theory and Methodology: Social Research in a More-Than-Human World. *Methodological Innovations Online* 6 (3): 108–119.

Niskanen, Kristi. 2017. Snille efterfrågas! Rockefeller Foundation, forskarpersona och kön vid Stockholms högskola under mellankrigstiden. *Scandia* 83 (2): 11–40.

Null, J. Wesley. 2007. *Peerless Educator: The Life and Work of Isaac Leon Kandel.* New York: Peter Lang.

Östling, Johan, and David Larsson Heidenblad. 2020. Fulfilling the Promise of the History of Knowledge: Key Approaches for the 2020s. *Journal for the History of Knowledge* 1 (1): 1–6.

———. 2023. *The History of Knowledge.* Cambridge: Cambridge University Press.

Östling, Johan, Erling Sandmo, David Larsson Heidenblad, Anna Nilsson Hammar, and Kari Nordberg, eds. 2018. *Circulation of Knowledge: Explorations in the History of Knowledge.* Lund: Nordic Academic Press.

Papanastasiou, Constantinos, Tjeerd Plomp, and Elena C. Papanastasiou, eds. 2011. *IEA 1958–2008. 50 Years of Experiences and Memories.* Nicosia: Cultural Center of Kykkos Monastery.

Pettersson, Daniel, and Thomas S. Popkewitz. 2019. A Chimera of Quantifications and Comparisons: The Changing of Educational 'Expertise'. In *New Practices of Comparison, Quantification and Expertise in Education: Conducting Empirically Based Research,* ed. Christina Elde Mølstad and Daniel Pettersson, 18–36. London: Routledge.

Phillips, David, and Kimberly Ochs, eds. 2004. *Educational Policy Borrowing: Historical Perspectives.* Oxford: Symposium Books.

Piattoeva, Nelli, and Galina Gurova. 2018. Domesticating International Assessments in Russia: Historical Grievances, National Values, Scientific Rationality and Education Modernisation. In *Assessment Cultures. Historical Perspectives,* ed. Cristina Alarcón and Martin Lawn, 93–97. Berlin: Peter Lang.

Pielke, Rodger A., Jr. 2007. *The Honest Broker: Making Sense of Science in Policy and Politics.* Cambridge: Cambridge University Press.

Pizmony-Levy, Oren. 2013. *Testing for All: The Emergence and Development of Student Achievement, 1958–2012.* PhD Diss., University of Indiana University. ProQuest (3599130).

Poli, Roberto, ed. 2019. *Handbook of Anticipation: Theoretical and Applied Aspects of the Use of Future in Decision Making.* Cham: Springer.

BIBLIOGRAPHY 197

Portelli, Alessandro. 1981. The Peculiarities of Oral History. *History Workshop Journal* 12 (1): 96–107.

———. 2016. What Makes Oral History Different. In *The Oral History Reader*, ed. Robert Perks and Alistair Thomson, 3rd ed., 48–58. London: Routledge.

Porter, Theodore M. 1995. *Trust in Numbers: The Pursuit of Objectivity in Science and Public Life*. Princeton: Princeton University Press.

Preston, John. 2021. *Fall: The Mystery of Robert Maxwell*. London: Penguin Books.

Primus, Franziska, and Christian Lundahl. 2021. The Peripherals at the Core of Androcentric Knowledge Production: An Analysis of the Managing Editor's Knowledge Work in The International Encyclopedia of Education (1985). *Paedagogica Historica* 57 (6): 1–17.

Randeraad, Nico. 2010. *States and Statistics in the Nineteenth Century: Europe by Numbers*. Manchester: Manchester University Press.

Rodogno, David, Bernhard Struck, and Jakob Vogel. 2015. *Shaping the Transnational Sphere: Experts, Networks and Issues from the 1840s and 1930s*. New York: Berghahn Books.

Ross, Jeffrey I., and Frank Shanty. 2009. Editing Encyclopedias for Fun and Aggravation. *Publishing Research Quarterly* 25 (3): 159–169.

Schopflin, Katharine. 2014a. *The Encyclopaedia as a Form of the Book*. PhD Dissertation, University College London.

Schopflin, Katherine. 2014b. What Do We Think an Encyclopaedia is? *Culture Unbound* 6 (3): 483–503.

Schriewer, Jürgen, and Carlos Martínez Valle. 2004. Constructions of Internationality in Education. In *The Global Politics of Educational Borrowing and Lending*, ed. Gita Steiner-Khamsi, 29–53. New York: Teachers College Press.

Secord, James A. 2004. Knowledge in Transit. *Isis* 95 (4): 654–672.

Seddon, Terri, Julie McLeod, and Noah W. Sobe. 2017. Reclaiming Comparative Historical Sociologies of Education. In *Uneven Space-Times of Education: Historical Sociologies of Concepts, Methods and Practices (World Yearbook of Education 2018)*, ed. Julie McLeod, Noah W. Sobe, and Terri Seddon, 1–25. London: Routledge.

Sills, David L. 1969. Editing a Scientific Encyclopedia. *Science* 163 (3872): 1169–1175.

Simonsen, Maria. 2016. *Den skandinaviske encyklopædi: Udgivelse og udformning af Nordisk familjebok & Salmonsens Konversationsleksikon*. Makadam: Göteborg.

Speich Chassé, Daniel. 2023. How the Global Became a Framework for Numerical Communication: A Comment. *European Review of History: Revue européenne d'histoire* 30 (1): 123–129.

Star, Susan Leigh. 1999. The Ethnography of Infrastructure. *American Behavioral Scientist* 43 (3): 377–391.

Steedman, Carolyn. 2001. Something She Called a Fever: Michelet, Derrida, and Dust. *American Historical Review* 106 (5): 1159–1180.

198 BIBLIOGRAPHY

Steiner-Khamsi, Gita, ed. 2004. *The Global Politics of Educational Borrowing and Lending*. New York: Teachers College Press.

———. 2009. Transferring Education, Displacing Reforms. In *Discourse Formation in Comparative Education*, ed. Jürgen Schriewer, 155–188. Frankfurt am Main: Peter Lang.

Steiner-Khamsi, Gita, and Florian Waldow, eds. 2012. *Policy Borrowing and Lending in Education*. London: Routledge.

Stone, Diane. 2013. *Knowledge Actors and Transnational Governance. The Private Public Policy Nexus in the Global Agora*. London: Palgrave Macmillan.

———. 2017. Understanding the Transfer of Policy Failure: Bricolage, Experimentalism and Translation. *Policy & Politics* 45 (1): 55–70. https://doi.org/10.1332/030557316X14748914098041.

Sundin, Olof, and Jutta Haider. 2013. The Networked Life of Professional Encyclopaedias: Quantification, Tradition and Trustworthiness. *First Monday* 18 (6).

Tröhler, Daniel. 2011. *Languages of Education: Protestant Legacies, National Identities, and Global Aspirations*. New York: Routledge.

Turchetti, Simone, Néstor Herran, and Soraya Boudia. 2012. Introduction: Have We Ever Been 'Transnational'? Towards a History of Science Across and Beyond Borders. *British Journal for the History of Science* 45 (3): 319–336.

Tveit, Sverre, and Christian Lundahl. 2018. New Modes of Policy Legitimation in Education: (Mis) using Comparative Data to Effectuate Assessment Reform. *European Educational Research Journal* 17 (5): 631–655.

Van Strien, Peter J. 1997. The American 'Colonization' of Northwest European Social Psychology after World War II. *Journal of the History of the Behavioural Sciences* 33 (4): 349–363.

Von Oertzen, Christina. 2023. Paper Knowledge and Statistical Precision. *Isis* 114 (2): 380–386.

Wood, Matt, and Matthew V. Flinders. 2014. Rethinking Depoliticisation: Beyond the Governmental. *Policy & Politics* 42 (2): 151–170. https://doi.org/10.1332/030557312X655909.

Ydesen, Christian. 2020. *The OECD's Historical Rise in Education: The Formation of a Global Governing Complex*. London: Palgrave Macmillan.

Zuccala, Alesia. 2006. Modelling the invisible college. *Journal of the American Society for Information and Technology* 57 (2): 152–168.

Index[1]

A
Academy of Pedagogical Sciences, 66
Ágoston, György, 67
Almqvist & Wiksell, 150
American, 1
American Educational Research
  Association (AERA), 83, 110
American support, 10
American Zone of Occupation, 17
The Americas and the Caribbean, 111
Anderson, C. Arnold, 39
Andersson, Lorin W., 120
Anticipation, 95
Anticipatory governance, 94
Anticipatory Systems, 94
Applied research, 73
Asia, 111
Aspen Institute for Humanistic
  Studies, 152
Aspen/Berlin seminars, 92
Authoritative knowledge, 87

B
Bank of Sweden Tercentenary
  Foundation, 55
Barrett, Barbara, 119
Becker, Hellmut, 141
Beeby, Clarence Edward, 72
Bereday, George, 140
Bergling, Kurt, 54n16
Berkowitch, Charles, 78
Bloom, Benjamin, 53
Bloor, David, 173
Boalt, Gunnar, 149
Botkin, James, 115
Bourdieu, Pierre, 79
Broadfoot, Patricia, 50

C
Center for Advanced Study in the
  Behavioral Sciences, 147
CERI, 150

[1] Note: Page numbers followed by 'n' refer to notes.

© The Author(s), under exclusive license to Springer Nature
Switzerland AG 2024
S. Grek et al., *The World as a Laboratory*, Global Histories of
Education, https://doi.org/10.1007/978-3-031-68090-8

199

200 INDEX

CES (later CIES), 138
CESE, 138
Chairman, 79
Chase, Francis S., 138n13
Choppin, Bruce H., 57, 118
Circulation, 4
Classificatory system, 114
Clifton, Rodney A., 54n16
Cold War, x, 65, 111, 112
Coleman, James S., 141
Collaboration, 158
Comparative education, 18, 39,
    167, 170
Comparative Education, 140
Comparative Education Center, 138
Comparative Education Review, 140
Comparative network, 158
Comprehensive school reform, 140
Computing, 55
Concoran, Ebba K., 151n50
Conferences, 72
Congresses, 5
Convention Against Discrimination in
    Education, 71
Coombs, Philip H., 72
Cross-border, 7
Cutler, Preston S., 148n35

D
De-authorisation, 129
Debeauvais, Michel, 79, 115
Decolonisation, 69
de Landsheere, Gilbert L., 115, 118
Democracy, 93
Department of Educational and
    Psychological Research at
    Stockholm School of Education, 3
Department of Psychology at Lund
    University, 166
Derrida, Jacques, 176
Development, 71

Directorship, 77
Disciplinary influences, 19
Discourse, 70
Disembedded, 11, 87
Disembedded laboratory, v, ix, xiv,
    3, 75, 112
Disembeddedness, v
Disembedded scientific laboratory, 9
Disembodied knowledge, 160
Distance, 4
Dunkin, Michael J., 118
Dunlop, Ian, 54n16

E
Economic crisis, 91
Economic prosperity, 72
Economy, 72
Educational Achievement organised at
    the Graduate School of
    Education, 83
Educational expansion, 71
Educational knowledge for
    policymaking, 69
Educational planning, 69
Educational psychologists, 23
Educational research, 170
Educational Review, 143
Education financing, 74, 81
Education number-making, 94
Education professionals, 80
Eidetic imagery, 135
Encyclopaedia, 112
Enkyklios paideia, 112
Entanglement, 4
Epistemic community, 3
Epistemic object, 129
Epistemic power of expertise, 88
Eraut, Michael, 118
Eriksson, Arvid, 135n4
Ethnocentrism, 114
Europe, 81, 111

INDEX   201

European laboratory, 25
Evaluation, 127
Expert education knowledge, 70

F
Factorial analysis, 28
Fellowship programme, 85
Financial resources, 83
The Finnish Academy of Sciences, 166
Fleck, Ludwik, 173
Food and Agriculture Organisation (FAO), 72, 86
Ford Foundation, 81, 152
Forecasting, 93
Foresight, 94
Foshay, Arthur W., 61
Funding, 81
Funds, 78
Futuramas, 92
Future of Education, 92
Future scenarios, 92
Futurological thinking, xv, 91–108
Futurology, 92

G
Gage, N. L., 115
Gal, Roger, 36
Gass, James Ronald, 150
General education, 170
Geographical representation, 80
Global expert network, 69–89
Global knowledge networks, 8
Global South, 69
Governance, 76
Governing Board, 76
Grundin, Hans U., 39

H
Halls, Wilfred Douglas, 49
Headington Hill Hall, 115

Headquarters, 82
Higher education, 170
History of educational research, ix
History of knowledge, ix
Hitler, Adolf, 135
Hotyat, Fernand, 35
Husén, Torsten, vi, 91, 109, 118
The Husén Archive, 171–172
The Husén Library at Växjo University, 113
Hylla, Erich, 21

I
IBM, 57
IBM 360, 56
The IEA archive at Stanford University, xiii
IIEP's Library and Documentation Centre, 86
Index, 114
Inflation, 82
The Institute of International Education (IIE), 166
Institutes, 35
Instructional materials, 81
Instrumentalisation of future imaginings, 95
Intellectual community, 27
Interdependencies, 70
International and comparative education, vii
International Association for the Evaluation and Educational Achievement (IEA), vi, xiv, 8, 124
International Book Market, xv
International collaboration, 76
International Council for Educational Development (ICED), 151
International development, 77
International education, 170
International Encyclopedia of Education (IEE), viii, xv, 12, 109

202 INDEX

International Examinations Inquiry
(IEI), 2
International Institute for Educational
Planning (IIEP), vi, xiv,
12, 69, 124
Internationalisation of education
research expertise, 81
International knowledge networking, 9
International Labour Organisation
(ILO), 72, 86
International organisations, 70
International reform agendas, 88
Interns, 78
Internships, 78
Inter-personal conflicts, 78
Invisible college, 3

J
Jackie, 152
Jaensch, Erich, 134
John Wiley, 150
Judge, H., 115
Jullien, Marc-Antoine, 48

K
Kagawa, Michi, 151
Kallen, Denis, 147n34
Kandel, Isaac, vii
Kärnell, Karl-Åke, 150n44
Keeves, John P., 54, 119
Kelly, Alison, 54n16
Kerlinger, F. N., 115
Kidd, J. Roby, 119
Knorr-Cetina, Karin, 173
Kogan, Maurice, 141
Kretschmer, Ernst, 134
Kuhn, Thomas, 173

L
Laboratory, xii
Laboratory studies, v

Labour market, 92
Lakomski, Gabriele, 120
Landquist, John, 135n3
Langeland, Alv Storheid, 36
Latour, Bruno, 173
Lauwerys, Joseph, 29
League of Nations, 47
Learning curve, 126
Legitimacy, 87
Leontiev, Aleksei, 65
Lewey, Arieh, 119
Lifelong learning, 130

M
Maheu, René, 78
Mählck, Lars, 54n16
Malmquist, Eva, 39
Manpower, 72
Materiality, 4
Max Planck Institute, 52, 166
Maxwell, Robert, 115
Measurability, 174
Measurement, 93
Measurement of outputs, 75
Merton, Robert, 173
Microplanning, 74
Military psychology, 135
Miller, Riel, 95
Monroe, Paul, vii
Multidisciplinarity, 72
Munch, Ingrid, 54n16

N
Narrative-making, 70
National commissions, 86
National Foundation for Educational
Research in England and Wales
(NFER), 53
National Institute for Educational
Research, 151
Nature of comparative education, 35
Negotiation, 88

INDEX 203

Networking, 5–8
Network of actors, 174
Neuhaus, Rolf, 149n43
Nicholas, Hans, 48
Nielsen, Dean, 54n16
Noll, Victor, 32
Noonan, Richard, 54
Nystrand, Raphael O., 119

O
OECD, 47, 150
OECD Scientific Affairs
  Committee, 83
Ögren, Gustaf, 52
Oral history, 176

P
Paradigms, 87
Passow, A. Harry, 119
Pergamon Press, 115
Perkins, James A., 141
Peterson, Alec, 140n15
Pidgeon, Douglas, 54
PIRLS, 46
PISA, 159
Place and space in research, 19
Poignant, Raymond, 79
Policymaking, xi
Policy networks, 8
Policy-orientated research, 33
Policy recommendations, 70
Poli, Roberto, 94
The Polish Academy of
  Sciences, 166–167
Postlethwaite, T. Neville, 12,
  109, 119
The print paradigm, 113
Probability, 92
Production of educational
  knowledge, 69
Production of expert knowledge, 87

Programme for International Student
  Assessment, 159
Provincial, 6
Provincialism, 39
Psacharopoulos, George, 119
Psychology, 170
Purves, Alan, 40

Q
Quality control, 128
Quality in education, 74
Quantitative data, 28
Quasi-autonomous, 73
Quetelet, Adolphe, 47

R
Read, Gerald H., 150n46
Re-authorisation, 129
Regional directors, 85
Research, 23
Research institutes, 18
Research networking, 3
Richter, Anders, 150n44
Robinsohn, Saul B., 51
Rosier, Malcolm, 54n16
The Royal Swedish Academy of
  Sciences, 166
The Russian Academy of Educational
  Sciences, 167

S
Sadler, Michael, vii
The School in Question, 92
School mapping, 74
School reform, 1
Science and Technology Studies
  (STS), v
Scientization, 87
Scottish Council for Research in
  Education, 64

204 INDEX

Secondary education, 157
Second World War, 153
Seminars, 85
SIDA, 55
Six Subject Survey, 49
Sjöstrand, Wilhelm, 161n10
Socialisation, 88
Sociology of risk and anticipation, 92
Social problems, 87
Social science laboratory, 172–177
Spencer Fellows, 54
SPPI, 64
State intellectual, 159
Statistical analysis, 91
Sutton, Frank, 152
Swanson, Gordon I., 119
Swedish Board of Education, 151
The Swedish comprehensive school
   reform, 165

T
Teachers College, 57
Technicisation, 87
Technologies of assessment, 1
Technology, 79
Terman, Lewis, 150
Textual analyses, 175
Textual ethnography, 172
Thomas, R. Murray, 119
Thompson, Hunter S., 146
TIMSS, 46
Titmus, Colin J., 119
Torsten Husén's archive, xiii
Torsten Husén's research archive, xvi
Training, 69
Training programmes, 74
Transnational connector of research, 43
Transnational history of science, ix
Transnational networks, v, xiv
Transnational projects, 4
Transnationality, 1
Travelling knowledge, 70

Tyler, Ralph W., 161
Tyler's rationale, 161
Typewriter, 145

U
UNESCO Institute, 25
UNESCO Institute for Education in
   Hamburg, 49
United Nations Educational, Scientific
   and Cultural Organization
   (UNESCO), 3, 81
United Nations (UN), 47, 72
United Nations Development
   Programme, 85
United States, 2
US Office of Education, 52

V
Vaizey, John, 78
Van Strien, Peter, 42
Vernon, Philip E., 36, 143–144

W
Wall, William D., 1
Wang, Margret C., 120
Washington Conference on Economic
   Growth and Investment in
   Education, 71–72
Weiler, Hans N., 78, 119
Wikis, 113
Williams, Shirley, 116
Wolf, Richard M., 57
Woolgar, Steve, 173
Worcester Training College, 142
Workshops, 22, 85
World Bank, 72, 125
World Crisis in Education, 74
World Health Organisation
   (WHO), 72, 86
Writing practices, 142

Printed in the United States
by Baker & Taylor Publisher Services